FROM LIMBERLOST PRESS

How to Sleep Cold
17 Poems & Related Writing Prompts
from the Outpost Writing Workshop
at Billy Meadows

By Kim Stafford

"*This book speaks from a place in far northeast Oregon, where time runs deep with stories. Wallowa County was the original home of the Nez Perce Tribe, and anyone who visits there will see, and feel, why it was, and is, sacred homeland. It is a place where the mountains are steep, the rivers clean, and history is yet a compass for navigating the mysteries of modern life.*"

Thus, from the "Foreword," Kim Stafford describes the place in 2009 where he met for a time with 15 "sterling companions" in a writing workshop they called the Outpost Writing Camp at Billy Meadows. Without electrical power or phones, many sleeping on the ground, the group immersed themselves in the writing craft for a week in a remote landscape, eating Dutch oven meals and exploring nature when not deeply engaged in writing. ***How to Sleep Cold*** is Stafford's collection of 17 poems, all written at the Outpost Writing Camp, inspired by the writing prompts (also described in the book) that guided and inspired the group of participants throughout their time at Billy Meadows.

Kim Stafford is the current Poet Laureate of the state of Oregon. He is the author of more than a dozen books of poetry and prose, and the director of the Northwest Writing Institute and the William Stafford Center at Lewis & Clark College in Portland, where he has taught since 1979.

Letterpress printed in a limited edition of 500 copies on Mohawk Superfine paper, folded and sewn by hand into Thai Chiri endsheets and Stonehenge wrappers.

$20 (*plus $3 Media Mail shipping; Idaho residents please add 6% sales tax*)
from www.limberlostpress.com, or send check to: Limberlost Press, Rick & Rosemary Ardinger, Editors, 17 Canyon Trail, Boise, Idaho 83716

FROM LIMBERLOST PRESS

Wild Dog Days
By Gino Sky

In this long poem, published in honor of the poet's 75th year, the indefatigable **Gino Sky**, author of the novel *Appaloosa Rising: The Legend of the Cowboy Buddha* (Doubleday, 1980), reflects on history, memory, and the power of poetry in bringing an end to the Vietnam War.

Publishing a 1960s underground literary magazine called *Wild Dog* that the FBI took notice of, Sky tells a story of all that swirled around the magazine during an eruptive time in America. First published by the poet Ed Dorn in Pocatello in 1963, *Wild Dog* was handed off to Sky who moved it to Salt Lake City and then to San Francisco's Haight-Ashbury District right at the moment of the counter-cultural revolution. Sky exuberantly chronicles the time, the place, and the peace movement with hallucinogenic clarity.

Illustrated with photos of some of the poets who helped hand-crank the small press literary movement, *Wild Dog Days* is dedicated to "every man, every woman, every kid, every dog who marched for peace and stopped the war."

Gino Sky has published two novels, a collection of stories, and a dozen books of poetry (including *Hallelujah 2 Groundhogs & 16 Valentines*, also available from Limberlost Press). *Appaloosa Rising* and his novel *Coyote Silk* (North Atlantic Books, 1987) have been translated and published in Korea. He and his wife Barb Jensen live in Salt Lake City.

Letterpress printed in a limited edition of 400 copies.

$15 *(plus $3 Media Mail shipping; Idaho residents please add 6% sales tax)*
from www.limberlostpress.com, or send check to: Limberlost Press,
Rick & Rosemary Ardinger, Editors, 17 Canyon Trail, Boise, Idaho 83716

LIMBERLOST LETTERPRESS

www.limberlostpress.com

THE LIMBERLOST REVIEW

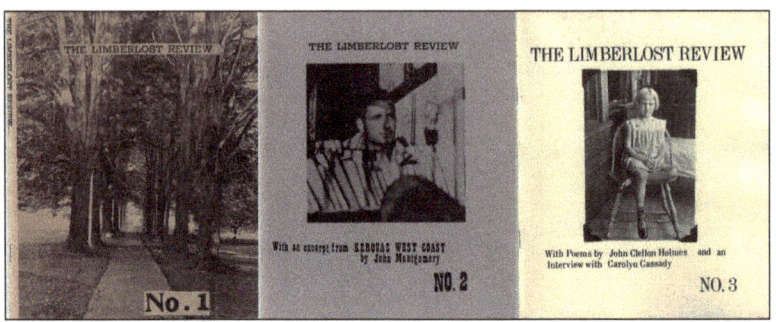

No. 1, 1976   No. 2, 1977   No. 3, 1977

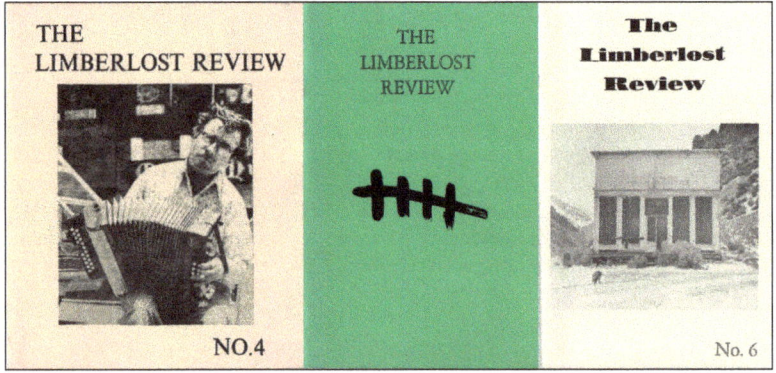

No. 4, 1977   No. 5, 1978   No. 6, 1979

No. 9, 1981   No. 13, 1984   2019

The Limberlost Review

A Literary Journal of the Mountain West

Edited by
Rick & Rosemary Ardinger

A publication of Limberlost Press
Boise, Idaho
2020

THE LIMBERLOST REVIEW
A LITERARY JOURNAL OF THE MOUNTAIN WEST

2020 Edition

Editors
Rick & Rosemary Ardinger

Contributing Editors
Chuck Guilford
Bob Bushnell

Sports and Social Media Editor
Jennifer Holley

Layout and Design
Meggan Laxalt Mackey, Studio M Publications & Design

Cover Illustrations
"Shattered Rainbow Ridge" (Front) by Royden Card
"Succor Creek Canyon" (Back) by Nancy Brossman

Limberlost Press
17 Canyon Trail, Boise, Idaho 83716
www.limberlostpress.com

THE LIMBERLOST REVIEW *is published annually by Limberlost Press. Copyright © 2020 by Limberlost Press, with all rights to the individual contributions returned to the authors and artists.*

ISBN 978-0-578-65575-8

This journal features some of the best writing from the Mountain West and beyond, including poetry, fiction, memoir, essay, translation, commentary about books we come back to again, interviews, artwork, and more. We welcome the submission of manuscripts, but can not accept responsibility for lost items or electronic correspondence problems. For copies of THE LIMBERLOST REVIEW, please email editors@limberlostpress.com or visit our website: www.limberlostpress.com. Printed in the United States of America.

LIMBERLOST LETTERPRESS

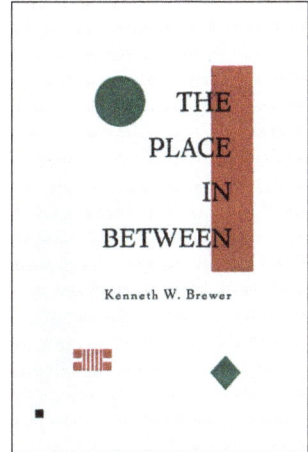

www.limberlostpress.com

LIMBERLOST LETTERPRESS

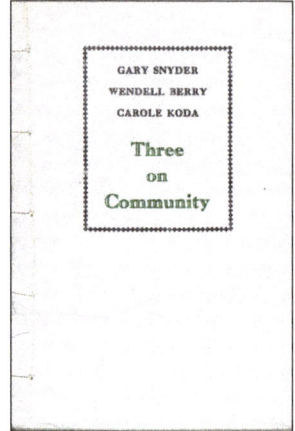

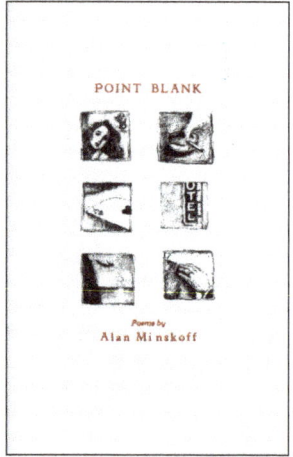

www.limberlostpress.com

TABLE OF CONTENTS

EDITORS' NOTE
Rick and Rosemary Ardinger 15

POETRY & FICTION
Ed Sanders, *Three Poems* 21
Jennifer Dunbar Dorn, *Two Poems* 31
David Lee, *Two Poems* 33
Judith Freeman, *Wyatt & Hela* 39
Robert Demott, *Christmas Tripytch, With Birds* 53
Ron McFarland, *Two Poems* 57
Judith Root, *Two Poems* 59
John Rember, *Getting Wood* 63
Chuck Guilford, *Two Poems* 75
Howard Wilkerson, *Dogwood Blossoms* 79
E. Ethelbert Miller, *Two Poems* 81
David Guiotto, From *The Distances* 83
Annie Lampman, *Two Poems* 97
O. Alan Weltzien, *Grande Ronde Suite* 99
John Garmon, *Light Morning Snow, We Wait for a Warmer Season* 105
Gary Gildner, *Jessica* 107
Charlotte Mears, *Two Poems* 117
Kim Stafford, *Two Poems* 119
Gerald Costanzo, *Election* 121
Bob Bushnell, *Wrath* 123
Danielle Beazer Dubrasky, *Shadow Prints* 129
Sherman Alexie, *Two Poems* 131
Jim Heynen, *Clarence* 137
Kirsten Porter, *Room* 153
Jay Johnson, *Mstislav Lovrek* 155
Sandy Anderson, *Three Poems* 175
Leslie Ann Leek, *On Lenin Peak* 181
Shaun T. Griffin, *They Must Get So Tired of Us* 195
Gino Sky, *Christmas Dog or A Silent Prayer for Hayseus* 199

INTERVIEW
Rick Ardinger, *An Interview with Gino Sky* 207

GALLERY
Glenn Oakley, *Where Music Lives* Photographic Essay 227
Nancy Brossman 38, 130, 194, 238
Royden Card 122, 128, 174
Jinny DeFoggi 136, 332
Dennis DeFoggi 80, 328
Greg Keeler 52, 96, 106, 116, 310
Alberta Mayo 56, 152, 334
Ray Obermayr 14, 30, 74, 180

ESSAYS & NONFICTION
Mary Clearman Blew, *Riding Horseback with the Midwife* 239
Mike Medberry, *Walking the L.A. River* 247
Tom Rea, *Remembering Marc Kashnor, 1951-2009* 263
Alessandro Meregaglia, *Vardis Fisher's Last Essay* 271
Vardis Fisher, *The World's Greatest Physical Wonderland* 275

RE-READINGS
Marc C. Johnson, On *Mari Sandoz* 295
Michael Corrigan, On *William Faulkner* 301
Hank Nuwer, On *Kurt Vonnegut* 305
William Johnson, On *Norman Maclean* 311
Grove Koger, On *John O'Hara* 315
Cameron Watson, On *Robert Laxalt* 323

LAST WORD
Three Short Poems by Ron Padgett 329

CONTRIBUTORS 335

LIMBERLOST LETTERPRESS

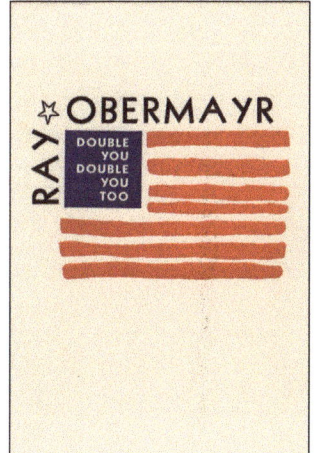
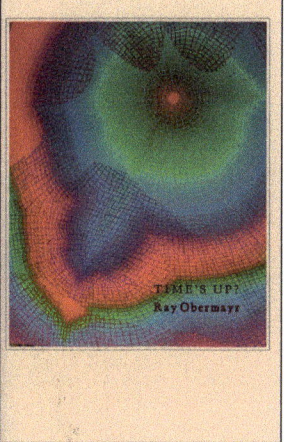

www.limberlostpress.com

"Scout Mountain #5" by Ray Obermayr. Oil on canvas, 40" x 32."

EDITORS' NOTE
Foreword and Onward!

The reception of the revived *Limberlost Review* in 2019 has been gratifying over the past year, and this new 2020 edition at 350 pages has been an adventure to pull together as word got around that this literary journal has resurfaced. This edition features work by veteran writers and new voices, and the artwork within by seven amazing artists and an award-winning photographer elevates the entire volume you hold in your hands.

Homage to the Poet-Editors
Several years ago, when we first imagined reviving the *Review*, we mused that we should simply pull together an 8 ½ x 11, photocopied-and-stapled compilation of work, similar to the mimeographed literary magazines of the 1960s in homage to the poet-editors of 60 years ago who ignited a revolution in poetry publishing. The inspiration for *The Limberlost Review*—especially the early issues of the journal that appeared in the 1970s and 1980s—came from several poet-editors whose work appears in this new edition of the *Review*. To them, we dedicate this 2020 edition of this journal.

We open with poems by Ed Sanders, prolific poet, Fugs founder, musical inventor, nonviolent political activist, and editor of the iconic 1960s mimeo magazine *Fuck You: A Magazine of the Arts* ("published from a Secret Location on the Lower East Side"). Typed on stencils and cranked out, collated, and stapled, *Fuck You* featured the work of some of the great poets of the era between 1962 and 1965, and while we all owe much to Ed for his belief that poetry can end wars and investigate history, we owe him for his work as an editor, offering a venue for poets during an eruptive American decade.

This *Limberlost* also features an interview with Gino Sky (formerly AKA Burt Gail Clays and Gino Clays) as one of the editors of another mimeoed 1960s literary magazine, *Wild Dog*, which was launched by poet Ed Dorn in Pocatello, Idaho, in 1963. Gino assumed editorship of *Wild Dog* in 1964 and moved it to Salt Lake City and then San Francisco, where the last issue appeared in 1966. Over 22 issues, *Wild Dog* featured work by a line-up of writers that reads like a *Who's Who* of mid-century American poetry (see interview with Gino on page 206).

And we close this issue by giving the Last Word to poet Ron Padgett, who, long before becoming a force in contemporary poetry, launched *The White Dove Review* in 1959, another seminal literary magazine of the era. Though it was begun when Ron was still in high school in Tulsa, Oklahoma, and lasted only five issues, *White Dove* published such writers as Jack Kerouac, Ted Berrigan, Paul Blackburn, and Allen Ginsberg, and featured artwork by Padgett's brilliant classmate Joe Brainard.

Copies of these three literary magazines today alone are coveted by collectors, dog-eared copies selling for hundreds of dollars each and especially treasured by the special collections departments of major university libraries.

Several other writers in this issue also know what it is to set your own work aside to stir the collaborative stew of a literary journal or press.

Jennifer Dunbar Dorn with her husband Ed edited the amazing *Rolling Stock* in the 1980s (Motto: "If it moves, print it."), and Jennifer later edited a couple of literary journals on her own, *Sniper Logic* and *Square One* in Boulder. Sandy Anderson edited *CityArt* publications as part of her organizing Salt Lake City's longest-running literary reading series. Shaun Griffin continues to oversee publication of the literary magazine *Razor Wire*, featuring writing by inmates of the Nevada State Prison in Reno, where he's been teaching for many years. Tom Rea and his wife Barbara published Dooryard Press in Story, Wyoming, producing beautiful letterpress-printed volumes of poetry for eight years in the 1980s. And Gerald Costanzo has published scores of books as the longtime editor of Carnegie Mellon University Press's widely respected poetry series.

These poet-editors deserve a shout-out—where would poets be without them?

And a blast from the past . . .
Another highlight of this issue is a recently discovered, unpublished essay by Idaho novelist Vardis Fisher (1895-1968). Fisher's name probably means

EDITORS' NOTE

means little to readers outside Idaho and the West today. But he was Idaho's most prolific mid-20th century writer, authoring more than two dozen novels in his lifetime, perhaps best known for *Mountain Man*, the historical western that inspired the 1972 Hollywood movie *Jeremiah Johnson*, starring Robert Redford. Boise State University Library Special Collections archivist Alessandro Meregaglia is doing some great work in his research for a book about the history of the Caxton Press of Caldwell, Idaho, a publisher for more than a century of much Western Americana, and a series of novels over several decades by Fisher. In unearthing the publishing history of Caxton, Meregaglia found an unpublished 1930s WPA guide to the city of Boise written by Fisher (recently published by Boise's Rediscovered Books), as well as the essay by Fisher, written shortly before he died, that appears for the first time in this issue of *Limberlost*.

What's Next . . .
Between publication of the 2019 edition of *Limberlost* and this new one, we also produced a music CD by legendary Idaho folk musician John Thomsen—*John Thomsen & Friends: Songs from Loafer's Glory*. Despite decades of playing and collaborating and mentoring, John had never released his own CD, and as he crested his 80th year, we thought we should remedy that. Without over-rehearsing or any over-mixing, the result is a memorable jam that John is locally famous for. Read about it in the last pages of this issue and get your copy of the CD today.

Beyond this 2020 edition of the *Review*, Limberlost Press this year also will complete letterpress-printed, limited edition chapbooks of poetry by two poets who have work in this volume, Sherman Alexie and Annie Lampman. Sherman's *A Memory of Elephants* will be the fourth chapbook Limberlost has published by the National Book Award-winner since 1996. Annie's *Burning Time* will appear on the heels of her first novel that also will appear this year—a big year for Annie Lampman.

Next Deadline
The deadline for the next *Limberlost Review* is August 1, 2020. See what we're looking for on the "What's Next" page at the back of this volume. We're especially interested in some interesting "Re-Readings."

Onward!

— *Rick & Rosemary Ardinger*

LIMBERLOST LETTERPRESS

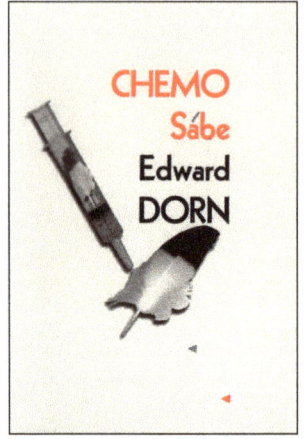

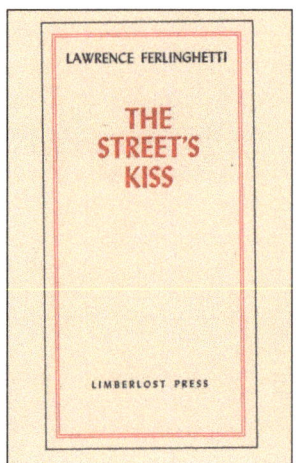

www.limberlostpress.com

POETRY & FICTION

Beckett in '51

Finally, when after many false-starts
Waiting For Godot began the rehearsals
                         for its first production
Beckett was there
arguing for this and that
        such as the stage set-up
& who Vladimir, Lucky, & shivery-w/-cold Estrogen
                                really were
Pozzo both director & Beckett agreed upon:
     he was an English gentleman farmer,
     hefting a case of wine bottles, and in a bowler hat

As for rehearsals Beckett wanted no observers
but the director convinced him to allow journalists
                              to visit now & then
so, as rehearsals progressed, there were
                          always viewers.
& a chain-smoking Beckett walked anxiously back & forth
           at the back of the theater
                during rehearsals

Heh heh, Beckett seemed to realize that if an actor
didn't really understand the play,
        then he would do whatever the playwright
                          told him to do!!

And then, before opening night, Beckett
retired to Ussy sur Marne
                to wait it out
—the first of his plays
     whose openings he deliberately missed

After the first rustle of its Thespis,
     Beckett, at 47,
          was "suddenly" famous.

E. S.
2-1-19

ED SANDERS

Beckett in '51

Finally, when after many false-starts
Waiting For Godot began the rehearsals
                          for its first production
Beckett was there
arguing for this and that
                such as the stage set-up
& who Vladimir, Lucky, & shivery-w/-cold Estrogen
                                      really were
Pozzo both director & Beckett agreed upon:
    he was an English gentleman farmer,
    hefting a case of wine bottles, and in a bowler hat

As for rehearsals Beckett wanted no observers
but the director convinced him to allow journalists
                              to visit now & then
so, as rehearsals progressed, there were
                        always viewers.
& a chain-smoking Beckett walked anxiously back & forth
              at the back of the theater
                          during rehearsals

Heh heh, Beckett seemed to realize that if an actor
didn't really understand the play,
            then he would do whatever the playwright
                                told him to do!!

And then, before opening night, Beckett
retired to Ussy sur Marne
                to wait it out
—the first of his plays
      whose openings he deliberately missed

After the first rustle of its Thespis,
        Beckett, at 47,
                was "suddenly" famous.

Ode to the Throwing Off of Debt
(Seisachtheía)

He came to power, Solon, about 600 BC
in a time of great debts & people
                        enslaved for debt
so Solon enacted the Seisachtheía
"the shaking-off of burdens"
nullified all debts
freed those who had been placed into slavery
                            to pay a debt
and he limited the amount of land
a person could own!

O, Forgiveness of Debts,
so Ancient, so New, so Now!
Ahh, let's do it again

O, shake off the mortgages!
Shake off the usurious credit card debts!
O Ghost of Solon, shake it!
shake that seisachtheía tambourine!!

All in an instant
(to prevent "shake-off scams")
annul mortgages, halt bankruptcy
then lift away
in one erasure
all debts & impoundments,

houndings by credit bureaus,
seizures by judges
dunning by electricity monopolies
trillions in so-called student "debts"

Lift away! Lift away!
O Ghost of Ancient Solon
No debtors' prisons
like in a
    Dickens novel
    such as "Little Dorrit"

Ahh! Lift away
    everyone's debts
on a regular schedule
    say every 6 years

Down with Usura
Break up the modern latifundia
    as Solon did!

Oh wipe away the evil-borne chalk
from the slate of Debt & Usura

O Ancient Shaker!

—Edward Sanders
2012-1018

Ode to the Throwing Off of Debt (Seisachtheía)

He came to power, Solon, about 600 BC
in a time of great debts & people
                        enslaved for debt
so Solon enacted the Seisachtheía
"the shaking-off of burdens"
nullified all debts
freed those who had been placed into slavery
                             to pay a debt
and he limited the amount of land
a person could own!

O, Forgiveness of Debts,
so Ancient, so New, so Now!
Ahh, let's do it again

O, shake off the mortgages!
Shake off the usurious credit card debts!
O Ghost of Solon, shake it!
Shake that seisachtheía tambourine!!

All in an instant
(to prevent "shake-off scams")
annul mortgages, halt bankruptcy
then lift away
in one erasure
all debts & impoundments,
houndings by credit bureaus,
seizures by judges
dunning by electricity monopolies
trillions in so-called student "debts"

ED SANDERS

Lift away! Lift away!
O Ghost of Ancient Solon
No debtors' prisons
like in a
        Dickens novel
           such as "Little Dorrit"

Ahh! Lift away
        everyone's debts
on a regular schedule
        say every 6 years

Down with Usura
Break up the modern latifundia
        as Solon did!

Oh wipe away the evil-borne chalk
from the slate of Debt & Usura

O Ancient Shaker!

Poem for Mother Mollie

I remember her making donuts
for my teenage friends
their hands and feet all cold from sledding down
                              Cemetery Hill
I remember how my mother created the
drum majorette attire for the
              high school marching band
& sewed for free
        the curtains for the new school cafeteria

I remember my father led the effort
to build that stadium for the high school
                  that stands to this day

I remember the orchards on Highway 7
                        at cider time
I remember the sparkling hill
    above the brick house
                  with its flashing stones

but most of all I remember my mother
(who designed the brick house)

I remember singing in the Glee Club
I remember the ups and downs and the angel sounds
I remember the thrilling times on Rabbit Road
I remember reading Ginsberg's "Howl"
to the bulls in Luther Hawes's field

I remember Larry Faeth in his '51 Chevy
driving us around the lonely streets
        with our flat-tops & duck tails

but most of all I remember my mother

I remember the broken piano hammers spread
on the living room rug, & my mother gluing them
and making the baby grand play again
so we could take lessons

I remember the yellow hedge apples in a driveway
            on Woods Chapel Road
I remember our victory garden by the cherry tree
I remember sneering at McCarthy
        with my mother
            during the phony Red Scare

but most of all I remember my mother

Mother Mollie, 1940s
with piano she repaired

Ed Sanders
2-15-19

Poem for Mother Mollie

I remember her making donuts
for my teenage friends
their hands and feet all cold from sledding down
                               Cemetery Hill
I remember how my mother created the
drum majorette attire for the
                               high school marching band
& sewed for free the curtains for the new school cafeteria

I remember my father led the effort
to build that stadium for the high school
                               that stands to this day

I remember the orchards on Highway 7 at cider time
I remember the sparkling hill
         above the brick house
                       with its flashing stones

but most of all I remember my mother
(who designed the brick house)

I remember singing together in the Glee Club
I remember the ups and downs and the angel sounds
I remember the thrilling times on Rabbit Road
I remember reading Ginsberg's "Howl"
to the bulls in Luther Hawes's field

I remember Larry Faeth in his '51 Chevy
driving us around the lonely streets
         with our flat-tops & duck tails
but most of all I remember my mother

ED SANDERS

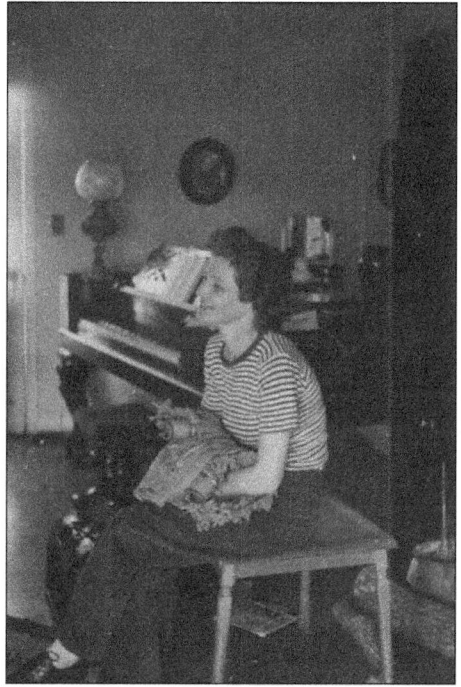

Mother Mollie, 1940s, with piano she repaired.

I remember the broken piano hammers spread
on the living room rug, & my mother gluing them
and making the baby grand play again
so we could take lessons

I remember the yellow hedge apples in a driveway
            on Woods Chapel Road
I remember our victory garden by the cherry tree
I remember sneering at McCarthy
        with my mother
             during the phony Red Scare

but most of all I remember my mother

"Mountain Rainbow" by Ray Obermayr. Oil on canvas, 19" x 24."

JENNIFER DUNBAR DORN

December 10, 2015

At Sloanes Lake today a goose swoops down over my head
honking its horn like a race car driver
or a bomber pilot making an emergency landing.
I think he's bearing a message from you, on the
anniversary of your death 16 years ago.
I come home and turn on the radio and there you are
reading poems on Joe's KGNU show,
your voice rings clear and strong until you get to
the last recording: "Sketches from Edgewater"
where like me now you start to weep
because you know you'll never be the old man
teasing Sheila at the checkout counter of what
used to be Cubs Food and now is Target
where I go afterwards to shop for new sheets.

I still sleep on my side of the bed where you
took your last breath and left through the skylight
even as I held you curled in my arms and
let you go into that dark night. Sometimes it seems
only yesterday, your sister breaking the silence
"I think he's gone," she said.
Your side long empty yet however
soft the down pillows
freshly dressed duvet, new sheets,
the spy glass in the roof above
brings the moon in on lonely nights
and you and my shadow haunt the banks
of the shimmering lake I walk around now
in the crack of the sun's last gleaming.

Crazy Horse
(after reading Mari Sandoz)

The rhythm of war changed after '68.
Until then fighting against the whites was
not so different from taking coup
or stealing horses from the Crow.
After '68 it dawned on Crazy Horse
that the old ways were dead
that a new kind of war was being waged
where there was killing every day, all the time
and no point in displaying subtleties of art:
now it was a question of survival.
The whites would come forever, digging
up the earth, laying immortal roads
buying up souls to save them from
falling into the pits they called hell,
slaughtering the buffalo.

There were no rituals for taking alcohol
no laws to protect against greed and lies
and nothing to save him from his sacred craziness:
a chief too wild and true to be trusted
who never let his picture be taken
for the files in Washington
or went to see the Great White Chief
to be decorated with top hat and cane
he was not one for vaudeville
even at home
he went to war without vermillion
only a stone behind his ear
a single feather in his loose hair.

DAVID LEE

Incident Based on a True Story Seen on Channel 7 Lubbock Evening News

Artists are here to disturb the peace
— James Baldwin

Harold Wheatley like Judas
thought he would go for a walk in his garden
being 80 acres of purdy good looking
August cotton on his birthday that morning
when he was struck on the very top metal button
of his Intermountain Farmers ball cap
cumpleanos gift from Ramon Martinez
who got it at a thrift store in Paragonah, Utah
by an ice ball falling out of the sky

Did it kill him any? sed Ollie McDougald
down at the Cotton Mill loading docks
Bobby Reid sed Killed him severely two days now
George Tillman sed he heard it was
a giant bluesky hail stone, a miracle
Hail ball made out of shit
sed Cephas Bilberry when it got through melting
I'll swan sed R. B. McCravey is that gospel truth?
That's what they say pure shit sed Cephas
pieces of corn in it you could still see
Busted his head open like a two penny party balloon
is what Dr. Tubbs sed in his own words
after the examination sed Travis Stribling
whose wife was the fatnurse at the hospital

We all agreed Rufus would have
a real hard time getting him reassembled
so there could be an open coffin funeral
we'd all have to get dressed up

and go see for ourselves
pictures being untasteful
therefore unlikely forthcoming
Harold would of done the same thing
in our place

2

Every airline from Lubbock to Dallas
to Albuquerque denied any flight
over the South Plains that morning
There was not at all no way
none of them could have had nothing
to do with it they were pure innocent
they would swear an oath to it
it must have been something picked up
by a careless tornado swooped
and held in the sky until it froze
then fell of its own violation and gravity
just bad luck he should of
stayed in bed that day
an act of God merciful in the suddenness

3

After the funeral the widow Mahoda sed
she was the unluckiest woman to ever live
and she didn't want to talk about it, but
now they would put it on the television
and then in the newspapers all over
with her picture of the grieving
all the rest of her life mired like a sow stuck sideways
in soured hogmud with the memory of being the wife
of the farmer killed by a thirteen pound turd
flushed out from a damn flying saucer
wandered off course and lost over the Llano Estacado

one hundred and eighty seven miles from the Roswell landing strip
undoubtedly accompanied by canned laugh track
when Jimmy Issacs the announcer sed her name
out loud on the six o'clock news showing her face
on the TV, not a thing she could do
but live with it, not one iota
to ever be thankful for the rest of her life
insurance barely even paid
for the funeral, goddammit
it was all just an embarrassment
a dammed crying shame

    Silver City, Nevada
    Thanksgiving Day, 2016

Monologue: Soft Focus Memory of Getting Drunk with a Scientist Who Actually Reads

Here are the data:

the half life
of a butter bean fart
is eleven hundred years
Now
if or when that figure
is bumped
by the factor of two Lone Star beers
the half life is not altered
but the velocity of impact
is increased by pi
to the tenth power

but I fear, amigo colleague of mine,
trying to impose advanced pedagogy
at this hour
is akin to catching piss in a basket
or moonlight with a fishnet

Nevertheless
I am ravished with admiration
for tonight's libation and discourse
while humiliated by the impossibility
of holding that same piss in
all night or attempting
to sleep in a hurried squatch
as I have a nine o'clock tomorrow
which will require an exuberant lecture
one of my self-reproducing
cyclical and incestual peccadillos
to stimulate young minds
to the Olympian heights of splendipity
in full knowledge

DAVID LEE

that I have been
a bell with a loose clapper
pealing at the incessant rate
of 768 miles per hour
or in a confined area
4.689 miles per second,
a grandfather clock stuck
on the perpetual monotony of twelve
a sot howling like a troglodyte
at the full moon

ergo now you must
push me out the door
and point me toward home
I will fall in that direction
at the speed of 32 feet per second squared
or prepare thyself
for permanent adoption
to the footsteps of infinity
of a pound dog genetic mongrel
of unidentifiable DNA

Good night sweet prince
and angels waft thee
as I make my way into dark matter
and the extreme possibility of black hole

Please call my lovely wife
tell her not to pay the ransom
I have escaped
and am in the tesseracting modum
turn on the goddam porchlight
which will broadcast its presence
at the velocity of 186,000 miles per second
I am coming, Dear!
Lead me gently home, Father
Prepare for re-entry and touchdown

"McConnell's Wheel Line" by Nancy Brossman. Linoleum block print, 6" x 9."

JUDITH FREEMAN

Wyatt & Hela

Editor's Note: *The following is an excerpt from* The White Mules, *a novel-in-progress.*

He woke up much later than usual, and now he was sitting in the shade just outside the back door of his house on a bench facing the creek, looking through the mail that had accumulated in his mailbox during the week that he'd been away.

There was a letter from his cousin Benny who still lived on the reservation, telling him of the annual reunion of the Intermountain Indian School where he and Benny had spent their junior high and high school years as boarding students, housed along with hundreds of other Navajo kids in the barrack-style buildings set up against the mountains near Brigham City, Utah. *You should come down for it,* Benny wrote, *it's going to be a great reunion and you can stay with us in the trailer and we'll all drive over to Wheatfields Lake together.*

He would not be going to the Indian School reunion, or seeing Benny, or driving with him over to Wheatfields Lake which, as he remembered it from the last and only time he ever attended a reunion there, had become one of the most depressed places on the reservation—and that was saying a lot. He'd have to come up with some excuse for why he couldn't come even though Benny would probably see through it. He put the letter aside and continued sorting through the mail. Utility bills, a plea from the local library for a donation, a postcard from his clients in Missoula thanking him for the willow chairs he'd just delivered. When he'd looked through all the letters and bills he opened up the latest issue of the weekly paper, *The Prairie Courier*. It was even thinner than usual—only six pages, three of them filled with obituaries. He read about the 5th District High School Rodeo taking place over the weekend in Cary and a cowboy tent revival meeting on Sunday, to be held in a field south of town. He briefly considered the ad for the old time fiddlers' convention in Shoshone and wondered if Hela might be interested in driving down with him for that.

He liked fiddle music. He decided he'd call her later and float the idea. He looked at the *Senior Center News*, not that he ever went to the center but he liked to peruse the menus listing what they served every week just to see what he was missing (fish sticks, beef stroganoff, potato bar, banana pudding, and something called Frogeye Dessert, whatever that was. He wouldn't have minded the banana pudding).

He noticed the new ad for North Canyon Rehabilitation Center in Gooding where he'd gone for therapy after the doctors had taken his left foot off last year, the result of his battle with diabetes. The ad showed a picture of a man who looked like a young Robert Redford being helped by a woman who looked a lot like Ali McGraw who was tenderly holding his arm and looking up at him. Not the kind of people he'd encountered, though his therapist, Nancy, had certainly been nice enough even if she did resemble Kathy Bates more than Ali McGraw. They'd been good to him there. He couldn't complain. He scanned an announcement for the 99th Annual Pioneer Picnic in the park—he wouldn't be going to that either—and then he read the 4-H News and the report of the last meeting of the Porky Pigs 4H Club: *Everyone was present. Kylie, Connor, Rayann and Cheyane did demonstrations. Kylie did hers on "How to Build a Pig Pen." Connor did his on "Pig Breeds." Rayann did hers on "How to inject a pig." And Cheyane did hers on "Things you can Wash your Pig with." We weighed our pigs and walked them. After that we had hotdogs and chips—yum, yum. The next meeting is July 11 at the 4-H park.*

He liked that *yum yum*. It made him smile. He wondered what exactly it was that you could wash a pig with.

There was nothing else in the paper to read except the minutes of the county commissioners meeting and he wasn't that desperate. He folded up the paper and put it on top of the pile he used to light fires.

He'd returned late the night before from a trip up to Montana and what he'd been thinking about as he drove back into Idaho via Swan Valley and Idaho Falls was just how different Montana was from Idaho. Heading up there, he'd gone over Chief Joseph Pass and dropped down into the Bitterroot Valley and entered a lush paradise, a world of rivers and thick forests, tall trees and little meadows pocked with ponds, water everywhere, flowing in clear streams and pooling alongside the road beneath the peaks still patchy with slubs of old snow, the whiteness standing out against the deep blue sky. Near Darby, the ridges of the Bitterroots had looked as sharp as pencil tips and in other places they formed massive granite plinths that rose almost vertically from the lower slopes. It seemed a world different in all ways than the landscape he'd left behind, with its treeless dry hills in hues of red and orange, the arid sagebrush valleys and sandstone scarps and the rock slides that came down to the edge of the road between Challis and Salmon where he'd driven along the River of No Return, following the same route once used by Lewis and Clark. Just south of Salmon he'd seen four bighorn sheep right next to the road—a buck and three ewes—foraging peacefully along the banks of the river and he'd pulled over in the truck and sat for a long while just watching them as they ate, occasionally lifting their heads to study him in return. The only trees in sight had been the blackened stumps of lightning-struck pines and little snags rising out of rocky crevices and the clumps of stunted yellow pines with their tops flattened by the heavy winter snows. The landscape had given off a terrible heat.

Then, Montana. So green and wet and piney, a beauty not to be found in southern Idaho with its high prairies and desiccated valleys— or not at least to be found in the parts he'd traveled through. In Challis he'd stopped at a café and flirted with a waitress half his age, a girl in skimpy denim shorts and a cropped halter top that revealed a belly-button ring, and she had played along with him for a while which lifted his spirits considerably. The trip had taken him in a big circle, from the prairie up through Sun Valley and over Trail Creek pass which was only open in the summer months, along the Lost River range and past Mount Borah, the highest peak in Idaho, and through Challis and Salmon into Montana. He'd delivered the chairs he'd made, a pair of willow rockers he'd worked on for the past several months. Then he'd spent the night in Missoula in a played-out motel and left the next morning at sunrise and made his way down through Yellowstone Park, its narrow roads clogged with dawdling Winnebagos, and dropped off two more chairs to clients in Jackson Hole before finally heading home across the Arco plain, the most desolate place he encountered on the entire trip, where in the 1950s the government had built fifty-two nuclear reactions amidst the spent cones of ancient cinder volcanoes, a landscape that appeared prehistoric in its emptiness. It was almost one a.m. when he'd pulled into his driveway, his headlights sweeping across the corral where he kept his mule Alfred and he was glad to see Alfred standing at the rail in the darkness, his big ears swiveling slightly as he watched him pull in, as if he'd been there for days, just waiting for him to come home.

The weather felt unsettled, like it might rain before the day was through but at this time of year it never rained that hard. There was a great depth to the sky this morning—a sense of a fractured dimension, one layer and then another layer of clouds stacked and sequenced and parting here and there to reveal a swath of blue and the beautiful infinity that lay beyond. The word *heaven* came to mind: he felt as if he were looking beyond the ordinary sky into the hallowed above. An old-timer had once said to him that in Idaho there were five skies every day. Five different skies, always in flux, never staying the same as the day progressed. It seemed to him this was true. And this was just the first of today.

He had begun to think about making another pot of coffee and getting some breakfast together when the phone rang. He thought if he just let it ring long enough it would stop but it did not stop and he finally realized he'd have to go inside and answer it since he had no longer had an answering machine to pick up for him. By and large he didn't care much for machines and owned as few as possible, limiting himself to those he considered essential, like his '69 Chevy pickup, painted forest service green, and the even older Indian motorcycle sitting out in the shed, waiting for repairs.

He headed inside, leaning on his homemade crutch and hopping on one foot since he'd not yet taken the time to attach the artificial one, and crossed to where the phone hung on the wall and picked up the receiver and said, Yup?

Wyatt? That you?

This amused him. Who else would it be? No one else lived at this number.

Who's this? he asked, which seemed the far more pertinent question.

It's Delbert, the voice said, then added, you know, J.R. This, too, amused him. His rancher neighbor Delbert, who sometimes called himself J.R. when he wasn't calling himself Delbert.

Oh Delbert-J.R., he said. Which should I call you today?

I think I'll call you Delbert because J.R. makes me think of that guy on the TV program with the big white cowboy hat and I have never seen you wear anything but a big brown cowboy hat. What can I do for you this morning, Delbert?

He spoke slowly and with a certain cadence, using his exaggerated Indian voice, just for fun.

Delbert, who had no sense of humor as Wyatt had long ago discovered, got straight to the point. He began explaining why he was calling. He spoke in what Wyatt thought of as his grave buckaroo voice, extra solemn but with an exaggerated twang. Here they were, Indian talking to cowboy.

Delbert said he'd just gotten a call that morning from a guy at an organization called the Make-A-Wish Foundation, a non-profit group that helped terminally ill kids realize a final wish. There was a fifteen-year-old boy with late-stage cancer who would be arriving in town sometime in the next few days, along with his parents, and staying in the local motel. The Make-A-Wish Foundation had arranged everything and they were paying for the trip but they needed some local volunteers with expertise to help them out and since Delbert was the president of the Chamber of Commerce they'd come to him. Delbert said he was trying to line up a few neighbors to work with the kid to try and help him realize his life-long dream and he was hoping that Wyatt would, as he put it, get on board.

And what would that dream be? Wyatt asked. He yawned loudly to let Delbert know he was very, very tired.

The boy's a hunter, Delbert said, and it's his dream to shoot a cougar before he dies.

Shoot a cougar? Wyatt asked, feeling suddenly more awake. He thought perhaps he had heard him wrong.

Yeah. That's right.

So the thing this boy would like to do before he dies is to kill something else? This is a strange wish, don't you think.

Well it's what he wants to do.

Has anyone tried to talk him out of it? Wouldn't he instead like to maybe meet a famous baseball player or go to Disney World and get all the free rides he wants rather than take the life of a beautiful cat?

Well the kid's a hunter so I can understand it. You gotta look at it from his perspective, Delbert said.

I don't think I own that perspective. You know us Indians, we got bad eyesight. That's why the government gives us free glasses. So we can see what you see. Heh heh.

Delbert made a little strangled attempt at laughter but squeezed it off fast.

The thing is, he said, Bill Daniels told me you mentioned to him that a cougar has been hanging around your place. This might be your chance to get rid of it.

What if I don't want to get rid of it? What if I think it's okay for a cougar to share this place of mine with me if he feels like it?

There was a silence on the other end of the line. By now Wyatt had gotten tired of standing on one foot: he'd drawn up a chair before the window that looked north toward Fricky Creek. This time of year the hills were red and green. Later they turned yellow brown. He liked the red green better.

I wouldn't think anyone would want a cougar hanging around their place.

No it's true I wouldn't think you wouldn't think that either. Wyatt held the phone away from his ear and made a face at the receiver then pressed it to his ear again and said, So Delbert, I guess what you are asking is if this boy can come onto my land and shoot my cougar.

Well it ain't exactly your cougar—

Yes yes you're right. This cougar doesn't belong to anyone but it just happens to like being near my place so I guess maybe that makes us kind of like family.

I heard it killed your cat.

Well it's true my cat has gone missing so maybe it was the cougar that got it but we have no proof that the big cat ate the little cat so we can't kill him for that.

I heard he's been hanging around your haystacks.

I think he likes the mice that live between the bales. *Yum yum,* he thought.

Well since Bill Daniels and I have both given the kid permission to hunt on our land and since your land is in between ours it only makes sense that we work together on this deal, especially since we know a cougar is here, in the area. I mean I think it's a thing we could do for this boy, don't you? Since apparently he doesn't have that long to live. And anyways, who knows if he'll actually be able to bag a cougar. It's not the easiest thing to do as you know. But if a fellow wanted to he could help give this boy a chance.

I'll have to think about this, Delbert.

You do that and let me know. We got a couple of other guys lined up to help us. The boy's dad apparently is a good hunter, and if there are four or five others out there working with the kid, maybe…well…maybe it could come out right.

When did you say he's coming?

Next couple of days. Don't have an exact date but I can let you know.

You do that.

Wyatt got ready to hang up the phone but before he could, Delbert said, I guess you heard about Len Peterson. It's a terrible deal.

No I haven't heard anything about Len Peterson. I've been away a few days, just got home last night.

Well he was killed a few days ago up at his golf course by some crazy kid he'd hired to help him put in a sprinkling system. Kid beat him to death with a shovel then took off toward the creek. Monty and the others are out looking for him, they figure he headed up Soldier Creek. They've been organizing different search parties and some of us are taking our horses into the hills to give him a hand. There's a meeting this afternoon at the senior center. Three o'clock. If you have any interest.

Wyatt sighed. This was terrible news. Len Peterson had not been a close friend but nevertheless he had liked him well enough. This was way too much strange news to come home to—that a dying boy wanted to kill a cougar, that a crazy boy had already killed a man.

Well I gotta run, Wyatt, Delbert said. I'll be in touch about this other deal.

Goodbye, Delbert, Wyatt said with exaggerated politeness. It suddenly felt that politeness might be a necessary means of getting through this day.

He dressed and made coffee and looked for something to fix for breakfast but all he could come up with was a package of Ramen soup and some peanut butter and crackers. The canned beets didn't count: who could eat beets for breakfast?

It was definitely time for a trip to Twin Falls to do some shopping. He felt suddenly cranky to think he'd let himself run so low on groceries but then he reminded himself that he'd needed to get paid for the chairs before he could do much of anything, which is why he'd taken the trip, so he could deliver them personally and get the cash in hand m*uy pronto*. It was also true that he didn't like shopping and tended to put it off. Life without a woman to temper your shortcomings was difficult. During his last marriage, to a mixed-blood Sho-Ban from Fort Hall named Winnie Dupree, he'd counted on her to do all the shopping and he'd gotten used to the idea groceries were simply something that materialized when you needed them, always there when you wanted to fix a meal. Not that he ever did the cooking himself. After Winnie left it had come as a great shock to him to realize that he'd have to shop for himself now or he'd have nothing to eat. It turned out he had no aptitude at all for this task. First of all he'd been stunned by the prices of things. How could a package of bacon cost over five bucks, or a block of Gruyere, his favorite cheese, run to nearly eight?

He'd go to the grocery store in the Wood River Valley and blow eighty or ninety bucks and come home with one or two paper bags and find he didn't have anything he knew how to make a meal out of. He'd never been a cook and he didn't know how to become one. During those first few months after Winnie left there had been some pretty disgusting attempts at dinners—undercooked chicken and overcooked rice, mushy vegetables and rubbery chops, until something had happened to change the course of things.

It was Hela who'd finally stepped in and helped him. This was maybe six months after Winnie had left. Hela had not only taught him how to shop but how to fix simple and tasty meals, as well as how to make his money go farther at the grocery store. He had not known her well at this time. She and her husband Phil lived less than a mile away but for all he socialized with his neighbors they might as well have lived in Tasmania.

It was the work on the anti-trapping initiative that had brought them together. Her dog, a little Sealyham Terrier, had been caught in a steel trap set out on public land while they were hiking in the national forest near Couch Summit and she had been unable to free him and had to leave him there for several hours while she hiked out and got help. The dog's leg was crushed and had to be amputated but by then he'd lost so much blood he never recovered and he died shortly after the surgery. She'd become so outraged at the idea that anyone could set out traps for anything, anywhere, at any time without regard for which animals might be caught or the suffering they'd inevitably endure that she had undertaken a campaign to outlaw all trapping on public lands in the state. Since Idaho was about eighty percent public land she felt this would solve a large part of the problem. But what she hadn't reckoned on, what she didn't understand as an outsider—-and not just an outsider but a foreigner—-is how her campaign would backfire, how the good old boys would band together to see that no woman and her pack of bleeding-heart cohorts were going to tell them what they could kill, or where they could kill it, and especially not how they could kill it, because to them killing was not only their God-given right but one of their very favorite forms of recreation. Of course the initiative hadn't passed: instead an amendment had been proposed to the Idaho constitution guaranteeing every citizen the right to set out steel-jawed traps on public lands.

Still, it was the poster she'd made showing a red fox caught in a steel-toothed trap that had gotten his attention when he saw it tacked up on the post office bulletin board. The fox had chewed off part of its hind leg in an attempt to get free. He'd stood in front of the picture for a long while, looking at the little fox whose eyes gazed out from the photo as if asking him for help. He'd written down the phone number on the poster and the next week he'd gone to the meeting at Hela's house—the first meeting she'd called about the initiative. Counting her husband, there were only seven people there—two of them high school students who believed in her cause but were still too young to vote. He knew then there wasn't a chance in hell her initiative would get any support. Still he'd been struck by her commitment, by the way she spoke about the cruelty of such traps, how the so-called hunters often never even bothered to check their traps with any frequency so that the animals died slow and terrible deaths and the carcasses were often simply left to rot. She talked about the moral obligation to act on one's principles, and the importance of standing up for what one believed was right and just even when the odds were stacked against you. She said that one measure of a civilization was how it treated its animals, and in that regard she felt the United States had a long way to go.

He felt a powerful moral presence as he listened to her talk. Had she been Navajo, she would have been the matriarch of a clan. She was cool, unemotional, yet he could feel the conviction and passion in her words. She never raised her voice. She didn't need to. She didn't become sentimental about what happened to the animals caught in the traps, not even when she spoke about her own dog, but instead addressed the issue with a kind of cold logic that emphasized the cruelty, the terrible suffering, the immorality of it all. He felt he'd never been around a woman like her. For one thing she was so tall she towered above him—and he was not a small man—and her German accent and proper bearing conveyed a dignity and quiet authority he initially found intimidating. He thought she was a handsome woman, not beautiful, definitely not that, but nice looking: he admired the way she dressed so simply in tailored pants and sweaters that looked as if she had knit them herself. She often had a pretty scarf around her neck. Everything about her was neat—her short gray hair, her clear face, and smooth skin. When she looked at you with her blue eyes she really *looked* at you, the way birds do. She was no longer young but he found her attractive anyway, even though he guessed she was close to seventy, at least fifteen years older than he was. He was drawn to her in a very strong way. From that first meeting he knew she was someone he wanted to be around, someone he felt he *needed* to be around. He was still drinking then and smoking dope. His life had gone downhill after Winnie left—it was Winnie who'd gotten him back into the weed again in the first place and it had helped to ease her absence once he was alone.

But lately, the truth is he'd begun to feel he was losing whatever hope he'd once held for his future. Only Hela had been able to help dispel the darkness by simply agreeing to spend so much time with him.

He no longer even knew who he was. A Navajo who couldn't return to his reservation. A fish out of water, an Indian in an all-white world, a one-footed creature. He had turned his back on his family and on all that had formed him, especially that place where he had been raised with so many unhappy memories. He felt the reservation was by and large a death trap, a gulag, a place of great sickness and no future.

He knew his own relatives disagreed with him, as did his friends who stayed on the reservation: they found his views heretical. They said he should be ashamed (and he was ashamed, no question, but still it was how he felt). For them the land was everything. How could he not see that? Without their ancestral land they had nothing: without their ties to the land of their ancestors they would disperse and become no more. But what he saw was overgrazed wastelands and poverty, children addicted to drugs and video games and violent movies, kids with drooping pants who had no interest in their culture but instead embraced gangsta rap, adults senseless with alcohol and dope, an unemployment rate that staggered the mind, lethargy, idleness, suicide and despair, a high school graduation rate of thirty percent, domestic violence, premature death. And so much fucking unhappiness.

And yet he knew his relatives were right, that he was seeing it only one way—*the bad way*—and that without the ancestral connections, without the land, without the tribe and the clan and the family and the community, he was lost. For a long while he had wanted to be lost. It seemed the best place to be, the place where no one would bother him anymore. Where he could be nothing. Where there was no one left to care about him, or for that matter, to care for him.

And then he met Hela, and he began to see himself differently. He found he could look at himself the way she might look at him and he didn't like what he saw. He didn't want her to see him as a loser even though he felt like one, even though he knew he was one. He wanted her to see his intelligence and dignity and his strength, his warrior *Dine* strength, and to do this he knew he would need to change because he no longer possessed those things in any great measure or at least he could not feel them in himself and nor could he make them visible. He would need some of her strength to change himself into a better person—in short he needed some of her power.

In the beginning, he thought if he spent enough time near her some of her strength and power might rub off on him. And it had. In some strange way it had. When he was with her he remembered why he had loved going to school. Why he hadn't minded being sent away from the reservation as a boy to live in the cold barracks in a distant place populated by white Mormons, with white teachers, required to adapt to their white world, studying both their white books and their white thinking, though later people would often pity him for being forced to do this thing. They didn't understand how he had loved those books. Those ideas they exposed him to. With Hela it was like going to school again. Once more he had found someone with whom he could discuss books and ideas. He discovered it really was much better to spend an afternoon walking down old stream beds with her (limping in his case), chatting, looking for arrowheads and glassing birds, rather than drinking himself into a stupor after a day of smoking dope. She seemed to give him something back that had been drained from him many years earlier when he had been fired from the only job he ever truly loved, teaching literature to high school kids, one of whom he'd made the fatal mistake of getting pregnant. For a long time he had thought he was finished. And then Hela, offering a new beginning.

He could call her now. It was possible she might invite him to come for lunch, as she often did. She might want to hear about his trip to Montana. He wanted to talk to her about Len Peterson's death. And about the boy with cancer who wanted to shoot the cougar. He didn't quite know how to think about these things. Yes, he needed to talk with her. He'd missed her this past week. Maybe she would even want to make the drive to Twin with him to do some grocery shopping. Or head to Shoshone on the weekend and listen to the old-time fiddlers.

He picked up the phone and dialed her number but he got only her voice on an answering machine. The thick German accent. The polite voice asking him to leave a message. The disappointment felt heavy.

He made the ramen and ate it along with crackers and peanut butter and felt satisfied he would not need to eat again until dinner. He found some frozen chicken breasts in the freezer and took those out so he'd have something to cook later. He cut some lettuce in his garden while it was still cool and it had not yet wilted and he cleaned that and put it away in the fridge. He saw the zucchini had begun to come on in his absence and picked two small ones. The garden was dry and he set out a sprinkler and then he got the wheelbarrow and loaded it with hay for Alfred.

Mules had been his passion for years. He had bred them and raised them and trained them and sold them. For a while it had been how he and Minnie had made a living, sorry as it was. That and her part-time job as a cashier at the market in town and the weed she sold on the side. Now all the mules were gone, only Alfred left. He'd sold off the two young white mules several years ago when he'd needed the money after the divorce. Gotten good prices for them too. A good riding mule wasn't that easy to come by and people were willing to pay real money for one. His neighbor Bill Daniels had bought the white pair and it had not been easy to let them go but Bill had given him a high price because they were so well trained. Trained to pull, and trained to ride. Mules you could trust if you knew how to treat them. He'd stayed drunk for three days after Daniels picked up those mules and took them away. Daniels had offered to buy Alfred as well but he could not ever sell him. Alfred was his one true friend and he would be until the day one of them died. He was the most intelligent mule he'd ever owned and he'd owned some very smart ones. His bond with that animal was something he could never have explained to anyone and would never have tried to. He felt that if he ever let Alfred go, a great hole would open up and this place where he lived would feel completely forlorn and so would his life. With Alfred to feed each day and look after, he never actually felt alone, though he almost always felt lonely.

The mule was waiting for him at the gate. He was a large mule with distinctive markings, a *gruillo* with a dark stripe running down his back intersected by another spanning his shoulders, as handsome a mule as you could find. He stood for a moment stroking Alfred's muzzle and then he massaged the place just beneath his eyes, the spot where mules loved to be rubbed, and Albert half closed his eyes with pleasure and let his lower lip droop, relaxing into his touch. He did not know what he would do when Alfred died, but he didn't have to worry about that for a while. Mules generally lived much longer than horses, sometimes reaching the grand age of 40. Cared for properly, Alfred might be expected to last longer than he would.

He threw the hay into the manger and filled up the water trough and then headed back to the house. He thought he'd give Hela another try. He hoped very much that this time he might find her at home. ■

"Magpie" by Greg Keeler. Acrylic on canvas board, 5" x 7."

ROBERT DEMOTT

Christmas Triptych, with Birds
— for Kate, always

I. Chickadees

Years ago, at dusk on Christmas Eve
in those few minutes of day left before loved ones
arrived for evening's ritual of giving and getting,
I walked outside, under a woolen batt of sky,
and hauled buckets of bird seed
to fill each feeder in our woodsy backyard—
black oil sunflower for one, thistle for another,
millett and pumpkin seed for a third. You
get the drift: I was spreading good cheer
as I dipped and ladled at each station
along my route, carefully stopping here and there
to sweep away empty seed husks and corn cobs
left by marauding crows and squirrels,
for once asking nothing for myself, when,
out of deepening shadows and *tick-tick* of falling sleet,
a pair of black-capped chickadees, dressed to the nines
in stylish evening garb, lit on my bare hand,
pecked seed from its open palm, and were gone. Friends,
they were so close, in that mindless moment, I swear
I heard only the thrum of their pistoned hearts,
but it has always been enough.

II. Cardinals

Afternoon of another waning year,
with dusk coming early and deepening fast,
my love and I trimmed front porch greens,
hung cheery lights and gayly striped ribbons
put up our share of bright bows and lacy tinsel,
draped our Christmas tree with shiny doo-dads
stored in our attic since last time, all the while
caroling giddily as we decked our halls in finery,
fal lal la, we sang, *fal lal la, 'tis the season*....
Then, just when we could not imagine more joy,
hosannas of birds—that's the right term, I hope—
chickadees, juncos, nuthatches, wrens, robins,
a whole gang of sprightly denizens,
swooshed in from nearby woods and fields
to feast on winter's banquet at our yard's edge:
scarlet holly berries, blue-black pearls of sour gum,
and those clustered morsels of bittersweet,
their orange globes shedding fractal light
on a pair of Northern cardinals, birds of soulful folklore,
visiting spirits of those we once loved and lost,
each an ornament aflame on bare limbs of shrubs,
there among fruitfall and a dust of snow.

ROBERT DEMOTT

III. Owls

Now, in deepening shades of rose and magenta,
evening steals across Appalachian foothills
in this tucked-away corner of Ohio we call home,
and a slivered moon, like a nail filing,
catches itself in the rude limbs of backyard trees
where last night in our grove of pines and oaks
a pair of great horned owls kept up their *hoo-hooing*,
the steady beat, beat of their bass drum carrying well beyond
our wrapping of presents and offerings of holiday cheer,
finally echoing at the margins of our sleep,
that moment before the moment after,
when the last stirrings of children in our house—
eager for what they hope dawn will bring—
settled to quiet and my love and I entered at last
a room inside a room, where we wondered
whether our life on earth was ever truly blessed
or only a brief dream, fearful and uncertain,
borne inward by a draft of chill wind
through an open window and more news
from our feathered pair, their dirge sent
across oceanic distances and blue-black star roads
this night of all nights, in this year like no other,
toward us, toward you.

"Family Album," No. 1 and No. 2 by Alberta Mayo. Gel pen on sketchbook black paper.

RON McFARLAND

Music before Dinner
— for Anna Fedorova

Just caught a black-and-white photo of the composer
Sergei Rachmaninoff out the corner of my eye,
and I noticed at once how thin-faced and bleak he looked
under his fedora, eyes expressively hollow,
his ears projected like a pair of jug handles but
not comical, more like absurd, like ears gone Dada
at the verge of the Movement and the Revolution.

His lips are turned down, perhaps contemplating his flight
from Mother Russia—he's in his forties but appears
much older and has not yet composed his *Rhapsody
on a Theme of Paganini*, which will cheer him up
temporarily.
                And this happened this afternoon
on the "light classical" music channel amid a
daylong snow, one of those fleecy events that look so
pleasant until you finally pick up your shovel.

When the phone rang, I informed whoever it was we'd
made plans for the evening, though I had nothing in mind.
The great composer's depression had proved infectious.
In the next room one of my wife's piano students
punished the F-sharp minor scale.
                The young Ukrainian pianist
closes her gray-green eyes and dreams of winter in Kiev.

Lost Knife

To him or her who found my fishing knife
Among the rocks and stones beside Priest River
Twenty-some miles west of Sandpoint, Idaho,
Please know that now I don't resent your luck,
Although I would have forty years ago
When eager rainbows battened on my flies
That fast fading afternoon, dazzling me.
They loved the Adams and the Renegade,
And I repaid their passion with my blade,
Slitting the largest pair from jaw to vent.
When was it that I yielded to my lust,
Abandoned common sense and left my knife
Among those stones where you have come upon it?
Don't cut yourself. It's awfully sharp, my friend.

JUDITH ROOT

Fireworks in June

Huge balls of light, seeded red and green,
explode, throw a line of palms into relief.
Heading for my window, they fall short behind
the hill, then rise as if they're starting
over, like water circling and spouting
in a city park fountain. I promised Michael
I'd check on you while he visited his parents
in Wyoming, far from your
disease, the constant feeding of its needs.

But these lights hold me to the window.
If I stop looking, they might leave the night
sky, move down the bay to Hayward, Fremont,
maybe San Jose, or inland farther south
to Gilroy, capital of garlic, whose blooming
heads, like these lights, burst and scatter
in the air. Or on to San Luis Obispo, past
fields of zebra to San Simeon, where even now,
glitter is a necessary part of daily life.

Here in Oakland, as everywhere in America,
it is too early for fireworks, too far away
to hear the whisper of a fuse. And you
at twenty-four are growing faster than the season
into your September death. I make the call.
Groggy but pleased, you bring up summer
reruns, a high school friend who stopped
to show you his new bike. I imagine its
leather seat throwing the streetlight's glare
back up and beyond. You ask questions that
keep me chatting until the cloud layer
catches red, spreads across the horizon like
a desert sunset or a forest fire out of control.
It will be at least a month before your talk

centers on disease, the way it's moved in
and taken over, every five lesions that slash
your face and neck, a sign of one more inside
where they can't be burned off, their numbers
greater than your age, or mine, though I am
old enough to be your mother. I have nothing
to tell you except that the sky is quiet now,
but sometimes I can see a star or the red blip
of a plane gaining altitude before it slides
behind clouds where I know it follows lights
that edge the bay to open sea, then moves on
out of sight.

JUDITH ROOT

Sunbathers at Mendenhall Glacier

In tiny swimsuits they sit on postage stamp
towels below an icefield bigger and whiter
than Rhode Island, as empty of culture
as the lookout parking lot where we watch
through a coin-operated telescope, a glass
they grow in until, like us, they're real.

A hand waving across the lake can pull reality
into the circle where one guy stamps
out a bossa-nova and gets in return our glassy-
eyed stare. To bring them close, we need a wide
lens, a zoom that tightens on the eye watching
us. If we let them blur to a culture

of rods and spheres, we'll be like cultural
anthropologists pondering rituals to reel
in a theory that salmon move the glacier watching
over the sunbathers like a mother who's stamped
them with defective genes. Maybe the sun, white
in the noon sky, warming the figures in our glass,

will melt the wall of blue ice, and panels of glass
will thunder and crack, breaking the cultural
barrier deep inside. The noise now is white.
No chunks calve, then drop into the lake, reeling.
To the sunbathers, though, danger's a handstamp
at a roving, illegal dance. So we listen and watch

the glacier's face as if someone's set it like a watch
we could stop and so stop time, hold it in the glass
until the tiny figures are safe from stampeding
ice, from nature's threats to anyone in our culture
who tests limits, who takes chances with reality.
Ice plunges in our minds—the water rising white

as a dream engulfs the sunbathers in the last white
water they'll ever see, a denoument we'll watch
in reruns all our lives—unless the wave takes us, real
people, not that far from them, as well. Our glass
will not protect us then, nor art nor culture
nor any manmade barrier to fate's indifferent stamp.

Ice retreating thirty feet a year whitewashes the glass
future generations will watch for clues to our culture
where the real heroes never appear on stamps.

JOHN REMBER

Getting Wood

I

Near the end of his life, my father told me if you have one good friend when you die, you're lucky.

We were out by his woodpile, which I had just cut and stacked in time for winter. There were ten cords in it, half of it in a shed I had built to keep the wood dry, half of it in a lean-to built against the shed, which my father had paid a contractor to have constructed. I had refused to build the lean-to because my parents, since they had installed a catalytic wood stove, had never gone through even five cords in a winter. When the lean-to had been completed and paid for—it had cost him considerably more than the shed—I told him he had come down with Old-Man-Can't-Get-Enough-Wood Syndrome.

I had more or less guaranteed I was going to be the one who filled the lean-to. If I expressed any more doubts about the project, he would put his chainsaw in his pickup and head into the woods for five cords of wood or a heart attack, whichever came first.

Over the next month, I felled dead standing trees, cut them into eight-foot logs, put them in the pickup, unloaded them near the lean-to, sawed them into blocks, and stacked them in under the slanting roof. You could see that the full lean-to pleased my father. It gave him agency in this world, even if I was his agent.

I didn't mind being his agent, because going out for an afternoon and cutting a cord of wood, loading it up and driving it home is a good way to demonstrate that even agents have agency, even if the agent in question has just spent more money and energy in saw and pickup gas than he brought home in firewood.

Keeping warm all winter wasn't the point.

The lean-to looked better full of wood than it had empty. I pointed this out to my father, thinking that if I praised its aesthetics he might wait a couple of years before deciding he needed fifteen cords instead of ten. If and when that happened, I would tell him that a lean-to tacked onto a lean-to would look ridiculous, all the while hoping he wouldn't think of the Sydney Opera House.

That was when he told me about being lucky to have one good friend.

"I'll be your friend," I said. "That way you can have two instead of one."

"Kids don't count," he said. "Kids have to be your friend."

I didn't point out the empirical falsity of his statement. Lots of his friends had died estranged from angry children. Those children, with successful careers and children of their own, were invariably reduced to helpless inarticulate fury when they occupied the same room with their parents. Not a few of them, as time had gone on, had reversed those bitter relationships and had become their demented parents' parents. In either case, what should have been dialog had become static and angry ritual.

I wasn't angry at either of my parents. I admired their courage and cheerfulness in the face of decrepitude. They appreciated their woodpile, and my efforts on its behalf.

They seemed to like my company, and I liked theirs. Even if I didn't count as a friend, I was still a friend.

The woodpile was only a part of it. We had conversations instead of talking-past-each-other shouting matches. We talked about my parents' disappointment that I hadn't given them grandchildren, my discontent with my envied-but-not-enviable job as a professor at a small college, their dismay and disbelief when George W. Bush was elected, their conviction that our country, at that moment, had betrayed its promise, and their worry that my career unhappiness indicated that I had betrayed my promise as well.

It's possible that I mistook their willingness to talk for empathy. My career unhappiness had taken the form of a morbid fascination toward my faculty colleagues, who seemed to have become the walking-around-dead. They had used good minds and good educations to turn their lives to routine rather than take the risk of reinventing themselves. They lived within the walls of their imaginations rather than looking at the beauty and tragedy of the world. To all appearances, they had decided their lives were complete the moment they had received tenure. Degrees and tenure and a full professorship hadn't completed me, and I didn't see how they could complete anyone else. I didn't have these words at the time. I just thought my colleagues had betrayed their promise.

My parents seemed sympathetic to this diagnosis. They became less sympathetic when I began to promote their own ongoing personal development as the purpose of their lives. You need to peak out at seventy-five or eighty rather than thirty-five or forty, I told them, which meant you ran up against the question of what useful thing you were doing with your time, no matter how old and sick you were. I see now why my parents flinched a bit when I showed up at their door wanting to talk about it.

That fall, in various ways, my father indicated that he had just about had all the personal development he could stand. He had begun to talk about the various times in his life that he had been betrayed, and about the people who had done the betraying. He spoke about friendships that had run their course because people started spending winters in Arizona. My mother was beginning to have moments when she didn't know him. Some of his friends had begun to drink too much. Friends had spilled the beans on the locations of secret fishing holes or hunting spots, places he was no longer strong enough to visit but still visited in his memory.

Other friends had simply died on him, acts which he was not inclined to forgive. Death had become a perverse choice for him, a deliberate insult. In his eyes, nobody he cared about ever died involuntarily.

Even then, he was planning on living forever. But a life of hard physical labor had begun to catch up with him. Old injuries in his back and neck and shoulders were causing him a lot of pain, and his doctor, whom I began to refer to as Dr. Death, had told him he had narrowing in his carotid arteries and needed stents in his neck, and probably, once they did an angiogram, in his heart.

Dr. Death had told him he was an old man now and had better start acting like one. My father reacted to his advice by refusing all further checkups.

Aside from me, there weren't many people who knew he had stopped trusting Dr. Death and everybody else. It was as if a street gang of former friends had jumped out of a dark alley and were standing around him, pushing and shoving him back and forth, getting ready to put the boots to him. I made the mistake of telling him that betrayal, just like any other hardship, was an opportunity for personal development.

I now know that my father's woodpile was starting to look like the one thing in his life that wouldn't betray him.

I told my father he should have a gas furnace installed in the house. I said that one of these days I was going to get too old to cut firewood myself, and I wouldn't be able to fill the woodshed or the lean-to, or even the wood box. When he agreed I realized that even though I was twenty-five years younger than he was, it was easier for him to imagine me getting too old and failing him than it was for him to imagine he was getting too old and failing me.

The furnace came with a five-hundred-gallon propane tank, which wasn't as much a comfort to him as another five cords of wood would have been.

II

That winter my father had a stroke and spent a tough month trying to stand or speak before he died. My mother, who had been showing signs of dementia for a decade, tried and failed to live alone, coming close to burning the house down every time she boiled a pot dry on the gas range in her kitchen. Within the year, we moved her into assisted living, then into a nursing home, and then into hospice.

For the remaining cold months, I kept their house warm with the furnace, but when spring came, I drained the water pipes and it's been empty and unheated ever since. I've had offers to rent it, but I don't like the idea of my parents' ghosts sharing the place they lived in alone for so many years. Judging from what I always start thinking in their house when I check on it—that I'd better sharpen the chainsaw and gas up the pickup—they're still there.

Over the next winter I burned the wood left in the lean-to in my own wood stove, and once the lean-to was empty, I tore it down. I used its lumber to build my own lean-to onto the side of my own garage, and it's got five cords of wood in it right now. I'll get five cords more to put under the eaves of the garage once firewood season starts, and that may feel like enough. If it isn't, I've got the five cords still waiting in my parents' woodshed.

For a decade my physician was Dr. Death—I had inherited him—but last fall I hurt my back after cutting and loading a big tree in the pickup. When I went to see Dr. Death, he told me I had Old-Man's-Back, and that I should quit cutting and hauling firewood. He gave me some exercises, which looked a lot like the exercises I did every firewood season, so I took the chainsaw and went back into the woods and for a while only cut down small and medium-sized trees. At first it felt like I was being broken in half, but eventually I could load the pickup with wood, albeit more slowly and with a few tics and anticipatory shudders when I bent to pick up a log.

At my age, I should be seeing Dr. Death for every little thing. Instead I've decided he's on the opposing team. These days I get my checkups from the Internet, and my symptoms indicate exotic and always fatal diseases, full of pain and delirium.

I have a limited amount of time left. At some point I will have no friends whatsoever, having betrayed them all by dying.

I've decided betrayal by itself isn't the issue. It's what will betray you—your body, your doctor, your friends, your thoughts, yourself, or something or somebody you haven't thought of yet.

A friend who drinks too much, who gets addicted to Oxycontin, who leaves a spouse whom you liked a lot, who retreats from the world and starts saving junk mail in boxes he gets from the liquor store dumpster, who votes for Donald Trump—the proper response, once you get over being angry, is grief. Nobody ever told me grief was going to be my route to personal development when I got old.

III

Recently my friend David—we've been best men at each other's weddings—got married for the third time. I wasn't his best man this time. I advised against the marriage. He got married anyway, in a county clerk's office.

His third wife doesn't speak English. She's a Chinese person, as David calls her, and highly intelligent and capable and beautiful—she's run businesses in China and has gone through the ordeal of emigrating to the United States without knowing its language. She's twenty years younger than he is. She was David's yoga teacher. She has raised two adult sons. They have moved into David's house because it's customary in Chinese culture for children to stay with their parents until they get married.

David doesn't speak Chinese. He and his new wife have developed a kind of pidgin for everyday life, and the translation app on their phones works to communicate grocery lists, furniture purchases, and vacation plans.

They're in love, I think. At least David is. He talks about her like he can't believe his luck.

Her two sons sit in his basement and play video games in their underwear, but their lack of interest in personal development doesn't appear to bother him. It also doesn't look as if either of them will get married anytime soon, but they use headsets and David has the whole rest of his house above ground level.

David likes taking care of people. He always has. At times, as when I resigned my tenured professorship and didn't know what to do with my life, he has taken care of me. He's a personable guy. He's smart. He's kind.

We haven't had an argument. He hasn't become an addict. He isn't showing signs of dementia or malignancy. He hasn't told me I need to see a doctor or a counselor, and he's seeing a counselor himself so there was no need for me to tell him to when he decided to get married for a third time. His counselor advised against the marriage.

His first two marriages were to two thoroughly unpleasant people. If someone, brought to spit-spewing rage by the cruel adolescent patriarchy running this country, slowly assembled a tit-for-tat facsimile of that patriarchy in her heart, you would see most of what David's first two wives were like.

He has a daughter by his first wife. I stood at a podium and read love poems at his daughter's wedding, which isn't like me, but his daughter had asked, and if she was going to see me that way, I was going to read love poems. None of the poems mentioned betrayal or death.

She's had a happy marriage so far, and David says he's glad about that, but he's missed the father-daughter relationship they had when she was young.

Now that David has married a Chinese person, he and his daughter are going through a rough patch. His daughter has told him she doesn't like his new wife.

"How could she decide she doesn't like her?" he asked me. "She doesn't even know her. She can't even talk to her." He was ignoring the question of how you could be in love with somebody you didn't even know because you couldn't even talk to her.

It might be possible. My father, a month before the end of all our conversations, said, "When I say friends, I'm not talking about somebody who talks about what you want to talk about—these big questions of yours. I'm talking about somebody who wouldn't ever bring them up and would tell you to shut up if you did."

When I sit in my father's house now, his ghost says things like, "I was old and tired and sick of you telling me I was in the most important stage of my life for personal development. You hadn't yet figured out that personal development has one purpose, and that's to murder the person engaging in it. If you had really been my friend, you would have quit talking, gone outside, and cut me a bigger woodpile."

I think David has picked someone with whom he won't have to talk to about the big questions. I mention this because it's clear to me that when you lose your friends, it isn't because other people betray you. It's because you betray them. You ask them questions about why people have to die, or why good people do bad things, or how you live a life of meaning in a world without it, and you insist they answer those questions in a language you understand.

Even if you're not that demanding, it doesn't matter. One or the other of you will die and those questions will show up as ghosts at the funeral.

I think David thinks marrying someone twenty years his junior is a way to avoid the language of grief.

I haven't told David what I think. I think he'll discover that the language of grief is the same in Mandarin and English, and pidgin, for that matter.

I also think that his daughter dislikes his new wife because you have to become someone new when you marry someone. When you become someone new, some people are going to miss the old you, the one murdered by you and your Chinese person co-conspirator.

I'm being unfair. I insist people continually reinvent themselves, but when they do, I tell them not that way.

David thinks his daughter is going to get over her anger, but she's angrier than he thinks she is. So many things in life are either/or land mines, and David has stepped on one. Bad for his happiness. Good for his personal development.

IV

The Top Ten Questions for Personal Development:

1. Why do we have to be born?
2. Why do we have to die?
3. Do good people who betray the location of your secret fishing hole become bad people?
4. How do you betray a friendship?
5. Will men and women ever share a common language?
6. Can they be friends?
7. How much wood could a woodchuck chuck?
8. How do you make meaning in a world that lacks meaning?
9. That's enough for now. These questions have no answers. My head hurts. Make it stop.
10.

I have not been married three times. I've been married once, twenty-five years ago, and I'm still married. I'm still in love, for that matter, in spite of Susan—my wife—an American person—knowing English, but continually twisting it. She prides herself on her plain-speaking bluntness, but there are always meanings within her meanings. She tells me that after twenty-five years she's still deciding whether or not she's in love with me. I've told her that if she comes down on the side on not loving me, please tell me in Chinese. She says that she'll love me unconditionally if and when I stop asking her personal development questions.

"If that's the case," I ask her, "why'd you marry me?"

"Your woodpile," she says.

We spend a lot of time talking about dinner, except in the morning, when we talk about breakfast. But now and then we talk about big questions, at my insistence.

I've decided life itself is a koan, and that the Buddhists are right when they say that you can benefit by contemplating life's lack of answers for as long as you can stand it, then going out and chopping an armload of wood, starting a nice warm fire, putting the tea on, and sitting in the rocking chair beside the stove with a mystery you've read before, maybe by Ross MacDonald, who writes about good people betraying their friends because basically there aren't any good people.

"Ross MacDonald has an answer for you," I tell Susan. "No such thing as good people. No such thing as a friend."

"Ross MacDonald is wrong," she says. "I'm your friend. One exception can sink a proposition."

"The old exception-sinks-proposition trick," I say. "Take that, Ross MacDonald."

"I've got other tricks," she says. "Your list of big questions is a list of big answers."

She proceeds to give them:

"*One*. We're born. *Two*. We die. *Three*. Fishing holes are the least of it."

"Fishing holes do not qualify as a big answer," I say.

"Don't interrupt. *Four*. You betray your friends when you die. Your father was right about that.

"*Five*. Men and women will share a common language when they share a common purpose. Don't hold your breath.

"*Six*. I've already told you I'm your friend. You need to return the favor.

"*Seven*. A woodchuck could chuck wood until the woodpile runs out.

"*Eight*. Meaning is what you make of the raw material you're handed. You start with dead trees and end up with a woodpile. The real question is the size of your woodpile.

"*Nine*. If your head hurts, getting outside in the cold air will help. Bring in an armload of wood while you're at it."

"I have questions. You have answers," I say. "But sometimes I wish you didn't know English."

V

I should say that I don't really believe Susan. Her answers are just attempts to stop my questions. The idea of turning the raw dead trees of existence into secure woodpiles of meaning is a good example.
Her metaphor is a brutally reductive conversation-killer. Contemplate it and you start thinking that turning reality into metaphor might be the point, which is way different from the point being felling, sawing, splitting, and stacking.

Fortunately, I can always change the subject.

"Have you noticed that we've never brought our personal development to a full stop by letting love be the answer to the big questions?" I ask her.

She looks at me sideways. "You're still thinking about David, aren't you?"

I nod. "He wanted me to approve of his new wife, whom he loves, and tell him that his daughter, whom he also loves, would forgive the person he's become. But I've realized that learning a language turns you back into an infant, and learning Mandarin at his age is going to keep him a baby 'til he's eighty. I think people should be able to marry anybody they feel like marrying, but not many people know how to be friends with a baby."

"So he's betrayed you," she says. "And you won't forgive him. You're going to betray him right back."

"Not really. Not now. Until I die on him, if David needs any help from me, he'll get it. I'll be there for him when he wants to talk, and I've thought that if and when he and his new wife learn one language or the other, he'll need somebody other than her to talk to. Finding out who somebody really was ended his other marriages."

"It hasn't ended our marriage," says Susan.

"Maybe you don't know me," I say.

"Better than you know yourself," she says. "And I'm still your friend."

"The exception that sinks the proposition," I say. "But do you love me?"

She says nothing.

"You're just waiting for me to die on you."
"Don't die," she says.
"I won't," I say, but we both know that's not true.

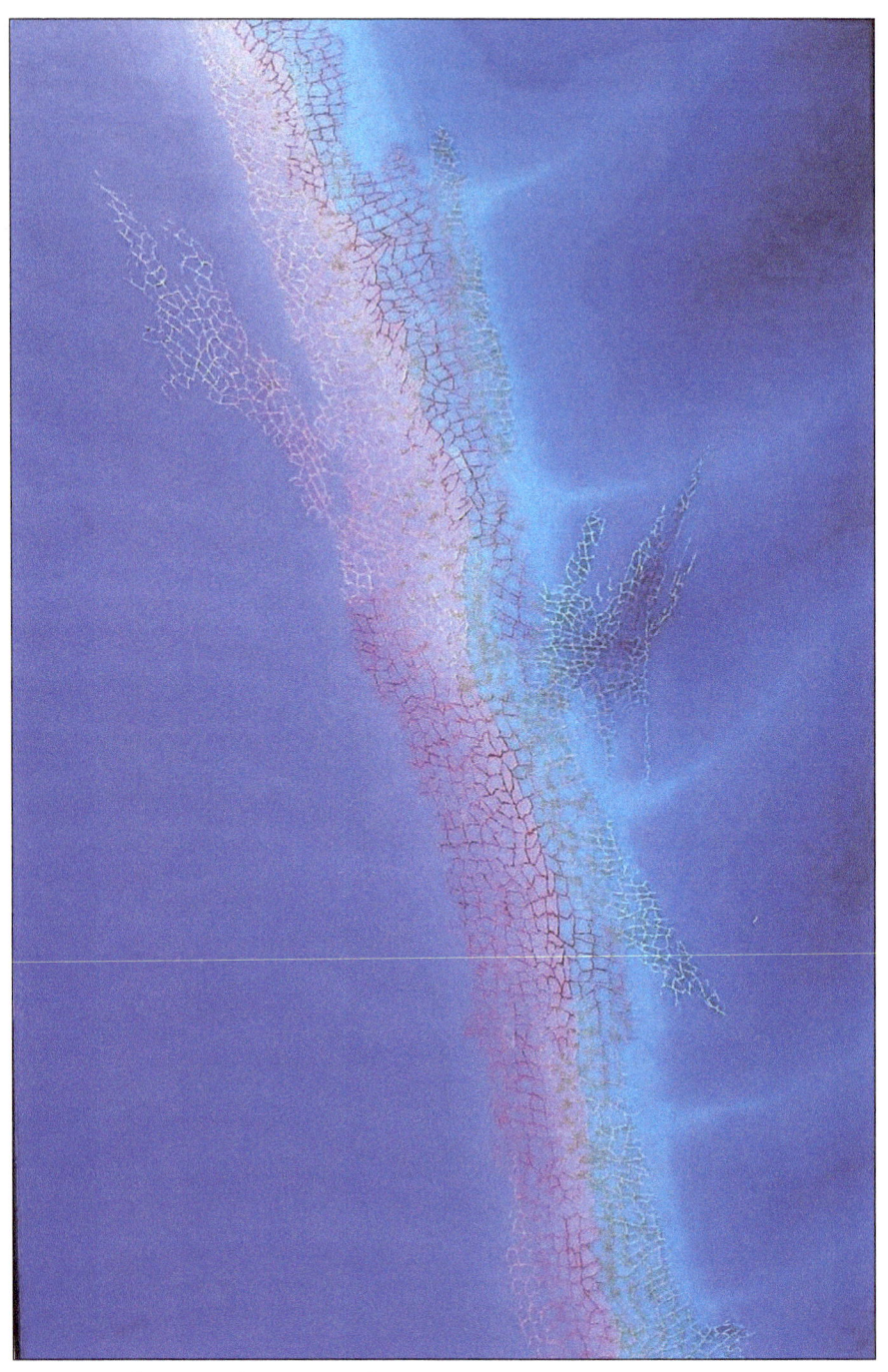

"Aqua #1" by Ray Obermayr. Oil on canvas, 31" x 37."

CHUCK GUILFORD

Forking Lightning
      at Lick Creek Lookout

We're pretty well grounded. Nonetheless,
when Thor starts heaving out big ones
from low hanging
pyro-cumulus,
slamming them out,
god muscle to iron on iron,
hammer on anvil,
what horse will wear the shoe
he fashions? What link in the chain
he forges will ever snap?

And he's heaving them now at 8,000 feet.
Big bolts of electromagnetic force.
The pure thing. The thing itself. *Das Ding an sich.*
No additives. No preservatives.
Just huge bolts of energy. Positive. Negative.
The *yin* and the *yang*.
The dark and the light.

Not to mention the rain.
Heavy sheets of it pelting the windows.
And ice chunks. And hail.

And all of it shouting, you fools,
you don't belong
on this rocky knoll. You humans,
with your contour maps,
your compasses and comforters,
your down sleeping bags.

THE LIMBERLOST REVIEW

I can take you down
any time I choose.
Blow you beyond smithereens.
You wouldn't even know it.

But I keep you around
for amusement,
for my entertainment. What fun,
after all, would it be
up here without you?

CHUCK GUILFORD

The Waves

Gulls, a crowd of them, patrol
the beach, now and then taking flight,
bellies just over the sea,
wings beating quickly at first,
then holding a slow, steady glide
while a few small wavelets bend
and curl along the shore,
describing the bay's long arc
with their ancient, informal rhythm,
reflections of light
on their slow undulations,
in their foam as they break,
in the traces of bubbly film
that they leave in the sand.

Did you know that a wave
is a circular pattern of energy,
force, not water itself, but a rhythm
that moves through the water
like shock waves in earth,
like sound waves in air,
like these words in the depths
of your mind.

In this quiet place
where the water stays or yields,
where it breaks or simply bends
at the waves' insistent bidding,
where it traces along the shore
in soft, unconscious concert
with the morning sun, with the fitful breezes,

in this quiet place past seeming,
past shaping, past conscious design,
in this force at the heart of the mind
we can think beyond meaning —
let a word become the throbbing of the water,
the earth, and the air, the pulse of one life
that we share.

HOWARD WILKERSON

Dogwood Blossoms

When dogwoods blossom in the woods as before,
men and guns resume
the sound of dancing over fields of war.

Only newborn soldiers wear their faces anymore,
dressed in homespun woven on their mother's loom
when dogwoods blossom in the woods as before.

She hears marching boots in rows of four
like water splashing down the wooden flume,
the sound of dancing over fields of war.

Men kneel in rows of corn outside her door,
she knows these fields will never bloom
when dogwoods blossom in the woods as before.

She crawls again in the mud beneath the floor,
hears the musket fire in her womb,
the sound of dancing over fields of war.

I raise my father's gun, sighting down the bore,
see a woman stacking empty boots
when dogwoods blossom in the woods as before,
the sound of dancing over fields of war.

"Untitled" by Dennis DeFoggi. Pencil, colored pencil, acrylic and thinset on mat board. 18.75" x 15.5," 2020.

E. ETHELBERT MILLER

1947: The Death of Jimmy Doyle

He stepped into Sugar when he
stepped into the ring. The sweetness
of the punch crazy against his head.
He fell hard to the canvas like it
was the bottom of a cup. Doyle
never saw daylight again. Robinson's
glove blocked the sun. One could see
death shadowboxing in the corner.

Free Agent

There is a silent divorce
heard between phone calls,
which soon becomes equal
to the distance between
the plate and the pitcher's
mound.

Listen for the first sounds
of spring in your muscles,
the sound of fingers grabbing
balls, fists pounding gloves.

Listen while you wait for a team
to remember your youth, wins
and strikeouts.

You wait like a confused bird
tucking your head under a wing.
There is a fear of flying
that comes with the night
sky, the wind's farewell,
the darkened scoreboard
and the empty bleachers.

DAVID GUIOTTO

From *The Distances*

Author's Note: *In* The Distances, *Mike and Sarah Vicenzo struggle to provide for their young daughter, Greta. After losing their house in the Great Recession of 2008, the Vicenzos decide to return to Italy, Mike's ancestral home. There, they live and work on an agriturismo now owned by old friends. At first, the Veneto is the ideal setting for this creative family. After chores are done, Mike writes, Sarah paints, and Greta explores. However, Mike is soon haunted by his family's violent history. Desperate to come to terms with his past, to finally resolve his issues rooted in anger and fear, Mike retreats into his writing. He searches for the truths that, he believes, will save his marriage.*

We had our little room with its view and its hissing radiator to keep us warm at night and for what felt like months, but was only weeks, we didn't need much more. The room was once a storage or livestock stall converted, like the others at the back of the house, into a guest room with a private entrance. The space was taken up by a big bed, an heirloom dresser that rocked on the uneven stone floor, and a tiny partitioned bathroom where we could wash away the dust and mud of the day. The room was small but all of the Veneto lay outside our door. In the early evenings, when the weather was good, we would put out chairs and sit and talk over a glass of wine while Greta and Lorenzo played in the yard among the chickens inspecting the packed ground for bugs. We'd savor the view, and say how lucky we were, and I knew we were truly lucky when Sarah would put down her glass and take up her sketchpad and begin to draw the barn and the bare fields, the trees thick along the canal, the dirt road and the wispy skies that spun off the sea and made a navigable ocean of the plain. It was only when she painted or drew that I knew she was content. Unlike me, she couldn't lose herself in her art until everything else was in place.

There was plenty of work to do around the farm and agriturismo. It was my job to feed the milk cow and goats in the morning, and nights I washed dishes or did prep work in the kitchen. Sarah helped Clara with housework, often going into town to shop for the needs of the guests. Some nights she took my place in the kitchen or helped serve dinner so that I could have time with Greta. We had a good routine, and we weren't overworked. Our afternoons were usually free and often we'd take a walk along the dirt road to Ceggia and there, among students in chatty groups and families on their strolls, have an aperitivo at one of the cafes on the piazza.

The days were still warm, though the nights were growing cold and damp. After the staff dinner we'd return to our room and the steaming radiator. Sarah and Greta might read a story in bed while I relaxed with the newspaper before my kitchen shift. My Italian was coming back, but it could take me nights to get through a *Corriere della Sera*, especially with the girls' soft voices tempting me to join them. Those short evenings together felt like home. Home is the right word simply because we had each other. There wasn't much money but we had the important things. The burden of trying to maintain a household was off my shoulders; Greta was, as always, eager for adventure; and Sarah was happier than I'd seen her in years. She had time to be a mother and time to herself. She sketched whenever she could—from the shaded side of the barn, from the canal bank, from different aspects of the property—taking a folding chair and colored pencils with her. She did well to catch the looming skies above the umber plain, or the sudden light that poured from late clouds and made the fig trees gleam like oil. I didn't know how long it would keep her. I figured it would be enough and perfect for awhile, and then like any season, its colors would fade, the light would change, and she would need another view.

On our days off we liked to get away, taking the bus or train into the nearby towns of Treviso, Caorle, Vicenze. But of course Venezia was our favorite place to wander. As I had been as a boy pulled along by my mother, Greta was mesmerized by the island city's crooked alleys and murky canals, its clacking piazzas and secret gardens, its dusty shop windows full of lugubrious gilded masks. We'd cross footbridges and take dank passageways into the perimeter neighborhoods, the Ghetto and Castello, getting lost among the listing buildings, the peeling peach and moss walls, following the sky as it slivered through touching eaves and buttressed corners and opened, like a deep breath, above some tiny lonesome square, crossed with laundry lines, shadowed by coppery light.

DAVID GUIOTTO

We made a point of getting lost, but we always found our way to Piazza San Marco, tourist signs leading the way. We were tourists too, on hard-earned holiday for the afternoon, disoriented, ridiculous, beguiled by the charms of Venezia, yet relieved when the moldering labyrinth released us into the grand white piazza, minareted and sparkling before the sloshing waters of the lagoon. And like proper tourists we'd buy a bag of seeds from a vendor, then take a table under the galleria and watch as Greta tossed handfuls to the pigeons. The waiter brought spritz and aperitivi and it felt good to be off our feet, taking our first fizzing sips of Campari. The crowds weren't so bad that time of year, the portici echoed pleasantly, and the cool autumn air made everything a painting you wanted to linger in. So we were happy to sit there and do nothing, to order another round and hold hands across the table and watch as Greta, having made some new friend, threw seeds into the air and ran circles under the thrilling birds.

Travel is a kind of dreaming in itself, and always on the train ride back, crossing over the lagoon to the flickering plain, I was glad for the farmhouse that would wake us. The routine of the agriturismo gave a needed structure to our days. The work was laborious and purposeful, yet it didn't demand the focus of our lives. We, each other, and our artistic efforts, were our focus. I didn't think we needed much more than that, other than some success in our mediums. Encircled by the Mancussos' kindness, by the sprawling countryside, by our work and our art, we were free of everything but our own expectations.

Tuesday morning, our first week at the agriturismo. I wake to the clanging of a tractor in the darkness: the bawling engine sounds as reluctant as I am to move into the cold. I slip from bed, careful not to jostle the girls, and pull on my work clothes. As the rumble of the tractor fades I imagine the old zio hunched at the wheel, woolen, muttering through damp whiskers, man and machine prying a seam between dawn and earth. The crazy old uncle, so manically industrious that the Mancussos joke he must be half-foreigner, the product of his grandmother coupling with an Austrian soldier when Caporetto fell. I both admire and loathe the man: at his iron core he's a laborer; I'm not.

I rinse my face at the sink, put on my coat at the door. Sarah, waking, waves from her pillow as I step outside. Woodsmoke on the damp air. A rustling sky and the uncut grass blown flat along the edges of the fields suggest a storm is coming, the first of the season. I enter the kitchen through the back door. On the counter breakfast is set out for the house: a platter of biscotti, a porcelain bowl of yogurt sprinkled with cinnamon, a canister of ground coffee beside the moka pot. There's a shout from the hall. In the dining room I find Clara pulling a shirt over her boy, Lorenzo. He teeters at the table trying to eat as his mother dresses him, tucking and tugging with harsh affection.

"Miki, puoi andar," she starts to say before catching herself and wishing me good morning. Finally she releases him, and he runs down the hall crying with relief.

"Senti," she says. "Can you get the wine this morning? Stefano must go to Milano suddenly."

"He won't mind?"

"Why would he mind?"

I push up my lips and shrug, suggesting ignorance. Buying the wine is, I always thought, a job for the man of the house.

"I'm sorry to ask," says Clara, hurrying to the kitchen. "I know you wanted the afternoon free. Tell Sarah I'm going to San Dona. If they want to come, it could be nice."

"I'll tell her."

I finish my coffee and breakfast. I'm searching for the bucket of kitchen scraps when Lucia comes in. She pauses to kiss cheeks, asks in polite English how my breakfast was. Taking off her coat and putting on an apron, she begins working at the sink. I'm always amazed to see her here: Clara's little girl now a young woman, pretty and vibrant, intelligent, confident with youth. Encouraged by Stefano, she studied law in Trieste, received her degree, but then returned home last summer to help in the kitchen, a job she doesn't seem to resent. When once I asked her why she didn't start her career in Roma or Milano, she replied, "Yes, that day will come. But after being away at university, it's good to be with family again."

I go to feed the animals: fresh hay for the milk cow and goats in the barn, a bucket of kitchen scraps for the solemn pig in his separate shed, bread rinds and corn kernels for the geese in the penned yard. I top off their waters, then return to our room. Sarah is propped on pillows in bed, reading while Greta sleeps. When I explain to her that Clara needs me to pick up the wine, she says with dismay, "I thought we were going to the beach?"

"Well, it's too cold anyway. She asked if you want to go shopping in town."

"With her?"

"Yes, with her."

"Errand shopping, or shopping shopping?"

"There's a difference?" I kiss her on the cheek, run my hand under the blanket to her warm waist.

"You're cold," she says, nudging me aside, then catching me before I can kiss sleeping Greta.

At the door I take up my rucksack. "Go," I whisper. "The kids'll have fun. And you will too."

The old Peugeot is parked on the gravel drive, keys in the ignition. It starts with a shudder and I drive down the dirt road and onto the banked highway and turn east for town. The car's tall rectangular windows give good views of the country, which is important in a vehicle that moves so slowly. By the time the speedometer reads ninety, it's necessary to slow down again into town. I ease through Ceggia, pass the benzina station, the algae-stained houses along the canal. After the walled cemetery I turn onto a road that runs through lanes of browning sycamore trees. On the right is the decrepit villa where my nonna used to send me to buy fresh milk from the family that worked the grounds. Then the short bridge leading to the chapel, then a cluster of houses close to the road. At the sight of my grandparents' place—a stout two stories under a tera-cotta roof, the rows of wooden shutters parted on rosy plaster walls—I imagine my nonna inside preparing breakfast, washing pears at the sink. My nonno, having had his coffee, is already at work in the shed, a cloth cap shading his eyes as he sharpens a blade against a grinding wheel.

The house looks both stark and cheery in the sun breaking through the low clouds. The pruned cypress and fruit trees reaching above the garden, the tile walkways hosed clean–everything in order now that the disorder of family life has passed from the house, now that the children are grown and gone, taking their shouts and laugher, their mischief, the arguments and revolts that throttled the place. The late nights as my nonna waited up for us, the hungover mornings when Nonno vengefully put us to work hoeing the fagioli beds. The merciful lunches, and afterwards, the deep naps that silenced the house.

    It pains me not to stop. But it's too soon, our relations too fragile. Maybe after another week, after a neighbor or a grocery clerk tells them they've seen us, the surprise news will soak in and by weight of formality, if nothing else, my nonno will feel compelled to put aside grievances and invite us over.

    I speed past the house, past the newer sixties-style houses of Gainiga with their shutterless windows and iron balconies, and into the yellowing soy fields to the east. Into the memory of riding this road on the back of a scooter driven by my uncle Claudio, my arms around his waist, his hair fluttering in my face, fear gripping me as we lean into a turn and charge for the secret meeting place of his friends. There at the edge of a field: Vespas parked under willows, teenage boys and girls in sleek boots sharing bottles of beer as a transistor radio plays The English Beat, The Cure. Everyone joking and arguing and flirting in a language that dizzies me as much as the cigarettes going round. They practice their bad English on me, offer me beer but, according to Claudio's orders, nothing of the potent cigarettes. He slips away with a dark-haired girl; half the gang are making out in the trees.

    Sei il nipote? some skinny guy asks me.

    Cosa? I say, not understanding him.

    Si, he says, squinting, amused. The mother leaves, but the son comes back.

    I want to talk to him more—he seems to hold something that's just beyond my reach. But suddenly, as if by a silent alarm, everyone is coming out of the trees, kick-starting their scooters, swapping kisses, speeding home for dinner and the cozy kitchens of their mothers, each guilty of being a good kid after all.

    At the rotunda I have to go around twice before reading the sign and recognizing the road north for Tore di Mostre. My nonno brought me here a few times: I should remember the way, know to stop at a certain cafe to talk with the proprietor about the kind of year it's been, the quality of the grapes, the local going price. After another kilometer I see a sign for the winery and veer left on a dirt road that leads to the vine-strewn neoclassical gates of yet another crumbling villa. A thick man in coveralls, seeing me step from the car, crosses a courtyard littered with rusting machinery and stacked, rain-bleached barrels. We shake hands. I mention the Mancusso family and he motions for me to follow him into the warehouse. The tart, wanton smell of oak barrels, of wine spilled on concrete, nearly makes me swoon to breathe it. He places a cask under one of the stainless steel tanks.

"Cabernet?" I ask.

"Si. Con Merlot."

As if to convince me of the blend, he twists the valve, allows a spurt of red into a drinking glass, hands it to me. The wine is young, still rough and tannic, but good.

"Si, bon," I say.

At that he fills the fifty-liter glass cask, caps it, and together we haul the cask onto a cart and push it to the car. Then we return for a second. As we load them into the back of the Peugeot, an old woman comes out of the house. She says something in dialect that causes the man to gruffly wave her inside.

"E lui?" she says, refusing to budge. "Il nipotino di Vicenzo?"

"Two hundred," he says, ignoring her.

"Two hundred?"

"The price has gone up."

"Even for Mancusso?"

"For everybody."

I pay him what he wants. If the price is unfair he'll hear about it from Clara. I get in the car. As I start the engine the vecchia hurries across the courtyard, waving at me to stop.

"Basta," cries the man.

But she's too quick for him. She reaches through the window and pushes something flat and metallic into my hand.

"E' di la, il campo," she says, "from the field where they found him."

When I return to the house there's a note from Sarah in our room. They've gone with Clara after all and will eat lunch in San Dona. I'm glad they'll finally have some time together. Until now a hesitation has existed between them: while Clara's been generous and Sarah's been cordial—while Clara certainly knows but Sarah only senses—they've been too busy to share anything more than our staff dinners together. I haven't brought anything up because I don't want it to get in the way. Not that they would discuss the matter. They wouldn't need to. Women like them don't need words. They need only an afternoon together, enjoying each other's company, watching their children play near a fountain as they sit on a bench in the sun, to arrive at a place of quiet understanding, of confidence between mothers, between experienced women, that that was then and this is now, and nothing else persists.

I go to the kitchen and call my old friend Jimmy Vialone, the skinny guy with the wry smile, the one with clues if not answers, and arrange for us to have lunch in town. As I leave, Lucia stops me. She puts a plate in the cupboard, then, hands on her hips, chides me in the floral English they learn at school here: "So where is the wine? Don't tell me you drank it already?"

"I'm getting it now."

"Let me to help."

We walk out to the drive, and between us carry one sloshing cask, then the other, from the car into a storage room adjacent to the barn. On a shelf stand a couple dozen glass bottles, liter and two-liter, green and brown, which the zio must have set out. We balance a cask on our thighs, tip its mouth into a funnel, and fill each bottle to the neck. Once all the bottles are filled we cap them with plastic corks and store them on a back shelf.

"Grazie," I say, starting to leave.

"But we didn't try it."

She opens a bottle, takes a sip, nods her head, then hands it to me. She draws in her damp lips as she watches me drink. She has clever hazel eyes, cute ears. It's a natural thought any man would have. Back of the storage shed, amid the sour odors of animals in their stalls. But I'm not any man in this case. I wonder how much she knows. Obviously, not enough. She has Clara's round face, yet softer cheeks, and her father's pronounced nose. Her chin, too, has a small cleft that looks familiar.

"E' buona," I agree. I cork the bottle with the heal of my hand, give it back to her, then dutifully take up three more bottles and carry them to the kitchen.

The dirt road into Ceggia passes a copse of trees that leans wildly out of the earth: a gangly vestigial forest resisting the combed fate of the fields. Amber and ruby leaves of alder and willow dab the sullen sky. Beneath dense branches, a sparrow hops among the leaf litter, searching for seeds. A shred of faded cloth hangs from a thorny olive branch; a mound of vines hides glass bottles and tin cans left by gypsies or immigrants sleeping rough. Nettles sting my wrists as I push from the copse and continue up the road.

Blackberry bushes along the ditches; pampas grass grows tall along the canal banks. The murky water slurps at the disappearing tail of a rat. A station bell rattles and then the powerful rushing whir of a train passes to the north, cars of teal and glass flashing over the countryside. Far-off farmhouses, painted or bare stone, gleam like pieces of seashell and coral in the cloudy light. Withered corn rows still standing, or cut and plowed under, the dark rows flecked with stalks and straw. On the cold air a burnt sugar smell from the burnpiles, here and there, loosing smoke into the sky, the last sweet draws of the season.

In a ditch beside the road float the green shields of drowned stink bugs. Even the sky returns to water. Each ditch and canal a slit in the land, a reflection of blue, a parting where the sea shows through. The tides they tried to bury: peasants and laborers hauling earth by the cartload to further their fields and finish their poverty. *Bonifica! Bonifica!* Even Mussolini couldn't resist. But all of this belongs below: the Veneto a skirt of sediments and backfill, of silts fanned by turquoise rivers from seabed peaks. All of this—the foggy towns and sinking cities, the lacework plain fringed by marshes and lagoons, the saline fields and watercolor skies—all a skiff on a patient sea.

After the ceramics factory, the storehouses at the edge of town, the neighborhood of close-built houses under magnolia trees, there's the slender church, then the cafes and shops along Via Marconi. The street buzzes with scooters and bicycles and cars, screeches with shutters being drawn down by shopkeepers and grocers as people going home for lunch pass on the narrow sidewalk. Near the piazza is a little restaurant called Gambero, where I find Jimmy Vialone sitting outside. Smoking a cigarette, looking aloof in a suede jacket, Levi's jeans and worn Italian boots, he seems the same as ever, only nineteen years older. He stands to shake hands, holding off my attempt to kiss cheeks.

"I'm not so Italian, remember?" he scoffs.

We go inside and take a table by the window. Jimmy orders for us and soon the waiter is bringing out a bottle of Roboso, steaming bowls of minestrone, boards of prosciutto crudo and cotto, aged cheeses from Friuli. Jimmy insists we speak "American." He tells me what he's been up to, how he's recently moved home with his parents after a summer in Prague where he worked for an Italian tourism company.

"And the girls, Miki. They shock with these blue eyes."

"Why didn't you marry one? Bring her back here, make your parents happy."

"I try, believe me. But they think Italian boys are only for fun."

"You're fun, aren't you?"

"I'm too much good at it." He smiles bitterly. He refills our glasses, then raises his: "To Claudio."

For the second course the waiter brings plates of fried potatoes and thin cuts of beef browned in olive oil and thyme. It's a delicious meal. Afterward we have coffee and Montenegro. Jimmy offers me a cigarette and, feeling in the mood, I accept.

"So tell me your story? You're married now? You have a sweet girl?"

I catch him up on our life, how I met Sarah, had Greta, been writing, surviving, all that. When I get to the part about losing our house, he shakes his head ruefully.

"Il Crollo, it's shit," he says. "The important thing is, you're here. So now what? You're living at Clara's? Milking the cows? Dodging the husband? Starting your beautiful life in Ceggia?"

"We're trying not to look too far ahead."

"You, no. Sarah, I'm sure she is looking ahead. Especially if you say she's German. You make a balance, I think. Tell her, in Italia it's better not to look too far ahead. It's why we have a good life here. Nobody look up the road. Except Berlusconi when a girl goes by."

"Naturalmente."

"Speaking of," he says, lifting his chin toward the door. A woman in her thirties, casually pretty, leans her bicycle against the curb and comes inside. She speaks with the proprietor—a rotund, black-locked, wild-looking fellow—then waves at Claudio as she goes out.

"Who's that?"

"Liza. She wave every time she see me, just to break the balls."

"You dated her?"

"Let's say we have a story."

"Let me guess. The story is, you're too much fun, but she wanted serious."

"No, the opposite. Believe me, Miki, now I'm changed, I become serious. I try to make a serious period in my life. Maybe I make a family, like you. But I'm not so sure about it. Why do I want this? For my parents, for me? Because it's getting late in the life? The problem is, the more you mix with another, the more you struggle. But also the more beauty you have. What you think, it's worth it? I'm sorry to spoil the mood."

"Don't apologize. It's not easy. All I can say is, Greta's the best thing to happen to us. And she was an accident. You can't plan it. Or if you do, you'll never do it. Just go knock up that girl Liza. Then you'll have a whole other set of questions to ask me."

"What about the wife?"

"What about her?"

"You're happy to be married?"

"Some days I am, some not. But you'll see. You just gotta go for it."

"Si, si," he says, tapping the rim of his glass. "When do I meet them?"

"Whenever you want. Come over for dinner some time."

"If Clara will have me."

"Of course she will. What, I thought everything was good between you?"

As if stalling, he slides his glass to the edge of the table. Seeing it empty, the waiter brings over the Montenegro and refills our glasses.

"Clara is hard," he says simply. "She doesn't forget."

"What's to forget? You got the business, right? And she got out, nice and clean."

"Money makes things not so clean, even when the scale is balanced. Anyway, tell her hello for me. Maybe she's happy enough now to remember we're old friends."

"I will. And I'm sure she'd be glad to see you."

"What do you know?"

"All I know," I say, rubbing out my cigarette, "is we're living on beans. Fagioli e radicchio. You need help with anything these days?"

"With what?"

"Anything. I could use some side work, if there's any."

"Miki. Senti. That era is finished. Why you think I'm working for a tourist company in Prague? The girls?"

He gazes at me cautiously, as though the matter isn't finished but he isn't sure what else he can reveal. "We made things even, yes? Also with you?"

"Si."

"Then what else you want?"

I don't say anything.

"It's finished, Miki. After you left, for a while, there was a need. But at a certain point it wasn't good anymore. When the police come to the house of your mother, you think, Eh, What the fuck? You think, Maybe it's enough now. You want the risk to stop. Basta," he swipes his palms together, "it's too much. So you take a job, any job, even walking old ladies in the museum."

"I thought they were pretty girls with blue eyes."

He doesn't laugh.

"I'm sorry I asked."

"No, no. It's natural. It's been a long time. But don't worry, Miki. What's important is you're here. The same old Italia. A good life if you enjoy the plate in front of you."

He finishes his glass, raps the table with his knuckles. "Have you been to your nonni?"

"Not yet."

"The other day I saw Marta at the cemetery. Keeping the flowers in water. She's always making his place nice, you know?"

"We'll go see them."

"Certo. You know your nonno is sick? Something here." He taps two fingers to his throat. "Your girl is what they need, Miki. Some life in the house. She'll make them laugh, and give them something to do beside sweeping the cemetery."

"We'll go."

"Mi promisa?"

"Ti promiso."

When the proprietor brings the bill, alongside two shots of limoncello, complimenti, he and Jimmy talk heartily in dialect. I can't quite follow them, except to catch allusions to the woman who came in. Perhaps they both have stories with her and need help with the endings, or the sequels. Jimmy introduces me. When he explains that my family is from Gainiga, the wild, black-locked man shakes my hand with a grave warmth.

"Vieni encora," he says, "piacere," and walks away with Jimmy's money on the tray.

"In San Francisco, it's your turn," says Jimmy, refusing my attempt to pay. "Only the finest diving bars in North Beach."

We go outside, walk across the quiet piazza to Via Garibaldi. We make a plan for him to visit us at Clara's.

"Oh, and Jimmy," I say. "I forgot to ask. Where was it they found Claudio?"

"Where?" He looks offended that I should ask such a thing on the street. "You know," he says curtly. "In Tore di Mostre."

"Near Morvetti, the winemaker?"

"Forse, si."

I know he's not going to like the next question, but I ask it anyway:

"Did they ever find the gun?"

He shakes his head slowly. "No, Miki. They found nothing. Not even the necklace she gave him."

"Sunwillows" by Greg Keeler. Acrylic on canvas, 30" x 24."

ANNIE LAMPMAN

Winter Hot-tubbing Guide for Northerners

Lie dormant in this hot effervescence,
head pillowed against your lover's chest,
arms and legs suspended, body aloft and floating,
anchored only by your hips in your lover's hands,
bubbles bursting against your face like fog or sea spray,
tepid gusts of wind like something you imagine—
a vacation you're not on, but feel as if you are—
a hawk kiting high on updrafts
wing-tucked into downward spirals,
tree limbs etched like art on bits of blue,
a scuttle of low-slung clouds,
a four o'clock sunset,
the Christmas lights swaying,
your squeaky-toothed feet as water whitened
and grooved as the yard full of snow and ice.

Independence Day in the Yard

Morning glory, button weed, bindweed winding
the trunks of our just-planted trees: hemlock, cedar,
larch, wilting in the heat of this summer pool,
tender leaders bent like captive orcas' fins.

Spruce needles skewer our feet in a yard of cracked dirt,
desiccated apples, and chicken poop, fur and feathers
banking lavender grown leggy and sparse,
the bug-eaten geraniums a still-life: Dried Flowers on Stems.
Lanky heat-struck cats and dogs lie about in a stupor,
the dust-bedded hens open-beaked and panting—

this air like a furnace, this heat like murder,
a theatrical set born on sweltering air:
Fire threat Stage I, Stage II, Stage III—
firecrackers and bottle rockets a prelude to the show:
torched trees that spark like tinder—a smoking
curtain call with millions of parched acres yet to go.

O. ALAN WELTZIEN

Grande Ronde Suite
 for James Nash

I

Prelude

North
West Company
voyageurs name it "Great
Wheel" in early 19th century "because
of [the valley's] circular shape." Though on
the river I don't trace a round. I roll the French r's,
weave through square dance's "grand right and left" as
the raft plunges northwest then northeast then east
from lower Wallowa River past Minam through
Wild and Scenic, tumble in lower canyon
past stacks of terraced basalt
to Heller Bar on the
Snake and curve
this diamond
into a
circle.

II

Minuet

A whitetail deer strokes
      across the current, west to east,
           only meters in front of the raft

her dark eyes and nimble legs
      sense an audience, possible predators,
           as she scrambles between short gray scarps

the first route a mistake
      when she tips backward, feet to sky,
           yet lands on all fours, a cat;

as the raft draws abreast, a frisson of fear
      ripples her muscles on a second
           chute of soil between rock

and she gains altitude and safety,
      a more composed fluid trot
           while I silently applaud, downriver

ALAN WELTZIEN

III

Air

The morning of our last camp
short miles above Boggan's Oasis
he spies a blond who forages in shrubs
above the pines behind camp.
"I've only seen four in my life"
admits this lifelong hunter;
neither my son nor I have seen
one. In their color phases, Jim
explains, black bears are sometimes
blonds. Through my binocs his caramel
coat shimmers as he stretches
hindlegs, gorges on leaves and grubs,
wallows about, sniffs for scents, nose
extended, occasionally resorts to four
legs as he shifts a few feet. We stand
in a row, rapt witnesses to a honey
bear who glistens in the day's
young light.

IV

Allemande

In interior Northwest river canyons,
        early season,
syringa, known domestically as Lewis's
        mock orange,
festoons rock outcroppings, cascades towards water's
        edge; thick petal
clusters spill, a floral cornucopia whose sweet scent
        perfumes eddies
where boaters pause before fast high water, inhale
        the essence of spring
from the sturdy plants that reach up and out and down
        in billowing white bunches.

ALAN WELTZIEN

V

Sarabande

                In the lower Grande Ronde canyon,
                thinning grasses tinctured green
                in late spring, Grande Ronde Basalt
              stacks higher as we drop below 1000',
              follow the diving water seam that
              exposes layer upon layer, according
           to a WSU geologist "three magnetostrati-
           graphic units and thirty-five flows."
           I roll "Plagioclase-phyric flows...
       with thick entablatures" around
       my mouth, geology's unwieldy
       word lumps as I taste an ocher
     layer cake far higher than that eight-
     layer jam cake in Tennessee, tallest
     I've ever et, or discern a more
    intricate series of parapets guarding
    a larger castle than I've ever seen, or
    a series of failed terraces that would
  rival any steep stacks in Nepal or Japan
  or Indonesia. But cake or castle
  or terrace fall short of canyon
as we sink deeper below tiers, test
geology's precision with our tongue
as they loom just above the river's

edge.

VI

Gigue

Near its mouth the Grande Ronde
constricts to less
than half its
width and surges,
two throats
between tumbled
basalt where
we walk
and scout.
A wood
cross above
a cairn,
memento
mori
and this
race's
caution flag.
Jim picks
our line
and in
the raft
we hunker
down
pitch and
yaw
whoop
pound
and slow
below,
wet and grinning
as the River opens wide,
re-composes itself in its stately
march to its union with the Snake.

—at the Narrows, the Grande Ronde River's only Class IV rapid

JOHN GARMON

Light Morning Snow, We Wait for a Warmer Season

How good we imagine it would be
To see blue breaking through,

To see the snow ease up, to see
The sun blaze, eating white.

I think of you in white. Your
Virgin days are gone,

But I enjoyed the spring, the
Quickening to fall after that

Bird and bush summer. We look
Into an older mirror this winter.

It's good to have this morning,
Its soft descending, its mute

Reminding. I stand at the window
In a room where you do not see me.

I am watching the soft falling
Of the pure snowflakes, seeing

As they settle
Into the earth's alterations.

Do not blame me if I stay here,
Falling, delicate, merging.

"Underpass" by Greg Keeler. Acrylic on canvas, 30" x 24."

GARY GILDNER

Jessica

I

Jessica Livingston was beautiful, people said, in the way that Jacqueline Kennedy and Audrey Hepburn were beautiful. Glamorous—with a hint of brittle. More lyrically, Walt Shuttleworth, Snake River's librarian and a published poet, said she was beautiful in the way an Idaho mountain river was beautiful, wildflower-fragrant and full of light.

Every December you would see Jessica on a ladder, snow in her hair, leading the volunteer crew that decorated our huge Christmas fir in Pioneer Square. In the spring you saw her dispensing apples and brochures at the town's annual Fresh Air Fair she helped organize, a Saturday when a good number of our doctors and nurses and technicians at the hospital took over the high school to draw blood and examine the hearts and other parts of the hundreds who showed up for this free assessment of their health. You saw Jessica walk on stage in the school gym, her red cheeks beaming, to receive a bouquet of roses from the community for single-handedly raising the money to send our Snake River Thespians to Washington to present, in one crisp act, their prize-winning rendition of Mr. Lincoln and a band of angels calling on the Republic to cultivate what was best in our natures.

But you could not see or ever imagine that generous, beautiful woman stealing one dollar, let alone tens of thousands, from the hospital's Foundation, of which she was the unpaid director. When the news broke people cried. If everyone in town, they said, had to be listed on a roster of potential embezzlers, from the most likely to the least, her name would be dead last—even after the Catholic priest who was suspected of drinking too much, the Episcopal rector who was *known* to drink too much, and the various protestant ministers, heavily Evangelical, who seemed to see the Lord's many enemies behind every gooseberry bush. Or she would not be included on such a roster at all if a spontaneous vote had been taken.

She grew up in Snake River, or a short bike ride to the outskirts, on a modest chicken-and-egg farm that she and her mother ran. Jessica's father, Sam Flaherty, perished in Vietnam on that frantic April day of the

Saigon evacuation; he was an enlisted man, a volunteer who managed to get in despite his advanced age and the fact that his left leg was shorter than his right: he'd contracted polio as a boy and the doctors put a pin in the good leg to slow its growth, hoping to keep it even with the afflicted one. Their science came close enough to satisfy the U.S. Army. Jessica's mother, Maureen, had not wanted her husband to enlist—she hated fighting, guns, and all music with a martial blare—and she crumpled the personal letter of condolence from President Ford and dropped it in the star thistles behind her roadside mail box, where Jessica found it. If you saw Maureen in town you saw a woman who had become old overnight (she was not a young mother to begin with, having married Sam Flaherty when they were both in their mid-thirties) and bent from grief, conducting her business at the hardware store or at the bank with an expression that suggested she took only the bitterest and most gnarled of roots for nourishment. The town forgave and tried not to pity this poor soul—largely because of the tall, slim, raven-haired daughter who was so optimistic and cheerful. She favored her father, no doubt about it.

After graduating *magna cum laude* from Snake River High School and then with honors from the University of Idaho in Moscow (where she had the added challenge of little Caleb), Jessica could have gone anywhere, been successful anywhere, but chose to come home to calm the usually unruly seventh-graders and charm them into mindful young ladies and gentlemen. She won the Governor's Teacher of the Year Award the first time she was eligible, and might well have continued to win it but for Major C.M. Livingston, Snake River's highest ranking military son, who came home from the first Iraq war with an artificial arm and captured her heart.

Twenty years Jessica's senior, the Major was balding and wore thick glasses but stood totem pole straight (as his sister-in-law put it) in the blue blazer and rep tie he always wore greeting his clients at Livingston Investments. Right away he did his part in helping retire his wife from teaching *and*—before you could say "Jack Robinson," it seemed—help her win Snake River's Mother of Pearl trophy and the accompanying $500 gift certificate from the Chamber of Commerce: they produced three baby girls in just over three years—all of them raven-haired and green-eyed like their mother. Add in Caleb plus her then modest volunteer work, Jessica had plenty to keep her busy without showing up at Hoover Junior High every morning. With each pregnancy the ladies at the Homegrown Quilt Shop on Silver Street were heard to say, like a Greek chorus, "The Major has no time to dally!"

Jessica had married into Snake River's most prominent family. Her father-in-law was Judge Cotton Livingston, the town's beloved magistrate for almost half a century before Parkinson's imprisoned his mind and stopped him from greeting one and all on Main Street; now he only waved feebly from the car as Jessica drove him to his medical appointments or to daily Mass at St. Joseph's. Emily, his wife, had been gone for a good decade—from a broken heart, the town believed. C.M.'s twin sister Rachel, her husband, and their two small adopted children had been crashed into going up the curvy Mountain View road by a drunk driver—a tourist from back east—on the Fourth of July. Exactly one year later Emily Livingston suffered the stroke that mercifully ended her grieving.

That left C.M. and his brother Jonathan, the oldest Livingston sibling. Jon, as he preferred to be called, had breezed through Snake River like a Hermes, Mr. Plath, the long-retired Latin teacher, said. As quick in the classroom as he was on the playing fields (his State record for the mile still stands), Jon went on to Williams, where his father had gone, and then to Harvard for his law degree. He married a daughter of the Boston family that claimed a cardinal, a U.S. Supreme Court justice, and the physician for whom Cushing's, the fatal wasting disease, is named. Jon and Abbey had been making their annual visit to Snake River during the summer Blossom Festival, spending most of that long weekend trout fishing at the Livingston retreat in the mountains; but after the terrible accident that took away Rachel and her family and then Emily's passing, they only flew in for the Judge's birthday on February second and usually left the next day. (Walt Shuttleworth referred to them as the Eastern Flying Groundhogs.) They had no children. Jon specialized in admiralty law in Boston and was himself a respected amateur sailor who once said in a profile in the Snake River *Republican Star-Ledger* that he enjoyed racing the yacht he owned a piece of far more than spending time behind a desk or in court. Of course we all took that comment as a joke. Abbey devoted herself to various Boston charities.

Jessica and Abbey became close, despite the considerable difference in their ages (almost a generation) and only that brief day or two each February when they could visit in person. (When the scandal broke, Abbey flew to Snake River as soon as she could.) Abbey adored Jessica's daughters, sent them presents and charming letters on every possible occasion—and on several holidays of her own invention—but her heart went out fully to Caleb, who was clearly struggling to find a place in his mother's new life in Snake River. He was nearly six the day she married the Major. His father, long out of the picture, was a senior engineering student from the Middle East when he met Jessica her sophomore year at the university. The Major adopted the boy. Insisted on it. Insisted, also, that should the biological father ever reappear, Cal was never to see him, have no contact whatsoever. This stricture, the fierce coloration of it, bothered Abbey in ways that forced her to believe later that her sister-in-law's trespasses were not exactly as the official charges presented them—that there was more to the story. Many others, even without knowing what Abbey knew, shared her opinion.

But I am getting ahead of myself. I was telling how Abbey's heart had gone out to this quiet boy with dark brown eyes and olive skin who sometimes stuttered. On one of hers and Jon's February visits Abbey heard Cal mention a dog he'd found that needed a home. Abbey wanted to meet this dog, so she suggested slipping out, with Jessica, to pay a call on Snake River's animal shelter, where Buddy, as Cal called the dog, was being kept. Buddy was a springer spaniel, black and white, and when Cal knelt on the shelter floor to embrace the dog, Buddy began licking his face and didn't stop until they delivered him to the vet's office for an exam and his shots. Next they stopped at the variety store for a nice leash and dog food. Cal also picked out a toy for Buddy, a rubber Elmer Fudd he could chew on. In the car, Buddy immediately ate Elmer Fudd. Apparently in one gulp. Jessica also saw that her seat belt had been mostly chewed off. At home, Buddy slept in a metal crate in Cal's room and during the day was carefully watched. But he couldn't be watched all the time and soon he had eaten a foyer rug, Cal's sneakers, that first nice leash and two more, a Raggedy Ann and several other dolls belonging to his sisters, and a portion of the walnut stock on the Major's 12-gauge shotgun. The Major had temporarily left it out after shooting clay pigeons at the Hunt Club, intending to clean and oil it later. His mistake, he admitted, but nonetheless Buddy had to go. He said the dog was untrainable and no good. He returned him to the shelter to be put down.

Abbey, hearing of this pronouncement, immediately sent the Snake River Animal Ark a check and arranged for Buddy to board there, as Cal's guest, until other arrangements could be made. Thanks to her, boy and dog saw each other every day; they took long walks and romps in the woods and on her lucid days went out to see Grandma Maureen. When Cal left for college, Buddy went to stay with Maureen, both of them under the care of Wanda Martinat, a retired nurse, widowed now, whose sweet Basque temperament completely won her charges over. She even brought some color to Maureen's cheeks in her last years. On a personal note, I grew up next door to the Martinats and learned as much about psychology babysitting those six clever Martinat boys as I did at the university.

Abbey Livingston once said she had a keen sense of time and of time's necessities. I didn't know precisely what she meant by this, but her account of how she came to behave toward the Major gave me some good clues. Whenever she and Jon came to visit after Jessica had pled guilty (and C.M. had been quoted on the front page of the *Republican Star-Ledger*, saying, "I turned her in as soon as I knew"), Abbey always brought up the subject—always in company—of how, exactly, the terrible accident happened that had cost him his arm.

"It wasn't enemy fire, was it, Curtis?"

"No."

"As I remember, the first Mr. Bush took care of his war in less than a week with no, or almost no, mishaps. But you, unfortunately—help me out, Curtis, please."

Everyone politely waited while C.M. explained, yet again, that a large crate of equipment slipped off the crane and just missed crushing him, but did catch his arm.

"You were counting the incoming supplies, wasn't that it, dear Curtis?"

"Among other duties, yes."

"Safely *behind* the lines, thank God."

"At the airport, actually."

"And what was *in* that crate of supplies, I never can remember."

The Major, no doubt feeling that he had gone through this grilling more than any man deserved, would glare at his sister-in-law, and eventually answer, "Foodstuffs."

"Yes, yes, frozen potatoes, I think you once said." After a pause, Abbey would always add, "What a dear, dear price to pay for probably tasteless government-issue French fries."

But she finally stopped this foolishness—and foolishness was her word for it. She also stopped reminding everyone how proud she was of Cal getting into Williams—"following in the splendid footsteps of his grandfather and his uncle"—where he had "found his legs" and "performed like the solid young man he always basically was." Perhaps she stopped praising Cal at gatherings because it no longer gave her satisfaction humiliating her brother-in-law, whose mediocre high school record had kept Williams from accepting him, a Livingston or no. She also stopped pretending to remember where he *had* gone for his higher education, forcing him to recite, numerous times, that he had received a degree in business and his ROTC commission at State College.

For a while Cal had not done well in high school either, caught by the police with marijuana in his pocket and banished from home by the Major for "insubordination" and other failures to measure up. He slept at his grandmother's house—or, in summer, in a tent in the woods with Buddy—until he graduated. It was during this period when Jessica began writing checks to herself from the Foundation's account, not even trying to cover her tracks. She had no plan, and no one was looking over her shoulder because she was so trusted. She simply withdrew money as if it were hers and gave some to her son and mother, some anonymously to people she knew were hurting, and some she just tossed in her car's glove box and forgot about or lost.

It was this cavalier manner that the Major's lawyer stressed to the court, drawing the portrait of a woman clearly beset with mental sickness. He brought forth two psychiatrists for their testimony, which included a discussion of the drugs she was taking in order "to simply walk from one room to another and lift up a fork." I dreaded being called for my observations, would wake in the middle of the night worrying about it, and finally could breathe when told I was not needed to testify. Like most Snake River folks I did not wish to see Jessica sent to prison.

But it's interesting, isn't it, how a very particular kind of worm will start to crawl around behind some people's eyes, a worm that can magically talk, or at least whisper, offering up opinions whose key words are *money, privilege, average citizen, what's fair, what is fair?*

Judge Livingston was still alive, but only biologically. At those gatherings in which he was brought out in his wheelchair, it was Jessica who, as before, wiped his chin. At Thanksgiving and Christmas and Easter and of course the birthdays—I am referring to those awful three and a half years between the charges and the sentencing—I was asked to bring Grandma Maureen, Jessica's nerves no longer together enough for her to drive a car. Abbey hired me, with the Major's assent, finally, to be a kind of companion-assistant.

At first he resisted having me in the house. He said he wanted to keep the family—and especially the three young girls, Emily, Constance, and Courtney, who were thirteen, twelve, and eleven when their father told the *Star-Ledger* that he had turned their mother in—"as protected as possible from the outside."

Abbey asked the Major—as if she were addressing someone slow-witted—how a long-time friend from childhood, a mature, university-educated, responsible professional such as myself, could possibly be considered a threat from outside?

"I can't," she said, "entirely grasp your logic, Curtis. *Are* you being logical?"

His lawyer, Mr. Finny, underlined Abbey's comments, saying that I could be useful in building their case. Not least *because* I grew up in Snake River with Jessica. Mr. Finny told me, in private, what I had not already heard myself.

Mr. Finny had a large, fleshy Irish face with many turns in it. He also let me know that the funeral of Grandma Maureen and Judge Livingston's only three months later were helpful. *Helpful* is my word, but there was no mistaking Mr. Finny's face registering rosy gratitude at the large turnouts for both events. I'm sure he was also happy to see the warm testimonials to the departed—and by extension to their families—in the editorials and Letters to the Editor of the *Star-Ledger*. Mr. Finny actually winked at me when he caught my eye during Father Welcher's rather long homily over the Judge's gleaming bronze casket.

At the reception he sidled up next to me and whispered, "Nice hominy."

"Pardon me?" I said.

He only smiled.

At Jessica's sentencing she looked beautifully alive, even glowing, and at the same time vacant, almost bloodless. You heard both descriptions in town. And then nothing. As if the whole drawn-out business had soiled us, reduced us, made us a party to her crime via our admiration and trust, and now all we wanted was to forget it. As if we could. The second anyone mentioned the Livingston name, a burst of bitter sighs could be heard, accompanied by hard looks at the speaker. That, to me, would always be Jessica's punishment. And the Major's.

The judge presiding over the case (there was never a jury), took into account Jessica's three daughters still at home (Cal was in Massachusetts) and sentenced her to a thousand hours of community service, three years of supervised probation and therapy, and restitution of all monies. A week after the judge's decision, the Major told me my services were no longer needed. I said I would be happy to continue helping Jessica without payment.

"I find your offer repugnant," he said.

Abbey called me that same day. "I'm so sorry," she said. "He has her now."

All I could see was the Major gripping Jessica with his artificial hand, which, instead of fingers, had a hook-like pincer.

"Why do you stay in Snake River?" Abbey's question startled me.

"You could do better, Jane, than part-time educational testing at the school. And the odd job or two."

"I've given it thought," I said.

"I could help you. With introductions, and so forth."

I thanked her, promising to stay in touch.

After hanging up, I felt I needed to do something physical—run across a field, or jump in the river, something. I remembered when we were young, Jesssica and I. Riding bikes down to the Snake on hot afternoons and dog-paddling around in our favorite pool. In the beginning, and even afterwards, she was never self-conscious about being one toe short on her left foot—not around me, that is. But when boys entered the picture and swimming came up, her spontaneity went missing. In the place for a second toe on that foot, she had a gap. Not a terribly big gap, but a gap nonetheless. Her parents, her doctor, a nurse or two, myself, Cal's father, and likely the Major had seen it; I can't imagine anyone else. (Nor, frankly, is it pleasant imagining the Major looking at her.)

In foolish moments, I wondered if Nature hadn't withheld that toe to balance out, in a way, the great many physical gifts she did receive. I hadn't thought about her absent digit in years. Now I thought about it almost every time I saw her in town or in my daydreams. I also thought about how, at the university, we would meet for fun with an informal yoga group; and the trouble she took to keep her feet covered. We loved the names of the positions we'd get into—downward-facing dog, low cobra, tall mountain, child's pose. Jessica, as in everything, was so good at all of them we wanted her to be our leader. But after she began seeing Yakub, Cal's father, finding time to join us was difficult for her.

Sundays during her community service period when I saw her at Mass—the times I could bear to go—she did not seem present at all. She went up for Communion leaning on the arm of Emily, her oldest daughter; otherwise she half-sat, half-knelt in her pew throughout the service like a woman twice her age with scoliosis, reminding me painfully of her mother.

Jessica performed much of her community service out of sight in the kitchens of the junior and senior high school cafeterias, cooking a little but mainly cleaning up. Some thought she might have handed out apples and brochures at the Fresh Air Fair—as a reminder of her former good deeds—but most people, including myself, considered that idea impossibly cruel, if not bizarre. She performed other service mopping and polishing floors at the hospital's hospice center, where Grandma Maureen had spent the last month of her life, largely in bewilderment. Jessica herself, whenever I happened to see her, seemed either bewildered or maniacally beaming. At the end, after her punishment was fulfilled, the money paid back by the Major, she was still so far away—at least it seemed so to me—that just holding my hands appeared to be a great success and the high point of her day. ■

"Deadfall" by Greg Keeler. Acrylic on canvas, 30" x 24."

CHARLOTTE MEARS

Early Morning

You, my mockingbird,
start your routine serenade
sweet and soft as sunrise.
By 5:45 you've flown multi-lingual
to perch on top of the lamp post.
What do other birds think of you?
Seen as an imposter, a loser, a vagabond,
a show-off, an irritant, a brash brazen braggart
your ego so big they scatter out of earshot?
Or perhaps you're regarded as star quality
for your virtuosity, a bird of many talents
deserving of high praises and prize perches
from which to express your wide-ranging talent.
Or maybe, just maybe, you're simply misunderstood,
an outsider wrongfully judged for being vocal
because you're actually shy, horribly shy,
your repertoire a succession of calls for companionship,
a kindness, a small interaction with another
to break out of your shuttered loneliness,
your utter befuddlement why
no one returns your reach.
I hear you as this, my mockingbird,
I hear you.

Time Heals All Wounds

The family who lives in the unit above
makes the ceiling creak at all hours,
and worse, drops ominously
weighty items, lifeless bodies?
So instead of my dark imagination
instead of the neighbor's activities
this, an attempt to speak of summer cicadas rising in concert
waves of castanets and their familiar falling away—
but the fear of him interferes, hisses, *Don't move or I'll shoot!*

Tight days then weeks turn into years with little improvement
because over time he had become potentially any man—
I pull out into traffic and a car appears too close behind me
swerves back and forth honking
follows me through two quick turns while I
ready to dial 911, look in the rearview again, and he's gone.

Fear doesn't disappear by moving into a house
into a better neighborhood or even another state.
A man is ringing the doorbell, his frame tall and waiting
on the other side of the obscure glass.
I crawl into the bathroom, hide panicked—
Silver gun hard against the back of my head again
Give me the password now! Doorbell rings.
This is where he'll kill me.

But some days zing by without trigger.
Out and about among strangers
I stop to take photographs of clouds
and wild violet, bluet, spiderwort, star
take walks among nesting geese
while all that he wants and forces me to do travels light
unpacks any time of day, outdoors, indoors, alone or in public—
at least one sanctimonious platitude shot to hell.

KIM STAFFORD

Why We Go to the Desert, the Mountain, and the Sea

In the desert, we seek the far horizon
of no road, the long look across rock and sage
where the evening stars glimmers alone.

On the mountain, we need rock and snow
above timberline, the peak thrust through
alpenglow belittling our plans.

Beside the sea, at the high tideline
strewn with salty debris, we find where
human comforts end and the wild begins.

We find where spirit walks unencumbered,
where all our intricate inventions pale,
where we are humbled into wisdom

and can be children of the Earth again.

The Turning

When they cut a tree, plant ten.
When they stain the river, welcome rain.
When they say no to wisdom, say yes.
When they say yes to greed, say no.
Comfort and convenience kill.
Economic growth withers earth.
How long shall we smoke the sky?
When they take the easy road,
choose the stony path.
If you cherish the children,
turn grief to gusto
and make sorrow sing.

GERALD COSTANZO

Election

In the midst of the packed
Convention Hall in Atlantic City,
New Jersey, a little man in a Panama hat
is making a motion with his fist.

Out of the demolished look of progress
vacant lots are filling with money! Just beyond
the Boardwalk, the ocean continues its
shabby threat of permanence.

Straddling cool glass palaces,
dilapidated lunch stands and the gift shops
of mafia baroque, who among us
can define the curio?

Even in a country
of vociferous Nay's
In the end the Aye's always
have it.

"Notom Lands" by Royden Card. Acrylic on canvas, 36" x 36."

BOB BUSHNELL

Wrath

I never knew why we stopped where we stopped. I never asked Mother since I knew she'd say he'd know where to stop and when he said stop we stopped. Or she'd say he was the one who decided to give up the parched farm in Nebraska and he'd decide where to stop.

And I never asked him since I knew he'd say he'd know where to stop and when we got there he said stop here and that's where we stopped. And if he'd been drinking he'd slap me and say I was asking things no kid of his should be asking. I'd tell him I wasn't a kid any more and he'd say you're still my kid and you'll always be my kid so shut your damned mouth and he'd slap me again.

And when I asked Mother why he was the way he was she said I should just be grateful. She said we were the lucky ones since other fathers saw their losses as failures and their failures as losses and they blamed themselves for the dust storms and the dead fields and for not being able to do anything but pack up and run and they were ashamed and defeated by their losses and failures and by their running. He lost and failed and he ran too but he refused to admit defeat or take any blame and he swapped resentment and revenge for the despair that ruined the others.

When he decided we should go, we went. We packed up what we had room for and neighbors took the rest. He drove us into town to fill the tank and all the gas cans we had. We watched our empty house disappear behind us. He looked straight ahead.

Mother's friends met us at Riley's General Store to see us off. He had no friends, so he waited outside. His face never changed and neither did Mother's till she had to say goodbye to her sister.

I thought we'd be traveling alone, but he wasn't surprised when we saw the dust cloud a mile before we got to the road heading west. Strangers caravanned like wagon trains since nobody wanted to break down with no help around.

We had piled our belongings on the truck, and when we looked at what others had packed up, we said to ourselves what a pity they're lugging those beat up chairs or worn out mattresses or burlap bags full of old Sunday clothes all this miserable way, while everybody else was saying the same thing about what we had tied down and hauled along. You never know what's important till you have to leave it behind or load it on top of some jalopy and drive a thousand miles, spending every dime you have left and not knowing whether you'll end up any better off.

We ran out of tears after a few days when there was no turning back and regret was a waste of effort. Then the futility of grieving won over all but those who never would forgive themselves for leaving a child or parent behind.

Families competed for the best campsites but shared their beans and bread with those who didn't have enough. It was different when someone ran out of gas money. Nobody could afford to help with cash for more than a day or two, so the caravan would give them what food they could spare and leave them some place where they might be able to eke out a living.

Sagebrush became the monotony that wheat fields had been back home. A few forests and green valleys were exceptions, but we sweltered through long, dry stretches that looked and felt the same at any place as they had thirty miles back or as they would thirty miles ahead. Whenever we met someone going east, we asked how far it was to California, then where the next water was.

He never looked back. Around the campfires other men talked about what they'd lost or left behind. He wouldn't say a word unless it had to do with where they were headed or what they'd do when they got there.

He never put up with weakness in others or admitted his own, but I saw him slip a dollar to a hungry family. He never told Mother and neither did I. And he never complained. Once, I heard him say, I guess it's better to go through this together than alone. I wondered how he would know. He was always alone.

We thought we were going to California like everybody else. But when we got to Utah where the others turned south, he told them we would go west to Oregon. Then he told us.

It was harder for me to part with the boys on the road than it had been to leave my friends back home who thought I was lucky to be going. The caravan was different. We were all hungry and broke and looking for a new start. That was all we needed to know about each other. We made friends riding together or gathering firewood while our parents set up camp and cooked dinner, so when we drove away from the others I hid in the back and cried.

None of us knew where we would end up, and goodbyes were forever. After living in the same place with the same friends for my first ten years, I learned to let go and hoped he would make good decisions for us. We all knew he would make decisions for himself first.

Everybody knew about California. We had talked for hours around dusty campfires about how warm and green it would be and how there would be jobs and how we'd have fresh fruit and vegetables year round. I didn't know much about Oregon and that worried me. Good thing I didn't worry a lot because we never made it there either.

We slowed down in Idaho. The roads were worse and it was hotter and drier. He took a hard look at every town we went through, but never said a word about what he was looking for and didn't see, or what he was seeing and didn't like. We used our last spare tire and I heard him tell Mother we were running low on money.

That afternoon we set up camp and he said he was going into town to take a look. He came back late, ate his supper alone and bedded down without saying a word. At dawn he told Mother, don't break camp till I get back.

When he was sure he'd found whatever he was looking for, he drove back and said, get in.

It was a house half the size of what we left behind and on a lot big enough for a garden. We called it a house because he promised Mother he'd fix it up from the shack that it was.

It was near the railroad switching yards in the middle of the town that had grown up around the tracks where men separated freight cars from inbound trains and rearranged them into out-bounds, or shoveled coal into the tenders and loaded water into the boilers, or cleaned the passenger cars—men he hated, he said, because they sold themselves to unions that fought with the company owners he admired: movers and shakers, men like him, he said, with vision and guts and the nerve to grab the land for their own, and who wrenched fortunes from the continent they believed God intended to be theirs to do with as they pleased.

The day after we moved in, he brought home some gunnysacks and marched us all to the switching yard. Starting now, he said, you kids are going to come here every day and walk these tracks and pick up pieces of coal that bounce off the tenders and you're going to take them home in these sacks and toss them in a corner of the tool shed, and when there's no more room, you'll stack them behind the wood pile where nobody can see them to steal. That's how we'll keep warm this winter.

Mother put her hands on her hips and said, Dad, you do whatever you want with the boys, but the girls are coming back with me. I'll be needing them to help with the baby and the house chores. They won't be picking up any coal. She always called him Dad and he got the message by the tone she used. So did we.

The first winter was the worst. He wouldn't pay for tarpaper to block the wind from coming through the walls, and that house turned out to be just a cold shack after all. Only the girls were allowed to complain. If he heard one of us boys whine, he'd give it to us good.

We learned to do whatever he said or we'd suffer the consequences. He chewed us out and slapped us around to keep our attention. And if we didn't satisfy him, he'd really let us have it. Mother said to him, you do what you have to do, Dad, but keep those hands open. I don't ever want to see any fists, Dad. No fists.

He worked all day every day. He soon built up a freight hauling business and that was all he thought about. We found other jobs for after school so we didn't have to work for him except on weekends and holidays.

Nothing I did was ever good enough or fast enough to satisfy him. When I finished high school, I got as far away from him as I could. I saved enough to buy a car and drove to California where we would have been if he hadn't changed his mind.

Then I showed him.

I showed him I could work harder and smarter than he could. He never said so, but I did. He wouldn't admit it, but I was better and faster and even meaner when I had to be. And I made more money than he ever dreamed of.

I showed him!

And I never laid a hand on my son.

From the day he was born, I pushed Buddy to be the best he could be, to work harder and smarter, just like me. But I never slapped him. I never touched him.

And when I told him to stay away from Buddy, he was mad as hell. He said I was being too easy on the boy, that I was letting him down, letting us all down, that Buddy would never be tough enough to be a man in this new and meaner world and that I would regret it sooner or later, and I laughed at him and said, I'll do it my own way, so just watch me, old man, just watch me. I said, I'm not going to have him hate me as much as I've hated you, and I said, Buddy will be stronger and do better than both of us put together, you'll see.

And even when he didn't do better, I just told Buddy, you need to do it for yourself, not for me. I know you can do it, Buddy, and I know you will.

But he never did.

And when I read his note that said he'd never be good enough for either of us on the day Buddy hanged himself in my den, I cried for the first time since we left the caravan. And when he said, see, I told you so, I knew he had gotten to Buddy somehow when I wasn't looking.

I promised Buddy I would kill him and I would have. But the dementia got to him first and there was nothing left worth killing, since by then he couldn't remember who I was, and I'd never have the satisfaction of his knowing it was me who was shooting him, so I didn't. When what was left of him died, we burned him and we threw away the ashes.

And Mother said, Amen. ■

"20 Mule Canyon V" by Royden Card. Acrylic on canvas, 30" x 36."

DANIELLE BEAZER DUBRASKY

Shadow Prints

My family waits to sight a black leopard beneath a constellated sky
after my father pulls the Land Rover up to a copse of moringa trees,

cuts the engine, shines a light into branches at two in the morning.
I am ten, fidgeting in the car, tricked into thinking I see a tail,

a sleek paw, but the dark body never shows itself.
I fall asleep as we drive back to our tent, and dream of Kebaki Kebaki,

the boy next door who pretends he is Sinbad to rescue me from sea monsters
swimming across his backyard to the rock where I stand.

Back in the states, you are already seventeen,
working your first summer job as valet at casinos on the Strip,

while I am a few miles away from the equator, skip over it like a jump rope,
in my British uniform, striped orange and white like a creamsicle,

recite the Lord's Prayer in Assembly, then pledge allegiance to the Queen.
We never find the leopard, but see cheetahs, gazelles on the savannah.

You spend nights cooling off in Las Vegas, a city called "the meadows,"
draw a high draft number, drag Tropicana with the windows rolled down.

This is years before I move west to your desert and bring the leopard with me,
watch with her eyes as you dive into a pool, glide the length of your body

over racing stripes before lifting your head to take a breath—
just as she had watched us from her branch, alert beneath the milky way,

camouflaged in the tree's canopy, muscles tense
and ready to spring if the scent of human got too close.

"Arizona Rain" by Nancy Brossman. Linoleum block print, 6" x 9."

SHERMAN ALEXIE

No

In the dark hours, I sometimes hold
An imaginary knife to my temple
And push it through. I have to grapple

With these terrible thoughts. My blood
Wants to become more blood. But, fraught
And fraught, one must unlearn what

One has taught one's self about escape.
Three times, doctors have burred
Into my skull. Three times, they've pushed

Their fingers into my brain and saved
My soul. Let every neurosurgeon be
The priest. Let every operating room

Be the chapel. Let my imaginary knife
Transubstantiate into a holy scalpel.
Let that blade remove the persistent

Tumors, flaws, and scars that whisper
Insidious commands. Sometimes, I will
Outlast the dark because I want to see

The decades pass, and sometimes
Because I know that my self-death
Would steal the breath of people I love.

So let the next day begin. Let the birds greet
The first light. Let me sit at the table
And break bread with this beautiful life.

Ode to Hospice

And so, day by day,
We help our mothers
    and fathers die.
And maybe we'll get the chance
    to say

What could never be said.
    Maybe we were always
    too afraid
To say "I adored you" or
    "Did you adore me?" or
    "You kept your promises"
    or "Why did you lie
So often?" Maybe we'll celebrate
    one particular day,

Like the day when my father
    challenged
    my brother to a foot race
    And ran so hard that his false teeth
    flew out of his mouth
    as he war cried
And won the sprint.
At that moment,
My family's collective laughter
    wobbled
    the planet's orbit.
But, in truth, I did not say

Such things to my father
    or mother
As they faded away.
No, I fled
    their bedsides
On their final days

SHERMAN ALEXIE

And have regretted it,
    in shallow
        and profound ways,
Ever since. My sisters
        stayed through the long nights,
As did other women, my aunts
        and cousins.
But I have to say—

I need to confess—
        that I made my escape.
I once spoke of my failure
        at a fundraising lunch
        for a hospice center.
        And, yes, I cried
As I thanked those hospice workers
        for helping us mourn
        our dead, for teaching us
        how to navigate
        the last days

Of our loved ones. And, yes,
        I thanked them for taking my place
During the Ceremony of Death—
        for staying
        through the grief-drummed night.
This is hard to say,

But I abandoned my parents.
        I didn't offer
        forgiveness
        and I didn't ask them
        for grace.
I gave them only my silence
        and absence
        and arid pride.
And so, now, day by day,

I'm the son
           with a price to pay.
I'm forced to say goodbye,
           goodbye, and goodbye
To the air—maybe for the rest
           of my life—
Because I didn't say goodbye
           to my parents
           when I had the chance.
I didn't even try.
But I am here now,
           on this grey Seattle day—
As if there is any other kind—
And as I write this poem,
           I hope that I'm building
           a hospice
           made of words.
And inside these words,
           inside these walls,
I hope I can lie down
           between my parents' graves—
           their final bed after their final bed—
           and thank them
           for creating me.
           I want to tell them how much
           I still grieve.
I want to apologize
For my flight away
           from the water and earth
           where my parents
           gave birth to me.
I want to again be the child
With the mother and father
Telling old Indian stories
           at his cribside.

SHERMAN ALEXIE

I want to listen to them.
      I want to listen.
I want to praise
      my mother and father.
I want to praise them
for their phenomenal courage
      and broken love.
I want to praise
      and praise and praise.
      Dear Mother, Dear Father,
      I praise you, I praise you,
      I praise you, I praise.
      And I hope that you,
            my favorite ghosts,
      can somehow hear
      what your inadequate son
            needs to say.

"Untitled" by Jinny DeFoggi. Ink on paper, 14" x 17," 2003.

JIM HEYNEN

Clarence

This story about Clarence happened back in 1957 and would probably be different if it happened today. But not much different: our people haven't changed all that much. There were ways in which Clarence fit in just fine: he knew better than to do unnecessary work on Sundays, he knew not to use blasphemous language, and he was a regular in one of the many varieties of Dutch Reformed churches in our community.

But then there was that other Clarence. Clarence the womanizer. He was admired for his slender shape, tall and gaunt, but with a bulbous butt. We called him by his ordinary name of Clarence when we were not joking around and calling him BB for Big Butt. Even though he was a John Deere tractor mechanic, his hard-working hands had long skinny fingers, knobby at the knuckles, like beaded hemp rope. He was, for reasons we didn't fully understand, alluring and sought after, probably because of his easy swagger and infectious grin. His face was long—like a butternut squash that had over-ripened—and was decorated with two squinting blue eyes that were shaded with blond eyebrows flaring out like sunbeams to light up his long forehead; and below, a long noble nose, with huge nostrils that panted suggestively when he breathed. He was, we all agreed, blessed with dangerous qualities. He was thirty-one years old, but his ring finger did not have a wedding band. Being unattached at thirty-one was another thing that made him different. The only other men among us who were single at thirty-one were the ones who didn't show any interest in women. And Clarence was not one of them.

Truth be told, Clarence was an excitable sort of fellow in many ways. He was attracted to anything that broke away from the smooth sameness of things. In the winter you'd see him tobogganing in roadside ditches, a barn rope attached to the toboggan and hooked to the rear bumper of a pickup going fifty miles an hour down the gravel roads. This was fast enough to launch Clarence and toboggan fifteen feet into the air over a driveway. In the summer, you might see him at a stockcar race sitting dangerously close to the fence, close to the exhaust, close to the roar, close to the possibility of having a close-up view of colliding stock cars spraying their fenders into the air.

Maybe the women just liked his craziness. Maybe they were trying to save him from himself. Hard to say. But word was that when he broke up with a woman, it was always Clarence who did the breaking. He seemed like a guy who always had to be trying something dangerous or new.

So it was strange that he was not cruising the gravel roads in his red F150 that Saturday to stare at what we all were staring at. We had just finished milking the cows and feeding the pigs and were about to go in for supper when an enormous cloud emerged on the western horizon. It had the shape of a football lineman's padded shoulders and it was headed our way. It looked alive, and it looked full of determination. It looked unstoppable, and it looked vindictive, like it was coming to avenge us for something. There was more than a massive shoulder, there was a loose appendage that dangled and swayed like a handless arm. That dangling arm was a bigger threat than the huge cloud that was its mother, and we knew it. The cloud and its ruthless offspring were at the South Dakota/Iowa border, eighteen miles to the west, when that dangling arm became a funnel that sucked up many thrusting tons of dark water from the Sioux River and wreaked havoc on all the people and buildings and crops and animals in its path.

We couldn't see where the twister hit the earth, but we saw the mud and dark who-knows-what spewing up and looking as if the funnel were trying to create its own shoulders made of masticated farms. It was impossible not to wonder if Clarence was watching what we were watching. That sky spectacle would have been right up his alley.

The first five miles on our side of the Sioux River were made up of German Catholics. The tornado would have five miles of Catholics before it went to work on our people. We watched and prayed. Accepting God's will did not mean we would not do what people do. Sure, we would run. Sure, we would hide. And keep praying.

The women and children were huddled in storm cellars when the miracle happened. The men watched the funnel lift off the horizon, dangling like a shaggy arm, but now it dangled above a band of troubled sky that separated it from the horizon of undamaged trees and barns. Our trees and barns. Our animals. Our crops. Our people.

JIM HEYNEN

We took shelter as the big cloud moved over us, but the funnel didn't assault the earth again. What we got was three inches of rain. We needed the rain because the fields were dry and the corn had not even dented yet. By midnight we were whispering prayers of thanksgiving and preparing our minds for the Sunday worship services. Our churches would be filled with thankful hearts. The ministers would be adjusting their sermons to accommodate the evening's Acts of God—and the miraculous sparing of our people and our farms.

"Have you seen Clarence?" a young woman asked after the church service at the First Reformed Church.

"Where is Clarence?" an elderly woman asked after church at the Second Reformed Church.

Nobody had seen Clarence at any of the churches. Not at the Trinity Reformed Church. Not at the Netherlands Reformed Church. Not at the Reformed Church of America. Not even at the liberal Evangelical Reformed Church that Clarence had been frequenting lately, largely, we figured, because it was known to be receptive to young widows or women who had put a profession before marriage and were stranded in singlehood in their late 20s and early 30s.

We normally didn't listen to the radio on Sunday mornings before church, but a few people had tuned in to the morning news on WNAX, the strong Yankton, South Dakota, station. The tornado had not killed any people, but dozens were injured. Five people were in a South Dakota hospital in serious condition. A dozen farms had horrendous damage. Cows had been killed. Pigs had been killed. The bodies and feathers of hundreds of chickens and turkeys had disappeared into the churning wind.

We wondered if Clarence had listened to the radio and decided to head out there. But why? Had he skipped church to drift into the easy pickings territory of the devastated Catholic community where there just might have been some fresh young widows to comfort and allure? But even if there were, they'd be Catholics, Clarence. Catholics. He should have known better than that.

But maybe Clarence did not know better.

After church, Gladys and Henry Kraayenbraak aimed their 1955 Ford Fairlane in the direction of the Sioux River, straight west down the new blacktop that would get them into the devastated Catholic territory in fifteen minutes. They were a couple in their sixties, empty nesters who moved from their quarter-section farm to a nice little yellow bungalow in town. Henry had thickened in retirement, now round in the belly, and his gray hair was still thinning. Under light, his large head looked like a moon rising through an oats field. Gladys was even thicker than her husband, but her mouth is what made you look at her. The corners of her mouth were always turned down in a way that made her mouth resemble that of a catfish. Together with her dark eyes and furrowed brow, she wore a constant look of disgust with the whole world. But we knew she was a woman of faith who looked for the Lord's purpose in everything that happened—or didn't happen.

Henry and Gladys wanted to see what the hand of the Lord had delivered to the Catholics. They watched the names on the mailboxes go through some changes at about mile twelve. Some Van-somethings and De-somethings were followed by some Von-somethings and something-bergs. What we called the mixed neighborhood. Then the tornado damage showed itself in bits and pieces of debris in the fields and ditches. Long splinters of barn siding, a whole windowpane, the red barn paint still on it but the glass gone. And there was a twisted metal cupola from somebody's barn, what once looked like a silver Indian tipi now looking like a crumpled pup tent. Then the strangest thing: a ball of barbed wire fencing six feet high, a fist of bristly wire the tornado had rolled up all by its vicious self.

"Henry, look at that over there." Gladys pointed and Henry pulled over.

Two Hampshire hogs, with their distinctive white stripe at the shoulder dirtied by mud, big ones of over 200 pounds each, lay dead in the middle of a green pasture. The tornado must have picked them up some miles away, flung them around for a while, and then slammed them down to their deaths in this pasture.

"My goodness, my goodness," said Gladys as they drove on and into the middle of it: the roof of a huge red barn torn off to show soaked mounds of alfalfa in the hayloft, a mattress and box spring lying in the filth of a hog yard, a two-wheeled manure spreader with its wheels on the ground but the rest of it twisted so that it looked as if someone had wrung it like a dishrag.

JIM HEYNEN

At the farm where Henry pulled over, box elder and ash trees still stood in place, their roots gripping the earth and keeping them upright, but they were stripped naked of their leaves and small branches which, as if gathered by some sky-monster, had been flung across the earth and against the standing buildings to spatter and stick there like a bowl of green porridge. And people everywhere, rummaging through the leftovers of the house and farm buildings. Seeing them out there—men, women, and children—so many children you had to wonder if they ever bothered trying not to have another one every year!—but still, the sad picture of them, working together like so many prisoners of their own beliefs, you had to feel something for them. At least Henry did. Gladys not so much.

Henry's reaction was an ache in his stomach, like a cramp after eating too much too fast. It was an agony he was feeling, not just for what the Lord had delivered unto these people with the tornado, but for these Catholics' own sad history. When they came here from Germany, we were already here and we had gotten all the good land, the rich loamy soil several miles back away from the sandy soil in the river valley. We had eighteen inches to three feet of rich topsoil, while they had skimpy sandy soil. In dry years, their corn wilted from thirst by the end of July, the leaves yellowing and curling, the tassels no bigger than wheat heads, while our corn flourished, the tassels shooting up like church steeples, and the ears forming big and round and firm as a boy's forearm. Year after year, their corn looked as if it had a curse on it, while ours looked blessed. We did not boast about this. We thanked God for it.

And now this. Why them, Lord, and not us? Henry wondered. It was not as if we had not had our own share of trials visited upon us. When we arrived here from Holland, the English landowners tried but failed to make us beholden to them forever. We outsmarted and outworked them and pretty soon towns had Dutch instead of English names. We kept our stores closed on Sundays and had church services in both English and Dutch—until World War II. That is when we stopped speaking Dutch in public because it sounded too much like German, and we did not want any strangers thinking we were Nazi sympathizers. We Americanized ourselves as fast as we could—and we prospered, praise the Lord! We prospered!

"They didn't deserve this," Henry whispered inside the parked Fairlane. Neither he nor Gladys had opened their car windows.

Gladys shook her head. "My goodness," she said. "Even after a terrible thing like this, they're still working on Sunday."

"They're staring at us," said Henry. "They know we're not from here. We should go." He put the Fairlane in gear.

"Look over there," said Gladys. "What's happening over there?"

A crowd had gathered around a grossly damaged corrugated metal building, most likely a machine shed. People were screaming and yelling. Arms waving in the air, some people running away from the scene as if it were too much to deal with.

"Something terrible is going on," said Henry.

"It's none of our business," said Gladys.

"I've got to see what's going on," said Henry.

"If you go, I'm going too," said Gladys.

They looked down at their clothing. They weren't dressed for any kind of rescue mission. Henry jerked off his tie and unbuttoned the top button of his starched white shirt.

"I'm leaving my hat," said Gladys. "I don't have shoes for all that mud."

"Me neither," said Henry. He already had his door open.

They made their way down the driveway toward the people gathered around the corrugated building. Mounds of splintered wood had already been neatly stacked. Kids' clothes had been scavenged from the mud and piled on soiled sheets. The gabled house they walked past had a huge section of the roof ripped off. Where the roof ended up would be anybody's guess.

Nobody stared at them suspiciously as they made their way toward the scene. The faces that did turn toward them looked bewildered—eyes wide open and faces with helpless expressions.

If something terrible was going on in that wrecked metal building, why wasn't anyone calling the fire department? Why wasn't anyone calling an ambulance?

The answer was in the desperate conversations around them: the tornado had wiped out electricity and telephones. There had been no ambulances or fire trucks on the scene, not even last night. People who were hurt were driven into the nearest South Dakota town by farmers in pickups. They had been taking care of their injured by themselves. There were bandaged hands in the crowd. Bandaged foreheads.

Henry and Gladys moved closer to the collapsed metal building, their arms out, their steps small to keep from slipping and falling in the mud.

"Somebody's trapped in there," said a woman's voice.

"Who is it?"

"Nobody knows. They just heard some guy yelling for help.'"

Big men with wooden fence posts were trying to lift sections of fallen corrugated steel. Nobody was in charge but everybody was trying to help.

"That big tall guy is trying to get at him," someone said.

Then a voice from under the rubble: "I see him. I'm almost up to him."

"That's Clarence's voice," said Gladys. "That sounds just like Clarence."

So one of us was already there trying to save one of them? Why not? That would be Biblical, what with Jesus helping strangers and all.

From under the rubble, Clarence said, "Keep lifting that section of roof where you've got the post. A little more and I can drag him out."

Henry grabbed a fence post and started giving orders to the others. Maybe it was his age, maybe it was because he wore the authority of his Sunday suit, or maybe it was because he had the voice of a foreman, but the other men listened to him. "You two lift there," said Henry, "and you two lift there."

There was a terrible cracking sound, a terrible collapsing sound. And then a guttural scream: "My hand! My hand!"

What followed was twenty minutes of desperation: men, women, and children, all lifting and scrambling.

"We need a big winch!" someone yelled.

"Is there a tractor with a front loader?" said Henry.

Indeed there was a tractor with a front loader on it. A John Deere model A came popping with its two-cylinder sound in their direction. The driver lowered the front loader and lifted a section of roofing off the ground. Other men had two-by-fours and wedged them in as support to keep the raised roofing from falling again.

There they were: two men on their bellies, Clarence with his big butt rising like a pocket gopher mound above his long legs. He was not wearing a Sunday suit, he was wearing his striped work coveralls. The middle-aged man beside him, whom Henry did not recognize, got on his hands and knees and crawled to safety.

"I'm all right," he said. "I'm all right. Thanks, folks."

Clarence was silent, his left arm stretched out to the side, a flat expression on his face, but he was not all right. A section of the corrugated steel roofing had come down like a guillotine on his right wrist. Henry crawled in beside him. Clarence's right arm appeared to be jammed against the section of metal roofing.

"Clarence," said Henry. "Clarence, can you move?"

Clarence pulled his right arm back. What appeared was blood and bone, but no right hand. Clarence got up on his knees and stared at his handless right arm. He stood up, grabbed his right arm with his left hand, and stepped, speechless, toward the crowd.

A young woman wearing jeans and a red, checkered shirt stepped forward confidently. "We've got to stop the bleeding," she said.

She was dressed like a farming woman, but she didn't look or sound like one. Too confident. Almost bossy. Clarence didn't look for a ring finger. He looked at her lips, then her squinting and determined eyes. Now he did feel a bit whoozy. No pain anywhere. He felt drops of his own blood hitting his coverall right above the knee. He stared at the woman's face.

Others stepped back and let her take charge. Clarence saw the three-foot piece of clothes line in the woman's hands, then felt her shoving it under his arm—and then a pleasantly sharp pain as she pulled the clothes line tight like someone who had done this many times before.

"Now we need to put some pressure on the wound," she said. She looked Clarence in the face. "Can you handle the pain?"

"I can handle it," said Clarence.

"You feel faint?"

"Nope. I feel weird. Like this isn't happening."

Gladys was the one who felt faint. Her face, with its usual expression of anger, had turned pale. "Henry," she said, "I'm going to the car to wait." Henry watched as she walked, in duck steps, away—and did not stop her. He went back to the scene of the accident. On the other side of the buried metal roofing lay Clarence's severed hand, its long fingers looking as if they had started to clench. Henry picked it up. Clarence's hand was cool in his hand. He held it tenderly and delivered it to the woman with the homemade tourniquet.

Clarence stared at. "That's my hand," he said.

"Maybe they can sew it back on," said Henry. The woman did not say anything, but she took the hand from Henry. "Get me something clean to wrap it in."

A pickup was already standing by. The driver said, "Let's get him to the hospital."

Someone came with a plastic bag. The woman dropped the hand in the bag, got in the pickup with Clarence, and they were off.

Henry looked around at the remaining crowd. "Who was that man we saved?"

"Somebody's cousin. He drank too much last night and everybody thought he'd gone home. He must have curled up in that metal shed to sleep it off and then the tornado hit."

Henry watched the rescued man slinking away. Clarence had lost his hand for a drunk. And the drunk had not even thanked them. Henry decided he would not tell Gladys that Clarence had lost his hand for a drunk Catholic.

The pickup with Clarence on board turned toward South Dakota at the end of the driveway. Clarence would be joining the other injured people in whatever hospital they were in. It no doubt would be a Catholic hospital, with nothing but Catholics around him.

"That's enough for one day," Henry said as he got in the car. "Let's go home."

Clarence was indeed driven to a Catholic hospital. With the young woman at his side, he walked past and under one crucifix after another, what we, in most situations, would call graven images, but Clarence was in no mood to call anything graven at a time like this.

The doctor on duty said there was no chance that Clarence's severed hand could be sewn back on. He would have to allow for a period of healing, and then he would have the choice of living with his stubbed arm or of getting a metal hand.

We all expected that Clarence would be coming back home the next day, but Clarence did not come home.

Behind the mystery that was Clarence was Clarence's own story, with his own reasons for driving out to the tornado-ravished Catholic neighborhood in the first place. He had not driven there out of curiosity, and he had not driven there in hopes of finding a young woman who might be especially susceptible to his gangly charm. He had gotten up that morning with every intention of going to church, but then he had listened to the WNAX morning news about the tornado. He heard that the tornado had brought the Catholic community together for a special mass to pray for the injured. That news gave Clarence an odd twinge that moved through his body like a low-charge electrical current.

Memories can be passed down for centuries, not that they are memories that come easily to mind. Some memories are much deeper than that and have sunk into parts of ourselves that we do not understand. Those memories will have their way even when the one with the memory is totally unaware of it. The buried memory that surfaced for Clarence that morning was of his grandfather's fear and hatred of Catholics. If Clarence's grandfather saw someone making the sign of the cross, he would break out in a cold sweat.

Clarence was nineteen and had dropped out of college after one semester because, he said, classrooms did not fit him. His grades had been fine, but he needed the freedom to work with his hands. His grandfather was already in a nursing home when Clarence had worked up the courage to ask him, "Grandpa, why do you hate Catholics so much? I saw how you acted when that Catholic school basketball team played our boys. When they crossed themselves before going out on the court, I thought you were going to have a heart attack."

"Crossed themselves?" his grandfather had said. There was a tone of spite in his voice. "Crossed themselves?" he had said again. "That's what they did before they killed us."

This led to his grandfather's account of their family history. "We were French Huguenots," he said. "We were fleeing from the Catholics. We weren't even fighting them. We were trying to get away from their evil ways! Away from their graven images! Away from their idolatry! Away from their heathenish worship of the Pope! On our way through Belgium and into Holland, the Catholics followed us and murdered us. Thousands of us. Before they murdered us, they crossed themselves, Clarence. That's what they did. They crossed themselves."

The diatribe had silenced Clarence—but it had also prompted him to read up on these French Huguenots. On his next and last visit with his grandfather, he brought up the topic of Catholics again and actually tried to lecture his grandfather that it was not Christian to hate people the way he hated Catholics.

"They crossed themselves and then murdered us! Don't you understand that, Clarence?"

"I read about us French Huguenots, grandpa. That was centuries ago! You can't blame someone for what happened centuries ago."

But Clarence's grandfather did blame them, and he went to his grave with that old hatred in his heart.

It was not as if Clarence was remembering his grandfather's words when he decided to drive to the tornado scene. Guilt had come at him in a more subtle way: he simply felt the urge to help the tornado victims so that he would feel better. The thought of meeting a young woman was not on his mind.

A few days passed and Clarence still had not come home. What we did not see was the friendship he was striking up with the woman who put the tourniquet on his arm and probably saved his life. She had stayed at his bedside through the night, left for a few hours to sleep, and then returned to be with him again.

Her name was Marie. She did not perform any nursely duties in the hospital, she just visited him. She was not only kind, she was also beautiful.

And modest. She wore no lipstick, though her lips were large and had a deep rose color. Her hair was dark and parted, with a smooth sweep of it arcing over her full, dark eyebrows. Her eyes! It was her eyes more than anything. The pure blueness of them. And the unapologetic directness of them, eyes that said, "I see you fully," eyes that said, "I am listening to you," eyes that said, "I understand you."

You can have what seems like the same experience over and over again—and then, without warning, that same repeated experience that you've had so many times in one variation or another, suddenly, without warning, that same experience is different. Clarence had been attracted to many different women in his life, and many women had been attracted to him, but this was different. Totally different. As different as night from day. As different as having a right hand and not having a right hand. When Marie visited him, the ache from his severed hand was overridden by the relentless ache in his heart. Clarence's life had changed forever, and he knew it.

He had lost a lot of blood from the accident. He still felt weak, and the doctors were having some trouble stopping the bleeding. He had two blood transfusions in three days.

"We'd better keep you here for a while," said the doctor.

That was fine with Clarence so long as Marie continued her visits. A priest stopped by one day, looked at Clarence's chart that said "Protestant," and immediately left. But Marie kept coming back.

What had he done to deserve this: a beautiful young Catholic woman sitting next to him, touching his long forehead, smiling at him even as tears swelled behind her eyelids. Was she pitying him, or was she feeling the same attraction toward him that he was feeling toward her? She had a rosary that she fingered with one hand. And, yes, she must have been feeling sorry for him because the tears kept growing in her eyes, and then one, and then two tears dropped down onto the rosary on her lap. he moisture of her tears brightened the little rosary beads. The rosary glistened on her lap.

"You are wonderful," said Clarence. He wanted to say more. He wanted to tell her that his heart had never before told him in such clear feelings that he loved her in a way that was different from any love that he had ever felt before. He wanted to confess that he had spent the last decade charming one woman after another, but that he had never felt anything like this. Not even close. The feelings of his love kept circling around inside him, the images of her beautiful face and caring hands kept playing in his mind. Finally, he let his feelings find words: "I have to tell you something," he said. "I've fallen in love with you. I mean totally in love. I have to tell you that I love you."

"I love you too," said Marie. She leaned toward him. A sad gleam appeared in Clarence's squinting eyes. He breathed deeply so that he would not sob. He breathed deeply several times, then he said, "But I can't marry you. I'm not Catholic and none of our ministers would marry me to a Catholic."

"And I cannot marry you," said Marie.

"Because I'm not Catholic?"

"Oh no," she said, "not that. I can't marry you because I am a nun."

He caught his breath. He stared at her, trying to understand her beauty in a different way. "What are you saying?"

"I asked for a leave, and they gave it to me. I thought I'd never go back to the order. I know they were expecting me to leave forever too. When they saw me caring for you, they were positive that I'd never go back."

"I think I could become a Catholic for you," said Clarence.

"No," said Marie. "No, you don't have to do that."

"You'd become Protestant for me?"

"No," she said. "Caring for you convinced me that this is the work I must do. I must serve, not marry."

"But you're so beautiful," said Clarence.

"Beauty is one of the burdens the Lord has given me," she said. "Many people have told me that I am beautiful, but I didn't choose my beauty."

"I don't know the Catholic rules. Is it a sin to love a nun?"

"Of course not."

"Should I call you Sister?"

"Not necessary," said Sister Marie.

Clarence put his chin down and shook his head very slowly. Marie put her hand gently on the arm with the missing hand. The tears that were forming in Clarence's eyes were like a magnifying glass between his eyelids. He looked up at her through the tears to behold her blurred beauty. "I have never felt this way about anyone," said Clarence. "I want you more than I've ever wanted anyone. Is the Lord playing a dirty trick on me? Sorry, Sister, but I can't think of you without thinking of being with you. Having children with you."

"You would like to live carnally with me?" She almost smiled.

"I guess so. Yes. I've never desired anyone the way I desire you."

"Sex is the natural flow of love," said Sister Marie. "And kindness is the natural flow of my love as I understand it."

"For you kindness is like making love?" Clarence's face showed his bewilderment. "So when you're kind to me you're making love to me?"

"That's a good way to think of it," said Sister Marie. "Exactly. You don't have to remove your clothes for kindness," she said.

"I get aroused looking at you," said Clarence. "I get aroused thinking about you. I get aroused about you in my sleep."

"You cause a deep stirring in me too," said Sister Marie. "It's a very profound feeling. I feel it in every cell of my body. But my desire is a desire toward kindness. I get my satisfaction through kindness. Can you understand that?"

"Not really," said Clarence. "Making love is a physical thing."

"Kindness is a physical thing," said Sister Marie. "You cause desire in me, believe me, and kindness toward you gives me a wonderful satisfied feeling. I'm feeling that satisfaction right now."

Her cheeks looked flushed.

"This is crazy," said Clarence. "I really would turn Catholic to marry you."

He stared at her and grinned. "Will you kiss me?"

She leaned over and put her soft lips on his. He moved his lips against hers, and she moved her lips back. He parted his lips and slid his tongue between her lips. She pecked his tongue with her tongue, and then sat back in her chair.

"That's all?" said Clarence.

"Anything more would be cruelty, not kindness," said Sister Marie.

She leaned toward him and rubbed his arm, then his forehead. She touched his cheek and rubbed it gently. "So beautiful," she said. "So beautiful."

It is hard for us to figure out what to do with a couple like Clarence and Marie. Sister Marie went back to live with the nuns after that week, and, to our knowledge, she and Clarence have never seen each other again. Clarence did come back home after that and made a notably quick recovery—if coming back into the world with one less hand can be called recovery. He was not the same mechanic that he was before losing his right hand, but people said he was getting better and better with his left hand. Farmers praised his work, even though they often had to wait several days longer than he had promised to get their repaired tractors back. Some of our young women still found Clarence attractive, but his desire to gain their attraction had faded. He started to go to the church of blue-haired women and bald men. He was in love with Marie, and he did not want to find another woman. He would be getting older like the rest of us. Perhaps his old desires and his old appeal would fade too.

There is nothing in our history or creeds that gives us an easy answer to how things might have turned out differently for Clarence and Marie. But our world is getting bigger, even if we do not understand it any differently than we did back in 1957. The Bible says, "Behold, I show you a mystery," and that is exactly what the Lord had shown us. There are some mysteries that we may never be able to understand until the Lord reveals all on Judgment Day. Meanwhile, we will have to live with what we know—and what we do not know. ■

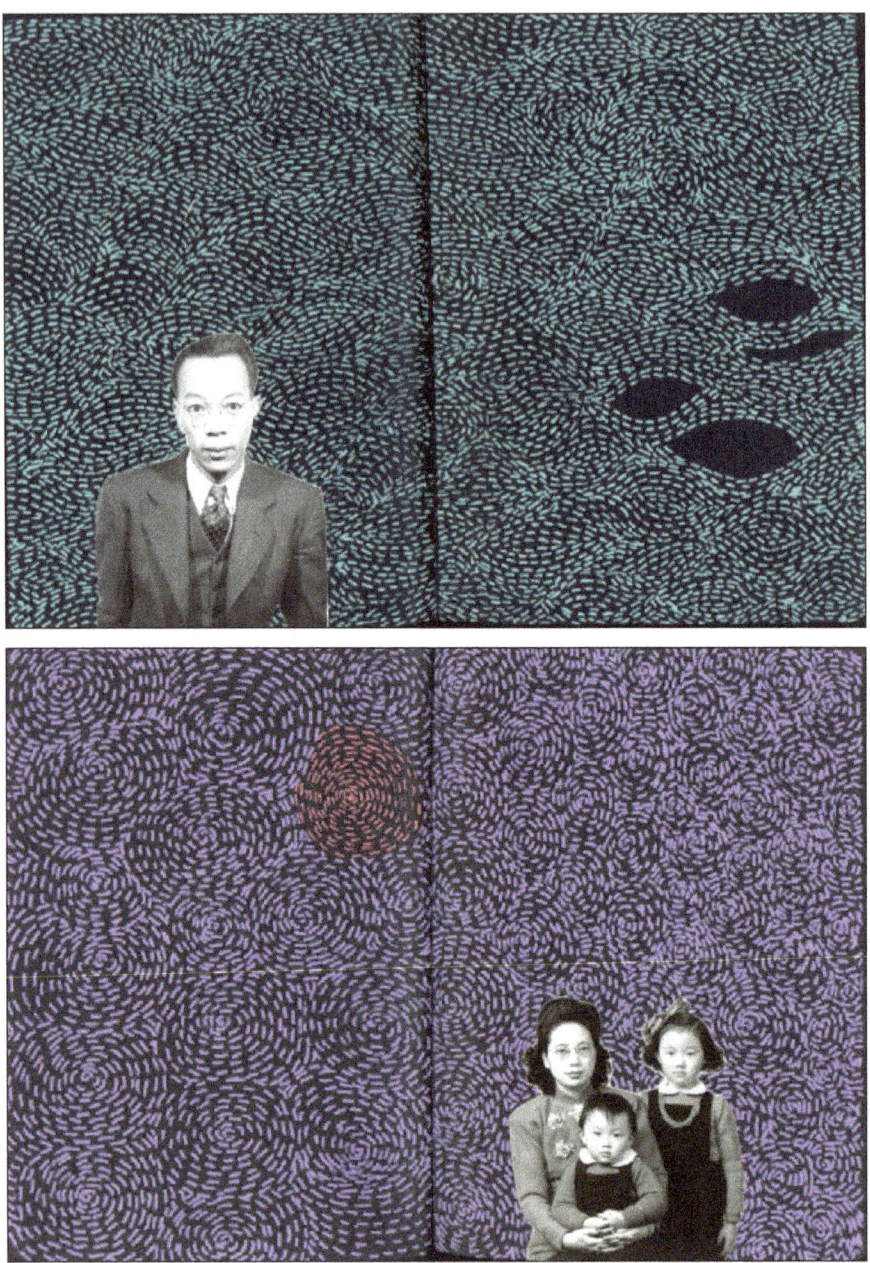

"Family Album," No. 3 and No. 4 by Alberta Mayo. Gel pen on sketchbook black paper.

KIRSTEN PORTER

Room

in this room
there is a window
of sky breathing blue
on my legs
on the pales
of unpainted walls
and all the hopes
in boxes
i'm afraid to unpack

in this room
the wooden spindles rise
up from the steps
like brown skeleton bones
and i lean my body closer
and closer
to some place
even quick hands can't keep me
from falling

in this room
the couch looks like a coffin
in its empty
black stare
and the air conditioner
is clucking its metal tongue
and someone is singing
aretha franklin outside

THE LIMBERLOST REVIEW

in this room
i'm sitting
to stop the spinning
and the April heat
is curled up in my lap
with some dream
warm on its lips
and i'm looking
for another day
in this room

JAY JOHNSON

Mstislav Lovrek

"Good one," Mike Smithson said. "You're telling me this guy is in jail for the crime of armed robbery when you have no proof of a weapon. He put his hand in his pants as if he had a weapon. The so-called victim walked with him for a half mile, arms locked together, then he turned over a coat and ten bucks. You must have been indulging in illegal drugs. That's about as nice as I can say it."

The prosecutor, Susan De La Rosa, extended her middle finger at Mike Smithson. "He is bad news. He is a menace."

"He is five-foot-four, weighs in at about one-fifteen, and does not own a weapon. He may have some mental challenges, but he is not a menace. Unless the person he befriends is just as crazy as he is."

"This is not befriending. This is theft, robbery. He scared the shit out of Donald Merrion."

"Donald is six-two, about one-eighty, and has studied martial arts. He is a wuss and a nut. Screw him. He had a butterfly knife in his pocket, the other hand entwined in my client's arm. The jury will not buy into this garbage. You haven't got a weapon, there is no weapon, and your So-called victim is unlikeable. And his story sucks."

"Your guy was going to rob a bank the week before."

That stopped him. Smithson had not represented a bank robber before—those were federal cases.

"Yeah?"

*****

Mike Smithson and Susan De La Rosa had squared off in the court-room, during a recess. Her office was efficient—the probable-cause affidavit and copy of the arrest warrant arrived in Mike Smithson's courthouse mail-basket on a Wednesday afternoon, shortly after the defendant had been given his initial appearance in court. Mistislav Lovrek. Smithson did not typically see Russian or Slavic first names, and the strangeness descended from there. It was four o'clock, and he read the affidavit quickly, then re-read it. The charge was strong-arm robbery, and the arrest occurred one week after the incident, and the overall circumstances were, well, crazy. The defendant was accused of stealing a leather overcoat and ten dollars. Smithson would spend another evening in jail visiting this client.

He set the case file in his briefcase along with a fresh legal pad. He would go home and prepare dinner, but this would have to be a post-two-beer interview. The story was too odd, so he might as well take it slow.

At 4:45, he received two new police reports by email from the prosecutor's office. Both of them involved the newly appointed client, Lovrek. The first report mirrored the probable-cause affidavit. The second was information on a different incident, equally bizarre. *Stack it on early,* thought Smithson, *fodder for plea bargaining.* The second report documented an event a week before the supposed robbery. That report suggested the perpetrator was crazy or foolish, and the subtext was that whoever called in these events was unreasonable. Supposedly, a week before the strong-arm robbery, the suspect had spoken of robbing a bank and had talked a friend into giving him a ride to the neighboring town, while hiding a Rube Goldbergesque weapon, the barrel of which was a kitchen mixing spoon. *Vigilant police work,* Smithson thought.

At 8 p.m., Smithson buzzed the entry at the jail's double-entry, and after a minute wait in the September night he was buzzed in, the door-latch solenoid slapping loud and hard. The halogen security lights blazed the night. He pushed through the first door, a gate in anchor-link fencing. The second door was steel, and the lock noise was more subtle; he tended to pull the door prematurely. It would not budge; he relaxed and silently chided himself. The latch released and he entered, and then he was allowed past a sliding barred gate. The jailer in the office, smiling behind the bullet-proof glass, mimed him pulling on the locked door.

"Patience, man, patience! Gotta learn a little patience! A man like you would never make it in here. Everything in due time! Not a moment too soon," said the jailer.

"Yeah. Thanks for the tip. Now here's a tip for you." He gestured obscenely.

"So. Who are you here for?" the jailer asked.

"Mr. Lovrek."

The jailer smiled. "*Okay* then. Coming right up. One crazy Russky."

Smithson made his way to the lawyer's interview room unattended, as was his custom in this small-county jail. He had been a regular there for almost two decades and always argued with the guards about guns, gun control, and his moderate politics. The jail personnel tended to agree with him about the realistic prospects for his clients, which of course he was not supposed to be discussing, and tolerated his occasional rants about whatever would strike his temper. More importantly, they trusted him.

The jailer led Mstislav into the attorney room. He wore the standard orange coveralls, oversized for his small person. He had rolled up his sleeves, but he swam in those coveralls. He had disheveled wiry brown hair, with a beard that had not been trimmed in weeks, and a sleepy but mischievous look in his eye. Guarded.

"Hello," he said. "Are you my wonderful lawyer?"

Smithson nodded solemnly. "Yes. That is who I am, Mike Smithson." He extended his hand. "You are Mstislav?"

"Yeah. They call me 'Slav.' Doesn't really mean anything to them, even though it might to somebody educated. Russian, Slav, whatever. Nobody even knows what that means here."

"Yeah. Well. I'm not really here to discuss ethnicity of Russians. You *are* Russian, right?"

"Yeah, by most any sense. I am an American citizen, naturalized."

"You are certain that you are a citizen?"

Mstislav laughed at the lawyer. "Of course? How could I not know something like that? That is important!"

"Yes. I'm asking you again, are you sure you are a citizen?"

The Russian's face clouded, and the eyes narrowed, nearly closed. "Yes, I am telling you I am an American citizen."

"Can I confirm your paperwork? Where are your citizenship documents?"

"My family has them. My American family. Over in Ketchum."

"Yes, of course. Does your American family—what is the name, and what is the phone number?"

"The American name is Aronson. I don't know their phone, I had it in my cell, which is gone. They have Europe in their veins, but Jewish eastern European." He giggled slightly. "Not Slav, not Slavic. Very nice people, they deserved better than me when they adopted."

"How so?"

"Well, I am trouble. As you can see."

"You are in trouble, yes. Do you have a record? Prior arrests?"

"Yes, sadly. And some other trouble, like, some people think I am mentally ill. But I am not."

Smithson observed the small man peripherally as he looked down at the police reports. The Russian was watching him intently.

"Mr. Lovrek. You did not change your name when you were adopted. You were adopted by this Ketchum family. The Aronsons?"

"That is their name, and no, I did not change my name. I was old enough that I wanted to keep my name. Why should I have to take a new name? I am Mstislav Lovrek. But they were nice people, and they did not insist, and now they should be glad, as I have not dirtied their good name."

"All right," Smithson said. "I have a couple of police reports here, and one doesn't charge you with a crime, although they might still charge it. It has to do with some bank robbery, reportedly with a mock-up of a gun. Lots of duct tape, apparently. Who is crazier, you or the cops?"

The Russian smiled. "Well, I guess that may be a matter of perspective, yes? I mean, I'm in jail, and they wrote some crazy report. But I have a reputation for being crazy. I'm not crazy. I wouldn't write such a crazy thing about another person."

"No? Okay, maybe not. Would you be crazy enough to perhaps talk about robbing a bank? Right before someone has accused you of attempting to rob him with a pistol stuck in your pants? So who is really the crazy one?"

The Russian grinned and his body rocked gently as he stifled some laughter. "Not me, Lawyer. Not me. I may be in jail, but I'm not crazy. The other guy, he's nuts."

"Yeah. Okay, Mstislav. Tell me what might have led the cops to think you were going to rob a bank with a kitchen spoon. They recovered a spoon with the tape adhesive on it and an empty detergent bottle, just like the report says."

His expression sobered. "Are you telling me that you think this makes sense? Are you telling me that a person could be charged with robbing a bank if he carried a kitchen spoon into a bank. Even if he said, 'gimme all your money?' Are you serious? Because if you are, I think I better get another lawyer."

Smithson stared back at him. "That ain't going to break my heart, Bubba. I've been called all sorts of things, and people wanted a new lawyer for better crap than that. And worse crap than that. You want a new lawyer, have at it." He leaned back in the straight-backed chair. "Maybe the judge will give you a new lawyer, maybe not. Maybe you can tell him I'm biased against your people. Which I don't even know what your people are. I clearly don't give a good goddamn." He leaned forward. "But I'll tell you what. Anybody who gets assigned to this case is going to be asking the same questions. You're a little bit off the beam, as we say in the hospitalization cases. If you don't want to go to prison, you might want to tell me what the hell happened. And yes, you can go to prison, even if you are crazy. Insanity is not a defense in this state. It's a little complicated, but you better come up with a better defense than 'crazy.'"

Mstislav stared ahead, then leaned back and sighed. "Yeah, people tell me I'm a little crazy, but they don't mean it clinically. Just, you know, kidding around."

"What kind of drugs do you take? How much alcohol?"

The Russian stared back again. "I don't drink. Nada. That's a long story. I smoke pot. I like smoking pot. So what?"

"So that little bit of information might go either way. How much, how often?"

"As much as I can, as often as I can. I'm homeless. No need to worry about the rent, and I get enough food."

"You look like you could use a few good meals, frankly. Jail food might get you up to normal."

"I'm normal now, thank you very much."

"Enough. Tell me about the kitchen spoon."

The Russian sighed deeply and told his story: it was just another of his little jokes, a scheme to get people to laugh, to delight people with an outrageous stunt. Again.

He had access to kitchens among the places he was crashing, and one of them had a surplus of kitchenware, and among the treasures was a hollow-handled serving spoon, just some cheap stamped stainless steel formed into a spoon, with a tubular handle. And the ammo magazine was a cardboard box, and the handle was the detergent bottle, all covered in duct tape. Who could take such a thing seriously? Well, a friend said something to the cops when they came looking for Mstislav, who fit the description of the person they were looking for; the "friend" told them about the trip to Granview, the next town down the little four-lane, and told about the rambling of his small hirsute friend.

Mstislav had been dropped off in the little town, a burg with another little college. Shortly he grew discouraged and lonely, since his audience for the prank was gone, and so he made it to a Harvest Foods supermarket, where he walked casually to the loading dock at the back of the store and looked for a dumpster. He found it, then broke down the ersatz gun and threw away the wads of duct tape and the garbage, saving the spoon, since it was functional and not to be wasted. He stashed the spoon beneath the dumpster, with the intent to return after dark and look for food and anything else of value. Americans discarded way, way too much of their produce and products.

Once situated in the asphalt and concrete backdrop of a retail outlet, he made his way outwards, to walk through the College Hill residential neighborhood. He had not ventured there in his wanderings, but he was comfortable as a hobo-tourist. He had no inclination to trespass on residential land, to cause discomfort, to do any more than explore. In the evening he would find shelter as needed, whether under cardboard at the dumpster or blanketed under a viaduct—he wasn't sure any existed here, but he had found shelter in those before-—or if necessary in an outbuilding, of which there were many in the surrounding lands. So he wandered, open-eyed and curious. It was still morning. The Granview cops eyed him, disheveled and out of place in the neighborhoods, weird even for a college town, but he broke no laws and confronted no one, deferred to strangers that he passed on a sidewalk.

In the autumn evening it got uncomfortably cool, and he wanted shelter again. As darkness fell he returned to Harvest Foods, found no canned goods, and the produce was not appetizing. A poor harvest for him indeed. The cardboard supply was good and dry. He looked around, gathered several broken-down boxes, and dragged them off to a wooded area just over a little rise to the rear of the store. He arranged them for cover, then noticed the rear-facing lights of a house. He gauged the distance, decided he was comfortably distant, and turned away to sleep.

"That's it, eh? Never brandished that bad-boy machine gun, Slav?"

The little man shook his head sheepishly. "Nope, Lawyer, can't claim any action on that one."

Smithson looked at him steadily. "Okay. Don't think they'll be charging that one, anyway. I don't think Ms. De La Rosa wants to go after an allegation that weak. So much for bank robbery." He continued to gaze at Mstislav. "She's got plenty of heartburn over this other one, though. She's gonna go on that one."

The Russian shrugged his shoulders and smiled optimistically. "Hey, we can't control that, can we? Let her do what she wants. Justice will prevail, right, Smithson?"

"You bet, Slav, you bet."

*****

Thirteen days after the jail meeting, Mstislav was escorted to a courtroom. He was prepared to listen to the worst, and Smithson told him to keep his mouth shut. He was about to endure the preliminary hearing for robbery.

The presiding judge was Robin Sanders, who had taken on the black robe just eight months previously.

Susan De La Rosa was the prosecutor, thirty-five years old and still unsure of herself. It had been just the day before when she interviewed the cop who had interviewed Donald the Wuss and the "friend," or Rat, as Mstislav termed him. Fortunately for her, the magistrate judge was usually swayed by the modicum of evidence that a prosecutor provided, often a policeman's testimony unrebutted by any defendant. At a prelim, every defendant was a one-legged man in an ass-kicking contest. No defendant would be called to testify for himself at this stage; once he voluntarily took the stand, he had waived his Fifth Amendment right, and he was fair game.

The first witness was Ethan Greene, the policeman. Susan dutifully guided the cop through what was a mildly creepy story—a little man who obtained a coat and some money.

"So what did you learn about the transfer of the coat?"

"The defendant told me he got it from the victim," Greene replied.

"Objection as to the use of the term 'victim,'" Smithson interjected.

"That's overruled, Mr. Smithson. You may continue, Ms. De La Rosa."

"And did you confirm the loss of the coat?"

"Yes, when I interviewed the victim he said—"

"Objection, hearsay."

"He hasn't *said* anything yet," De La Rosa stated.

"He was just about to quote from somebody else," said Smithson. "And he gave us hearsay in his last answer."

"We don't know who yet," said the judge. "And the late hearsay objection is too late."

"Yes, he was about to quote the so-called victim. He said as much."

The Judge hesitated. "Fair enough. Careful how you phrase this, Madam Prosecutor."

"What did you confirm?" she asked.

"That the victim had given up his coat under the threat of bodily harm, by the little Russian dude."

"Objection, objection. Use of 'victim,' hearsay, nothing in the record to support any threat, and characterization of Mr. Lovrek as 'the little Russian dude.'"

"Overruled," said the judge.

"By 'little Russian dude,' you are referring to the defendant?" De La Rosa asked.

"Objection. Leading."

"Overruled. Foundational," replied the judge.

De La Rosa rustled some paperwork on her table, and produced a photo and shoved a copy of it at Smithson. It was a photo of pieces of leather and fabric, labeled with an evidence sticker. She moved from around the prosecutor's table and approached the witness box. "I'm showing you what has been marked as State's Exhibit One. Do you recognize it?

"Yes," the cop replied.

"What is it?"

"It is a photograph, of what looks like cut-up leather and fabric."

De La Rosa moved to admit the photo into evidence, Smithson objected on foundation when Officer Green admitted he did not take the photo. The prosecutor tried again, but the judge sustained Smithson's objection. It was the smallest of victories:

"If you get the right cop, it comes in," Judge Sanders said. "You haven't got the right cop. Are you done with this witness? May this witness be excused from his subpoena?"

De La Rosa looked startled. "Sure. Yeah. No problem."

Smithson looked steadily at the judge. "No objection, Your Honor."

"Good, that's really great. You are excused, Officer Greene. Thank you," said the judge.

Sanders smiled wanly at the young officer, then waved him to get down and move along. "Next witness?" asked the judge.

"The State calls Daniel Merrion." Judge Sanders looked at her quizzically, then shrugged and looked down at his notes.

A minion from the prosecutor's office scurried out to the hall and soon re-entered followed by a man a bit over six feet tall with long brown hair and dressed entirely in black: long leather coat, dress slacks, and a dress shirt with a black tie. He carried a black Stetson, and his hair was slightly compressed where the hat had been.

Under oath, Merrion repeated the tale that he had given to law enforcement—that he had been accosted by an acquaintance, a person he knew from attending classes, yet the person had a gun stuck in his trousers and wanted Merrion's coat. He testified that he saw "just a flash" of the butt of the handle of a revolver, possibly a .38, maybe bigger, and he saw no more, but it was not the handle of a semi-automatic, and he was pretty sure it was a gun.

"And what was your reaction when the other man demanded that you give him your coat?" De La Rosa asked.

"Well, it wasn't phrased as a demand. But there was a definite threat to what he said."

"So what was it he said?"

"He said, 'That's a pretty nice coat.'"

"And how did you respond to that statement?"

"Well, I kind of nodded hello and said, 'Yes, thank you.'"

"And were you frightened by what he said?"

"Objection, leading."

"Sustained," said the judge.

"So what did you feel when he said that?" persisted the prosecutor.

"So, I could see he was underdressed for the inclement weather, and it was a peculiar thing to be commenting on, since I was warm and he was not warm, and I figured he wanted me to give him the coat."

"Did he say, 'Give me your coat'?"

"Objection."

"Sustained," Judge Sanders said.

"Well, what did he say?"

"What I just told you."

Smithson was openly smiling at this point. The judge intervened.

"One of the things that the State is trying to establish is whether or not you reasonably felt fear. I cannot tell from what you have described if you, or anyone in your position, would have felt fear."

Smithson looked pained. The judge was stepping in and taking care of the prosecutor's mess. But it was impolitic to object to a judge's comment.

"Well, yes, of course I felt frightened. This cold and desperate man comes up and says, 'Hey, I like your coat,' and he's got a gun, aren't you supposed to be scared? Yes, I was scared."

And so what did you do next?" coaxed the prosecutor.

"Well, there was some further discussion, and obviously he wanted a coat, and I was scared, but my training calmed me, and I kept a fairly cool head, and I offered him a different coat that I had at home."

"And can you describe this other coat?"

"It is quite similar to the one I'm wearing, only perhaps a little more worn."

"And why would you have two coats that were so similar?"

"Just, well, you know, I like this style and I found this coat, and it is a little nicer than the other, and it seemed like it was prudent to have a spare coat"

"And it certainly proved to be handy in this case, didn't it?"

"Yes, it turned out to be especially handy given the fearsome situation I was put into," the witness stated. He shuddered slightly.

Merrion described his walk up the street, arms locked with a odd little man he had met in a class, and then getting to his apartment, where the man did not want to disengage his arm to enter and walk up the stairs, so they struggled up the narrow stairwell to his bedroom, where his girlfriend was asleep. It was then 4:00 p.m. He retrieved a second coat, and also a ten-dollar bill from a paperback copy of *The Fountainhead,* and gave it to the little crazy foreigner.

"Did he say anything else at that time?" the prosecutor asked.

"He said not to leave the building or call the cops, because he knew where I lived."

"No further questions, Your Honor," De La Rosa said. The judge looked at Smithson.

"Cross-exam, Mr. Smithson?" he asked. Smithson snapped open a binder and glanced down at his notes, then looked hard at Merrion.

"But you called the cops, didn't you?"

"No. I did not."

"Why not?

"Because as he said, he did know where I lived, and my girlfriend and roommate, and I didn't think it would help, and he would leave us in peace."

"What did you do?"

"I armed myself with a pair of sai, and armed my roommate with a katana, then we waited, and then scouted through the house, and then finally my heart slowed down, and eventually I called the cops."

"I'm unfamiliar with what the heck you were just talking about. A pair of what?

"Sai. S-A- I."

"And what was the other?"

"Katana. K-A-T-A-N-A."

"And there is some martial art these are associated with?"

"Yes. Kyokushinkai. K-Y-O-K-U-S-H-I-N-K-A-I."

"Okay. Kyokushinkai." Smithson cocked his head and sighed, and the judge stared impassively into space. "Have I got that right? How long have you studied this Kyokushinkai?"

"Six years."

"And you were also armed with a butterfly knife in one pocket during the entire arm-in-arm walk up Third Street, weren't you?"

"Yes."

"Okay. Let me get this straight. You look to be about a foot taller than the defendant. You have six years of some exotic martial art, and you have a knife." From the corner of his eye, Smithson saw Slav, head down and shaking, trying to suppress laughter. "You have imagined that this little guy has a gun, but he's walking up the street arm-in-arm with you."

"Is there a question here?" challenged Merrion.

Smithson looked over at Susan De La Rosa, who had not objected to his supposed question, and he smirked slightly. Judge Sanders glared at him.

"Yeah. What is wrong in this picture?" Smithson asked.

Mstislav started laughing out loud and slapped the table three times in succession. Smithson shushed him, and his client continued shaking with laughter.

"Mr. Smithson, perhaps you need a moment to exercise some client control here."

Mike looked up to see the judge, caught between anger and compassion.

"Perhaps a moment, Your Honor." He leaned and whispered to Mstislav, laughing, tears forming in his eyes. There was a pause punctuated only by the Russian's squeaks of laughter. "A short recess would be helpful," Smithson said.

"We'll take a recess. Back in ten minutes, everybody," said the judge.

The bailiff escorted Smithson and his client through the door to the hallway, where Mstislav burst into laughter, and Smithson let it play out. "Look, you got to work with me, Slav. Poker face, man, poker face."

Slav hooted aloud again. "Okay, Lawyer, okay. Poker." He laughed again. "I hardly know her." He laughed.

"Terrible, Slav, terrible. Shut up."

Slav wiped his tears with the sleeve of the orange coveralls. They returned to the courtroom and waited.

Ten minutes later, Smithson got the answer to his question.

"Nothing. There is nothing wrong with this picture. As you put it," Merrion said.

"When is the last time you saw a similar scene unfold on Third Street in this town?"

"Objection. Relevance," Susan De La Rosa broke in.

"Counselor?"

"Oh, come on. There is nothing wrong with what they have described? It would only occur in a bad dream."

"What is the relevance?" the judge asked.

"He indicated it's normal, and he can't possibly say he's seen it before."

"You are impeaching him?"

"Yes, Your Honor, I am impeaching him."

"Go ahead and answer the question, Mr. Merrion."

Smithson knew it would not matter what the answer was. He bent low over the counsel table and wrote down notes for a full minute. He looked up and faced Merrion.

"I don't think I've ever seen anything like what I experienced," Merrion said evenly.

"Thank you." Smithson paused again, then stood straight and faced Merrion. "When did you call the cops?"

"Two days later."

Smithson looked at the judge. "No further questions at this time."

"Ms. De La Rosa? Re-direct?" Judge Sanders looked directly at her.

The prosecutor looked puzzled as she hastily wrote notes. "Thank you.," she said. There was a long pause. "Why would you wait two days?" she asked Merrion.

"Well, my father said I should call the cops, because I had a civic duty."

Susan paused. "I'm sorry, I did not understand your answer. Why did you wait?"

The witness glared at her. "It wasn't safe. I was advised that it was not safe, and I concurred."

Smithson suppressed his smile as he looked up at the tense interchange. Ms. De La Rosa didn't like the complaining witness any more than he did.

"All right. Who gave you such advice?"

"My father. I trust his advice."

"When did he give you this advice?"

"He has always given me that advice. If an assailant has a gun, the odds are in his favor. He wins. Even if he doesn't kill, he wins."

De La Rosa smiled, almost genuinely. "Thank you. Nothing further."

Judge Sanders looked to Smithson. "Re-cross?"

Smithson rose. "Okay. Did you ever hear from the defendant again?"

"No. Have not seen him until today. Thankfully. Would not want to deal with that again."

"Objection. Non-responsive." Smithson interjected.

"Sustained," said the judge.

"You never saw a gun, did you, Mr. Merrion?" Smithson said quickly.

"I did see a gun."

"You are familiar with firearms, aren't you?"

"Yes."

"And you can't tell this court if what you saw was a revolver, a semi-automatic, or a squirt gun, can you?"

"It was not a squirt gun, and it was not a semi-automatic. It was a revolver."

"How much of this revolver did you see?"

"The butt of the handle."

"How much of the butt?"

"Just a flash, just enough to know . . . if you know anything about revolvers, you know the handle."

"I'm not convinced you know, and neither is anyone else. But did you show him the handle of your butterfly knife? Like, you know, you show me yours, and I'll show you mine?" Mstislav smiled, then laughed, and slapped the table. Smithson gripped his client's hand, hard.

Merrion coolly answered. "It was a revolver handle. Wood, it appeared. And no, I did not show him the butterfly knife. That would not have been a good strategic move."

"Well, what would have been a good strategic move?"

Merrion did not answer.

Smithson looked up at the judge, then over to Susan, then winked at her, unseen by the judge. She hid her hand gesture with a legal pad, as she extended a finger again. Smithson gave Merrion a pass on his question and continued:

"Okay. You got a knife, you got six years of some martial art, and this small man is shivering. You are convinced that he has a gun. Were you shivering?

"No, I had a good coat." Merrion said, then paused. "I was pretty agitated right in the beginning."

"Because a little shivering man admired your coat?"

"Because an armed man wanted the coat off my back."

"And you had training, the 'moves' so to speak, and a knife."

Merrion did not answer, and Smithson let that pass.

"Are you fearful now?" he asked.

"A little bit, yes. I don't know how the court will treat this mess, and you are mocking me."

"Okay. I'll stop." He looked at the prosecutor. "Nothing further."

Susan took his lead. "Mr. Merrion, are you afraid of the Defendant right now as we speak?"

"No, I'm confident he is not armed now. I am somewhat apprehensive that he will be turned loose. He is . . . weird. Menacing, in that other context."

"Nothing further," she said.

Smithson glanced back at the father, catching a slight nod of approval, and a look at his son. "No questions in re-cross, Your Honor."

"All rightee then. Next witness?

"Nothing further, Your Honor."

"State rests?"

"Yes, Your Honor, State rests."

The judge sighed and looked over at Smithson.

"Mr. Smithson, witnesses? Some defense?"

"No evidence, Your Honor. Just argument."

"Fine. Defense rests then?" the judge asked. Smithson nodded. "Ms. De La Rosa, argue your case."

Susan ran down the elements to prove her case and then gave examples of threat, fear, theft, and concluded that there was only possible outcome—that the defendant be bound over on the charge of strong-arm robbery.

Smithson contained his sarcasm to the best of his ability and hid his scorn for the complaining witness. He had played this hand at preliminary hearing many times, although not before this judge. He knew that understatement was the safe play, and he played it. But it was hard to ignore the difficulty of the small man threatening the larger man who had been trained in the martial arts. And there was no gun recovered, and the only one proven weapon was on the person of Merrion. His problem was that Merrion had stated definitively that Slav had threatened him, and that he was scared, and that he gave up his property as a result of the threat and fear. It was preposterous, but not to be hammered on at this stage of proceedings. He asked that the judge find the evidence too specious to be given enough weight to burden the next court with, and knew it was a dying argument, as the magistrate would not have the power to make that call.

"It is so absurd that I ask the court to dismiss. There is no weapon, the size disparity is obvious, and the State's evidence does not match the story. They have naked testimony, unsubstantiated."

Judge Sanders looked pained as Smithson sat down.

"So Mr. Smithson, you are asking me to find that the evidence presented by the State is so weak that it to be disbelieved?"

"Yes, Your Honor."

"And yet you presented me no evidence to the contrary, anything to show that Mr. Merrion was either delusional or mendacious in his testimony."

"I'm not about to ask the court to order a mental evaluation on the State's complaining witness, Your Honor. Nor am I about to subject my client to cross-examination at this stage of proceedings. But yes, I am asking you to find the witness not credible. Incredible, if you will."

"I'll concede that some of this is incredible. Perhaps in a different sense. Unfortunately, you have left me nothing in the record to support your claim."

"You have the power to assess credibility of the witnesses as you sit there."

"I am well aware of my position in the system, Mr. Smithson. I think you know I have to have some evidence in order to make a ruling, even one in your favor." He removed his glasses and wiped his face with a tissue. "I can't exactly sit up here and say that Mr. Merrion is anything less than credible, when he took an oath to tell the truth, and the police recovered goods he said were his, from your client's abode."

"Alleged abode, Your Honor."

"He's homeless, Counselor, but he's staying with a friend."

Smithson started to respond, thought better of it, and declined to challenge the judge on a trivial point of his client's residence, which at that point was the county jail.

The judge then stared at Susan De La Rosa. "Well, based on the evidence before me, I have to say to a standard of preponderance of the evidence, the State has shown that Mr. Lovrek took ten dollars and a black leather overcoat from Mr. Merrion by the threat of force or violence. I find the circumstances as described to be highly unusual, but many things that get described in court are unusual. And we can thank our lucky stars that they are unusual. Sometimes impaired people are dangerous, and Mr. Merrion said under oath that he was scared.

"But I'll add this, for Mr. Merrion's benefit, and for Ms. De La Rosa's benefit. And that is: this court is not established to hear cases, especially those charging felonies, when the characters are something out of a TV show. Some sitcom. We come to sit in judgement of people who have disputes. Sometimes people have wronged other people, or are reasonably thought to have wronged other people. Sometimes events in civil cases are utter rubbish. We try to restrict those cases to Small Claims Court. But they are meaningful to the litigants. We try to cull out the rubbish. I trust this case is something other than utter rubbish.

"Mr. Lovrek, my disdain for this case does nothing to relieve you of the responsibilities in front of you. You are bound over on a very serious charge. You will be held in custody, unless the District Court decides to lower your bond." He glared at the Defendant. "Arraignment in the felony court next Monday at 1:30."

"A.m. or p.m., Your Honor?" piped up Mstislav. The judge did not answer but stared back.

The Russian smiled wanly at the magistrate, then turned to face Smithson. He thrust out his hand to shake and smiled confidently. "We got them where we want them, Mike," he said quietly. "I can feel it. The judge hates those other people."

Smithson motioned to the Russian to stand up for the departing judge, and chairs scraped backward. "You are right, he didn't like the Merrion clan."

"No, he disrespected those bastards."

"You sound pretty cocky for someone who just got bound over on a felony, and you have to park your butt in jail for a while longer."

"Justice will prevail. It is my destiny, and it is my culture. The artists suffer, and the art is great."

"Whatever. Your artwork needs a little polish."

"Hey, Lawyer, your craft needs a little polish. The judge hates the opposition and still found in their favor."

"Bite me, Russky. I need a better clientele, and then I'll get the rulings."

The bailiff moved to Slav and motioned him into the hall. Smithson heard the ratcheting of handcuffs.

*****

Four months later, Smithson walked back to his office from lunch at his favorite upscale joint. He was nearing the old city Carnegie Library, and noticed a figure approaching on the same sidewalk. He slowed and moved to his right, and the figure passed. The man's head slumped down, but the hair and the gait were clearly the Russian's.

"Hey, Slav," he said loudly, as the small man had passed him.

The small man drew up, turned, and smiled shyly. "Hey, Lawyer. I see you are still out walking around free," he joked.

"Yes, I am. And so are you."

"I am a free man, Lawyer. I am a free man. It is a free country. I am happy."

The felony charge had resolved as a misdemeanor, with an agreed bargain—Mstislav was admitted to Mental Health Court. There was no such court in their county, and the next county to the north accepted him as a courtesy. But the oversight was tight in mental health court, the accountability was enforced, and Slav would not be an easy client. Smithson had washed his hands of him when it transferred to the next county. But he inquired, since he knew the players in the next county. Slav would have a hard time giving up marijuana, and he would challenge the rules until he jeopardized his long-term freedom. Short term periods of jail, a week or two at a time, might be imposed until he incorporated the concept. The threat of losing his spot in a specialty court, and returning to do a year in county jail on the original misdemeanor, might dry him out.

Mentally ill people found it difficult, mentally ill people with drug habits found it very difficult. Russians with attitude . . .

"So, Slav, how are you doing, really?" Smithson asked.

"I am a free man, Lawyer. Life is great. Life is beautiful."

"There is a court proceeding I want you to see."

"Yeah?" Mstislav asked warily.

"Yeah. Meet me up in the courthouse at two." Smithson said. The Russian looked wary. "Two sharp, don't be late." Mstislav shrugged.

*****

Mstislav sidled up to Smithson in the back row of the gallery of the courtroom. Judge Sanders was presiding, and Susan De La Rosa had her back to them. Smithson gestured with his head to a tall man in orange coveralls seated beyond the gate, but Mstislav's view was blocked.

"Next case, State v. Daniel Merrion," Judge Sanders announced. "Are you Daniel Merrion? Go on up there and take a seat." The tall man shuffled the to defendant's table and sat. Mstislav jerked in his seat, and nudged his attorney. Smithson suppressed his smile. The judge gave a long look at Merrion, and almost imperceptibly looked to the back of the courtroom.

"The first charge is aggravated assault, Mr. Merrion. And there is a second one, carrying a concealed weapon without a permit. Ms. De La Rosa, what are the maximum penalties for these charge?" The prosecutor answered quietly, and the judge continued:

"I'll enter a plea of not-guilty, bond is set at $5,000. Preliminary hearing is set for ten days from now, at 10 a.m. Are you going to get a lawyer, or should we appoint a public defender for you?"

There was a long pause.

Mstislav whispered, "That guy is really crazy, Lawyer. I told you."

"I thought this would be worth seeing," Smithson replied.

He motioned to his client to leave, and they moved in unison. The judge stated loudly: "Mr. Smithson, not so fast. We may be needing your services."

Smithson halted. "I'll stay if you tell me to, Judge," he said. "But I'm pretty sure I won't be taking this case."

"View from West Virgin" by Royden Card. Acrylic on canvas, 20" x 20."

SANDY ANDERSON

Dogless

There will be no dogs in this poem.
No tales wagging eagerly
waiting to be let in,
no eyes begging.

This poem will be stuffed full
of many other things.
Clouds bursting with rain,
screwdrivers blessed with an infinity of screws,
empty puppet stages with boxes of puppets
ready to enact whatever scenes
you wish to indulge in

JUST AS LONG AS THERE ARE NO DOGS.

This poem has it all,
flamenco music that builds to a frenzy
before the lolling cadenza,
canopeners set before all the cans
of delicacies you have ever
wondered to taste,
scrapbooks stuffed with pictures
of all the magic you are ever present in,
Rolls Royces and designer labels
under giant blue spruce umbrellas.

This poem is stuffed like a holiday pig
and invites you to feast
like a Hawaiian princess
before the Christians arrived,
no taboos on words you can use
or places you can enter,
larger than Bosch's "Garden of Earthly Delights"
framed in an absence of dogs.

The Closet Is Stuffed with Shoes

Walking shoes, running shoes, shoes with gum
on the soles so they won't fly off the earth.
Stilettos with heels in the clouds, tattered shoes
stuffed with too many steps to part with.

Potato shoes that are sprouting, pomegranate shoes
with sections for each moon toe. Slinky shoes with
no molars, letterpress shoes with distinctive footprints.
Nomad shoes full of sand and dance shoes overflowing
with stardust. Banks of pennies in loafers,
and saddle shoes that trot off escarpments.
Ancients shoes without fingerprints.

An infinite variety of shoes from which one can
not choose. There are silk slippers that sigh om,
old women's shoes with so many children gone.
The toddler's shoe that expands, the balloon shoe
that floats and the cement shoe that sinks.
Thongs which leave the feet with no imagination.
Track shoes with records, reed shoes that replant
themselves and grow roots, and papyrus shoes
that are undecipherable.

Army boots that kick the shit out of themselves.
Alligator shoes that swim and scarecrow sneakers
longing for crows. Snakeskin boots that rattle
and avalanche boots that thunder. Space boots
that cocoon one in and bronze shoes that support
legends of birth.

A harvest of shoes,
A cemetery of shoes,
A possibility of shoes,

SANDY ANDERSON

A haven for the winged foot
      and the clubbed foot
      and the foot without form.
There are antlered shoes that remembered deer,
riding boots that gallop off the horizons
and shoes to die in.

Clogs made of music, tap shoes with a pulse,
Rubbers lined up like ducks in the empty tub.
Cartoon shoes batting their eyes, glass slippers
fitting no one as well as the prince shoe

complete with shoe mega horn. The blessed shoe
and the cursed shoe with bruises.

The party shoe drunk on itself, the Santa boot
emptied out. The hungry shoe that wanders streets
and the narrow shoe that winces. The winged
Hermes shoe whose message is forgotten
and the nurse shoe that bandages everything.

The shoe that wants you like a whore.
The cowboy boot grazing on herds of sheep.
The club boot which shuffles and the peg leg shoe
with a huge imagination. The borrowed shoe
that runs home in the night and the refugee shoe
that longs to run home. The tyrant's shoe that
stands on your head and the victim's shoe
you trip over. The dry pump and the soggy sneaker.

The smart shoes that lead us around with tongues
that babble on like we know where we're going,
but forget where we've been. Nuclear shoes
lying dormant like threat, and suicide shoes
blowing themselves up. The first shoes that
were expelled from the garden: apple shoes
that know everything.

Cancer Sestina

In the past year my memory has lost
its keys, perhaps melted in the supernova
that started as rain in radiation, when earthworms
climbed out the ground searching for my keys in the garbage,
finally finding them on the counter, in the open,
but they were the wrong keys, & I threw them to the pavement.

My mind used to follow the pavement
between houses to find home, but now it staggers, lost
between cracks that grow in my steps to open
pits I fall into, dark so I fail to notice the supernova
that I mistake for the garbage
truck rumbling past, yell for it to watch the earthworms,

there is sacred in every creature, even earthworms
have the right to a memory paving
their tunnels, are not to be treated as garbage,
they are to be picked up and put back on grass when lost,
not to be stepped on when my mind supernovas,
learns to remove myself from the open

field when lightning strikes, blinding my open
eyes, my mind cowering like earthworms
trying to escape rain, no supernova
of thoughts, easy words on the pavement
like pennies ready to be picked up, lost
change like words turned moldy in the garbage.

But suddenly I behold the garbage
as a gold mine in the dump, open
to scavenger minds looking for lost
keys, lost words, lost memories, earthworms
burrowing into insides that have been paved
over during the radiation supernova

SANDY ANDERSON

that saved my life, the supernova
that incinerated the tumor like garbage,
left me raw, taking months to pave
the skin back to smoothness, to let my mind open
to daylight after snuggling with my earthworm
self as if everything worth retrieving was lost.

And so I pave over the lost year that supernovaed
into the future, lost like the keys in the garbage
to be dumped out, unlocking myself to broad fields,
                                      no longer the burrowing earthworm.

"Scout Mountain 2" by Ray Obermayr. Oil on canvas, 40" x 35."

LESLIE ANN LEEK

On Lenin Peak

The winter I was obsessed with climbing expeditions on Mt. Everest, I tracked you to the narrow foot bridge over the river. Your arms were splayed against chain link stretched above the bridge rail to prevent dogs and children from falling into the water; your fingers awkward in thick gloves poked through the diamond shaped wires making it impossible to hold on for dear life. It wasn't clear if you were trying to get in or out of a desperate situation. Though I'd been confident I'd find you and take you home, the sight of you felt like the misfortune of bad weather at high altitude.

*****

After reading your note, I rushed out of the house we shared to catch sight of you laboring against the blowing snow. My grip on the yellow notebook paper contorted the ink of your scrawl: "Clarissa," then phrases: "exhausted. . . can't . . .can't go on," and finally, what I'd wanted all along: "I do love you."

Yeti, I thought as I watched you, already a block away, bent and shuffling under the bulk of your down jacket and wool pants. But as you moved into gray distance, it became clear you were a man laboring up the South Col of a legendary Mt. Everest, with no choice but to strain against ghost shapes roped behind him. I thought to call after you but knew you wouldn't hear or comprehend the syllables ripped and torn by relentless wind. The letters of your name: M-a-r-c-u-s shredded like old prayer flags dangling by a thread. You wrote it all in the letter, a yellow slice of resignation.

I'd shoveled the walk that morning while you negotiated your crowded space at the dining room table: 52 papers from your art appreciation class to grade, a book of Frida Kahlo paintings, coffee-stained copies of poems by Anne Sexton, two number-six brushes, a tube of vermillion paint. Exhilarated by the outside work, I barged into the house full of health and good cheer to find you staring at the spindrift of steam curling up from your coffee. You seemed a large heavy shape against the dull light from the window. The words *thud of gray light* came to me. I was still writing poetry in those days.

"You can never trust this western light," you said as if you were sick of it and I to blame. A few hours later, time means nothing, let's face it, I watched your form diminish, a speck of red cap, vague movement against the weather; others watching from, let's imagine base camp, might take it as a good sign. My bare feet burned on the ice covered sidewalk. I looked down to see I'd forgotten my shoes

"Damn you," I said, and imagined you navigating the crevices off the perilous Khumbu icefall as I hobbled to the house to prepare the expedition to bring you home. I assumed rescue was my calling. I wonder if you knew that but wouldn't admit it. As a child I rehearsed with my friends. We were the cavalry ambushed by Apaches and I was the handsome and fearless lieutenant who rallied the men to safety. I was the sheriff leading the posse at full gallop to capture the gang of desperados who held up the stage and headed for Robber's Roost to stash the loot.

"I'm pretending I live in the West," I once told my Dad who laughed and said, "But you do live in the West." If the boys insisted I play the little lady in distress, I'd say, "Like hell," and decide whether to fight them or go home. By the time we were teenagers, I refined my technique and counseled troubled schoolmates, mostly boys, to take heart. Summer evenings heavy with the smell of Russian olive trees and June grass, we'd talk for hours outside of the church, ball park or rodeo arena. I was sure of my power to convince them life was precious.
"There's so much to live for," I'd say earnestly. "You've got your life ahead of you. Consider your blessings and the people who love you."
.

*****

You seemed like a foreign shape on the foot bridge, not far from the railroad tracks and within sight of the rundown house where you once lived. I was sorry the river below had been channeled in cement by the Army Corps of Engineers after the flood in the sixties. I didn't want you to think badly of us and felt the urge to remind you of the natural habitat both up and down stream and that the modest flow was a tributary to the mighty Snake River and had been named Portneuf by a French

Canadian voyager who must have known something about survival. I had to concede that lifeless brown water moved sluggishly beneath you, not deep enough for a grown man to drown in or to get carried away. How can you get in there anyway? I wondered at the time. You're too big and bulky to climb around the protective fence and even if you do, the fall, the jump, will be humiliating. Your heavy clothes and thick boots will suck you down but not under and I'll call 911. A fire truck and ambulance will arrive, sirens blaring, neighborhood alerted, and good natured EMTs will rush into the water and drag you out. You might suffer hypothermia or a sprained ankle, might develop pneumonia later, but you won't die and you'll have to face the consequences. I knew you wanted the Atlantic Ocean, or at least a swollen reclaimed eastern river, the Raritan, the Ohio.

Finally, I stepped onto the uneasy sway of the bridge and inched carefully toward you until I was close enough to place my hand on your broad back. But I was repelled, shocked by a vision of you spinning around, grabbing my arm, swinging me high over the protective wire and letting go. I imagined I flew above you. Entranced by the sensation of old flying dreams, I laughed and was about to say thank you for the launch, you always know what I need, when I realized the imminent fall, the plummet into brown water and cement. You were a man going down and one way or another I'd go with you.

You might despise the people who try to save you.

Only a few nights before we found ourselves on the bridge, let's say after midnight, January, end of the nineteen eighties, we were in our cluttered bungalow close to the university when you frayed all hopes of safety by introducing me to the Adrienne Rich poem about the team of Russian women dying in a raging snow storm on Lenin Peak; not Everest, but close enough. I was curled up in the red wingback chair in a pool of yellow light from the antique floor lamp, Chris Bonington's Everest book open on my lap and red wine in a ceramic goblet, a relic from my marriage, on the table beside me. I wasn't reading; I was contemplating the labor of breathing above 24,000 feet: human systems breaking down, the heart giving up. How do some people know their limits and have the sense to turn back while others push against the odds, one foot then the other: one-two-three breathe, flesh turning black, toes and fingers destined for amputation, snow blind, and all the tricks the mind must play? You might make it to the top climbers warn, but do not celebrate until you survive the descent.

"Here's a little something to cheer you up," you said. You'd been working late in your in your art department studio and had come home silently and gone to bed. I assumed you were sleeping and was surprised and delighted to hear your voice. You cast a huge Prospero shape in the middle of the hallway arch with your dark hair loose from its braid and charged with electricity.

"Phantasia for Elvira Shatayev," you announced. Though you held the fragile paperback reverently, *The Dream of a Common Language* seemed threatened by your large hands, traces of blue paint you called lapis lazuli visible under your thick fingernails. You read the poem aloud in what felt like an eerie lip-sync of your own warm voice, driving images like an ice ax into the space between us.

"We had no need for words," you read.

I held my breath.

"Until now we had not touched our strength," you continued.

You had your mojo working; shaping energy, charging the atmosphere. You were known for wooing your art history students with compelling stories about painters and models in detail so vivid they forgot the lecture hall. You entranced your painting students with the possibilities of color and technique until they lost their own vision and followed you into perspectives they hadn't imagined.

"We will not live to settle for less," you read, then looking directly at me delivered the last line, "We have dreamed of this all our lives." You paused to savor the impact, marked the poem's place by turning down the corner of the page which seemed careless and mean to me. Then you closed the book, walked heavily across the room, bowed, and placed it on top of the Bonington book on my lap.

"Enjoy," you said then laughed as you transformed into king's fool and capered out of the room, apparently unaware or unconcerned that I struggled for breath. I was stunned by the image of women frozen against their passion, Russian women, a team of climbers, dead on Lenin Peak. I envisioned them: one frozen in the posture of sleep, another reaching toward an image of her lover or a blue cup steaming with hot tea, Shatayev, the leader of the expedition, clutching her diary, knowing her husband would reclaim her body and break it from her fingers.

You and your male friends delighted in encouraging emotional upheaval in the women around you, especially those teetering on a precipice of change: naïve Mormon wives and daughters or small town girls sensing their power but not sure what it meant; women driving over Fish Creek Summit or past Massacre Rocks to take college courses, secretly questioning their culture, religion, marriage, sexuality. You were there to greet them, us, as professor or teaching assistant from exotic universities: Princeton, Oberlin, Brandeis, Ohio State. We practiced pronouncing your names and smiled at your slight accents. Some of you had long hair or beards and were irreverent and ill kept which was exciting. We assumed you were caught in intellectual or creative pursuits and paid no attention to convention or grooming. Over coffee at the student union or beer in a downtown bar you'd engage in verbal arm wrestling to establish the week's champion of enlightenment.

"Now she's heard Patty Smith, she won't be the same."

"She hadn't read Anne Sexton, imagine that."

"Then I showed her the Frida Kahlo paintings."

You saw yourselves as the gurus, professors, Prospero's of transformation.

"Here's where it's at, baby."

"Here's the world. Move into it. Move on."

But you were seldom husbands or fathers and not likely to risk yourselves to reclaim your women. When I found my way to your studio, you allowed me to nap on your bed while you painted. After you left me incapacitated by the image of Lenin Peak, I pulled your fisherman's sweater from the back of the sofa and wrapped the arms around me. Your once intimate voice had been hard as a warning. I wasn't sure who you were. Some painters only speak clearly through the laying on of color or the shaping of form, but your repertoire included thrilling discussions of poetry, music, secrets about the language of math, or most intriguing, the mysterious vision of your own art and the sacred territory of your next painting. You were the voyager bringing news and experience from other worlds to our village, mesmerizing us with tales around the fire. We plied you with food and drink and a warm place to sleep to keep you talking. You know, I once found a note you'd scribbled that read: "Why do I always lie?"

In our early days, you were a charming, dangerous host who welcomed me into your run-down house by the river. You opened the door into a space of light or dark depending on your mood. I'd been searching for it. As an undergraduate, maybe I was twenty, I was compelled to explore the evening streets of tree lined sidewalks in the oldest neighborhoods. Who lives there? I wondered. What are they crying about? Why are they laughing? What does it mean that in the front room, one chair faces out, the other in? What conversation was there? What would it be like to live in that room where the lamplight forms a yellow circle around a red chair? Even after I married, though I never mentioned it, I knew there was a room somewhere where I belonged and someone waited for me with answers, or if not answers, a gift for finding them myself. Not until I entered your space cluttered with books, paints, sketch pads; with paintings and a map of the Greek Islands crowding the walls, where plants were well cared for and coffee went moldy in forgotten cups and a jug of wine was kept on a shelf beneath the sink, did I feel I'd found it.

"Clarissa, my friend, come in," you said. "Let's have a cup of coffee. I've got something to show you."

I couldn't resist the threshold, even when my husband and child said, "Come home. We need you."

Every expedition is about limits, the test of them, and some people going beyond for reasons of their own.

*****

We weren't in Nepal, no Everest base camp, not even the Tetons, though we don't have to drive far to get there. When I told you, the valley was formed by prehistoric floods and the movement toward Yellowstone of ancient volcanic unrest that was due to erupt again this century or the next, you said that suited you just fine.

In the early days of our cohabitation, Union Pacific still ran the hump yard and everyone joked about the lusty banging of freight cars and we woke with the taste of chemicals on our tongue from the fertilizer plant west of town. Climbing Everest wasn't big business: the mountain not yet a garbage dump, climbers not hoarding their precious breath while trudging past men and women dying along the trail.

*****

Once I understood the danger of being too close to you, I backed off the bridge and moved to the channel bank. The phrase *weak in the knees* came to mind as I sank into the snow, brought my legs in wool army surplus pants up to my chin, wrapped my arms around my knees and dropped my head on them. My breath formed frost beads on the alpaca sweater you bought for me from a Nepalese vendor who set up shop in the student union every November.

I couldn't see your face but imagined your mustache and beard frozen with snot and tears and your eyes unfocused or focused on a distance I couldn't see. Did you know I was there?

"I'm just so fucking tired," you'd written. It was your mantra.

I sought refuge in memory, a scene at the Lost Horse Saloon. We were vivid and full of ourselves, caught up in laughter and word play, riding the undercurrent of John Coltrane, Miles Davis, Leonard Cohen: "Jazz police are going through my folders." The regulars joined in a sing along: "Jazz police are going through my things," or they rode Patty Smith's cadence: "horses, horses," voices raised: "horses, horses" to the rhythmic thump of beer mugs on the bar. Sometimes we read our poems or played music at the open mic. You were a force at a drink stained table, a package of Terrytons and a paint brush in your shirt pocket, sketch book and pencils in the bag at your side, engaged with cohorts in serious conversation, argument, or absurdity. We women clustered at the edge of male ego and claimed our independence. "We don't need them," we asserted with beer and our own good conversation. We shook our heads and exchanged knowing glances as you men raised your voices to recite a poem by Ezra Pound or told a yarn about a backcountry adventure. In the rural county where I grew up we'd make a special trip to see the sage grouse *drumming*, puffing out their chests and prancing around to attract the females. Often weeks after one of these nights at the Lost Horse we might be secretly pleased to find ourselves represented in a poem, or sketch or even a painting created by you men. I shouldn't say we as I never recognized myself in the art. One night I realized three of you had depicted in poems or in your case sketches, Theresa, the most enticing among us. At the Lost Horse we heard stories about the legendary *Wild Dog* poets and hippies who came before us and christened this town, the Karma Debt Center.

People were drawn to you, especially women, especially me. You were the leader of the expedition and I wanted you to choose me to go with you; me a curious yet inexperienced small town girl, a western girl, though I wasn't a girl anymore. I'd never heard of Cohen, Trane, or Rich. I was happy to rope up behind you as if getting to impossible heights was all that mattered.

"Meet me for coffee" you'd say, and I'd do anything to get there. One night, not long before our expedition to the bridge, you'd been listening endlessly to the Cohen song, "Suzanne": "Suzanne takes you down to her place by the river. . ." and you said: "I wanted you all in those days. You'd go out the studio door, Julie or Shaleen would enter, each of you a fusion of light and possibility framed in the doorway before entering and creating an atmosphere I could explore in broad or subtle stokes."

"She brings you tea and oranges that come all the way from China," you whispered.

"I wanted it, them, you, with all my senses." You laughed, "I had a grand time in that little house by the river."

I hadn't realized I was one of a group in those days. I could see nothing outside of my desire; foolish to think I could be the one who mattered most.

*****

The heat was relentless the summer I moved into the bungalow by the university. I told you it was a good sign to start a new life in a house on a one-way street that led out of town. You warned me not to get too excited as the speed limit on that street was only twenty-five miles an hour. Though you often visited me you seemed increasingly distant.

One day I received a call from the nurse from the university health center.

"Clarissa," she said, "don't leave Marcus alone. Whatever you do, make sure there's always someone with him. The depression is severe. No telling what he'll do to himself."

"Marcus," I said, "come stay with me." I thought there was no choice.

One day not long after, you stumbled out of the bathroom with a towel printed in zodiac symbols wrapped around your lovely body and another of blue and gold stripes around your head like a beautiful Sultan. I first thought of snatching the zodiac symbols away from you and replacing them with my hands but then realized your face was contorted as if in pain.

"Couldn't do it," you said, "took the razor blades in, waited, too fucking tired to do it." You slid to the floor, sobbing. I thought I could take care of you.

You asked me to drive you to the psychiatric hospital, State Hospital South; you needed a rest, you said. You carried only your sketch pads and pencils and a book of poems, Anne Sexton's *To Bedlam and Back*; she'd been crazy too, you said. When we entered the locked door to your unit, a man rushed up with documents concerning patient rights. I assumed he was a nurse or ward clerk, but he was a patient. "Read this before you do anything else and see me for questions," he said. He'd gone right to you rather than me though we walked in together. You said I shouldn't visit, but I had to see you and went there twice a week. You had a protector who said she could see people for who they were and wanted to have your baby. She made it clear that if I were your girlfriend, she had no choice but to beat me up. She made you promise to put her in a painting. I'd watch the two of you in the day room, close as any couple. She leaned into you and whispered into your beard: "John is a woman. He shouldn't be in the men's quarters. Beatrice is the Virgin Mary. Her son is a rodeo cowboy." She whispered urgently, rhythmically while you kept pace with your pencil scratching across the page. You didn't put her in a painting, but I was compelled to write her into a poem. She had taken care of you; we owed her something. You were the favorite of hospital staff who came to you to discuss their problems.

*****

I raised my head to check on you and a swirl of wind pelted my face with snow crystals. I had to squint to see you hadn't moved on the bridge. In the beginning of our cohabitation, I was out of my mind with wanting you. You set the rules: a caress was lovely, a hug could be had though I should learn to ask for one if I needed it, a back rub could be offered. We held hands at the movies and shared the bed. We were the best of friends. I kept hoping you'd lose yourself in a dream some night and reach for me. It's such an old ache; I guess I can tell you.

Your sketch pads were covered with exquisite charcoal renderings, details of the human form: the crook of an elbow, curve of thigh, ankle arched in pain or pleasure, a hand and arm reaching. None of the forms were mine. Remember the nights you'd conjure stories about them? Details whispered so intimately; I felt your tongue rake against my nerves. You insisted I stay in the red chair.

"There, I've given you some images to dream on," you said. "Have another glass of wine." Then you'd go to bed and leave me stranded. I think you were trying to help.

"Is it me?" I asked.

"I don't think so," you answered.

Can you call it love when a man knows you're the woman to aid and abet him? I'd haul the oxygen canisters on my back for you.

My throat was raw with cold and words I couldn't say. The present situation was dire and I had nothing to bargain with. Your stories about religion were clichéd tales of altar boys drunk on the wine at Christmas mass, terrifying nuns in grade school and the Jesuits beyond in your school for the smartest boys. I wouldn't dream of suggesting your family was a reason for anything other than escape, your father's violence causing you to avoid looking in mirrors for fear you'd catch a glimpse of him in your own face. I might have considered your art as an enticement to live until I remembered that evening after your show in the university gallery.

"You must be happy," I said. The scene was so vivid that now I'd call it *high definition*. We were home celebrating with the expensive red wine I bought for you.

"Why?"

"The gallery was full. Everyone raved about your work. 'The use of light,' they exclaimed, 'the mystery of atmosphere. You get lost in it.' One of your students was weeping in front of the canvass you call *Nights Like This*.

"They don't know."

"Your colleagues, other artists, don't know?"

"A real painter doesn't waste time teaching kids who think art is the easy "A.""

"It supports you for now."

"Nothing supports me. If you think you're on solid ground, what's the use of it?" You emptied your wine glass and poured yourself more. A ruby drop of cabernet caught in your mustache and I fought the desire to lick it off.

"Think you're supported, you're in trouble. Falling through, constant falling, that's what I know; what I trust."

I poured my own wine, the only place to go from here, I thought. I also cried the first time I saw *Nights Like This*, an exquisite rendering of our house, the room where we sat, the red wingback chair, a pool of yellow light surrounded by shadows that seemed to have a life of their own; no sign of me there.

A gust of wind brought me back to the bridge. I thought: *the last sigh of wind*. It was dusk. I became aware of a voice which might have been speaking for some time but I'd failed to pay attention. I looked up but it wasn't you. It was a woman's voice. My head throbbed as I tried to make sense of it until I understood it was my voice, Clarissa's voice, coming from a distance of time, as if from behind a theatre scrim or a thin membrane in my head, a future self, warning me.

"Don't," were the words I heard. "Don't make the next move."

Train cars concussed in a violent chain reaction along the valley. The metallic scream of steel on winter track made me flinch as the train slowly struggled south toward the Portneuf Gap. It left behind the echo of two blasts from the horn and the inevitability of our situation. A small patch of sky cleared above us and stars shown brilliantly, sharp as surgical instruments. Yet there were the smells of wood fires and dinner cooking and the glow of warm light through windows of modest houses. Are they happy, I wondered, that couple in their small kitchen fixing dinner? Is it pasta sauce he's stirring? Are they trading stories about their day? An old woman peered out of her window as she closed her curtains. Did she see us? What did she think? Finally we were enclosed in the night. The wind died and the cold air turned to ice crystals.

Don't be stupid, I admonished myself as I pushed the voice, my voice, away. Maybe hypothermia was setting in. Though I couldn't think clearly, I knew I was not a frozen woman on Lenin Peak or Everest.

Too long in the cold, not sure I could move and not at all sure you could, I stood up and limped painfully toward you. The phrase, *on her last legs,* came to mind as I cautiously approached the bridge.

"Marcus." I was scared you couldn't hear me.

"Marcus." I inched onto the bridge.

Finally you made a sound, testing breath over vocal chords.

"We have to go." I moved closer, as if to secure the jumar onto your belt, as if the slightest change in pressure would cause the ice shelf to fracture and we'd be lost. "It's too cold."

Minutes passed, I was lightheaded and couldn't think what to do next.

"Not worth it," you rasped.

"You have to come now."

Please, I thought, please, don't ask why.

Stiffly, in slow motion and with terrible effort, you pulled your fingers from the wire and dropped your arms. If you could feel at all, it must have been excruciating. I thought of the Kurosawa film we saw: Butoh dancers enacting an assent of Everest, contorting their bodies in the nuance of muscle and tendon stretching and retracting; revealing the intimate detail of each step and the tortured motion of inhalation and exhalation.

"Let's get a cup of coffee," I said.

You turned slowly to me as if looking up from what they call the balcony at 27,600 feet on Everest and knowing the summit was still a thousand feet away. I felt you understood my presence.

"Coffee," you whispered.

I extended my hand in its thick wool mitten, and you accepted it.

LESLIE ANN LEEK

    I was grateful to strain against your weight, short roping they call it. I knew we wouldn't always be this lucky as we staggered three steps through the snow then stopped to catch our breath. In the wind wraiths of time, I recognized the moment when I sent myself the warning; twenty years in the future, you are irrevocably still but not yet cold, no need for oxygen. Light fades slowly from your brown eyes as I repeat this story but can't hold on.

    The night at the bridge, with you close behind me and my mind caught by stories of Everest and Lenin Peak, I convinced myself I had no idea where we were going, and you followed because you had no choice. ■

"Redfish Lake" by Nancy Brossman. Linoleum block print, 3.25" x 5."

SHAUN T. GRIFFIN

They Must Get So Tired of Us

I

walking around their lives,
the indolent stares, the formal
chaos of living beyond the border,
where a border is little more
than a moustache, a drawing
of two countries sleeping together.

This morning in the *correo,* my wife
needed to wipe her brow. A woman
opened her purse and handed her
three white roses. The colonial visit
to places south becomes a suture
in the hail of truncated speech.

I have no wall, no authority to believe
in rust. I left before Columbus,
but the anchor chain trails behind.
I think of the Allende Bookstore in La Paz—
not Salvador, not Isabel, but the last
modifier in descriptive space: beyond,

as in beyond the venal thirst of nations.
This is home to a child
in the bougainvillea, and the frigate
birds circle overhead, unsure
of the cross floating in the palms.

II

At the *joyeria*, Noe Segovia
soldered the severed heads
of my glasses for two hundred pesos—
about ten dollars. Perhaps a lens
will drape the wall with carnal vision—
perhaps it will lure a surfeit of lives
to its corrugated skin.

Outside his store, I ride an old
bicycle to the intersection
of lazing gringos in golf carts
and mostly tolerant residents:
without trying we have become
a land of two stories—a gurney
of greed topples mid-street.

III

At the El Moro Hotel
Americans sit by the pool,
read Kindles. Our neighbor
confides, "I only have four more days,"
like being here is a sentence.
A jewelry salesman, he frequents
flea markets in So Cal—
a silver scorpion crawls his wrist.

In the bar, a retired hospital exec
genuflects to the New World Tequila.
He lost a hundred pounds
after the stroke. He is kind,
a fragrant noun in the idyll
that is Baja California Sur.

IV

The newspaper erects eight prototypes
of border walls. They look like abstract art
trying to find an audience.
Nothing has a point of view,
I think, unless it ceases to exist.
Mexicans sit by the installation, read ladders.

V

At coffee this morning,
admonished by the newly retired
to avoid the hungry young man,
I pay the bill. The change
rattles my pocket like a visitor
from the day of the dead.

All the way to Misión San Javier,
they chant *hombre con nada.*
Perhaps he will grow food in his pockets,
make a rosary of centavos,
hang it over his head and disappear
like the scent of the accused.

VI

In the body shop, a woman
straddles a hill in the dust.
She tapes the bumper with news—
the PRI rattles to an election win
and sands the plastic *defensa*—
a bumper with spots like old skin.
She has bent for seven years

since *secondaria*. Each time it
brings her closer to what seems
like rent. Maybe it is food she paints
or a lawn on the dirt floor. At night
a dog soldiers from the patio
of tools. An acetylene torch
sleeps in a shawl of moonlight.

VII

In a hotel in San Felipe,
first sun through the window
to a *panga* in another dawn—
I fished until my hands hurt.

We cross the perforated steel into
America. The tattooed ICE agent asks
in her best, tendrilled English,
"Are you trying to escape?"
as the drug dog prowls the Subaru.

Hours later, in the Sonoran Desert,
the saguaro signal that we're free
from the helicopters, the burrito
captors, and I wave at the cholla,
the saltbush—perennial shrines

to the sudden eclipse of borders.

GINO SKY

Christmas Dog
or
A Silent Prayer for Hayseus

My cousin, Taylor Riding, was close to forty years old when he became a Born-Again. His conversion happened on Christmas Eve somewhere in the deep snow of a mid-life crisis. But, as I understood his miraculous change, it wasn't Jesus who was the catalyst, but a beer-drinking, black Labrador hunting dog who had been born in a bar in Pocatello, Idaho.

Taylor had won her playing liar's dice at a bar called the Bomb Cellar. It was Christmas Eve, and he was on his way home to finish his daughter's Christmas present he had started in October. That had been his intentions, but somehow his pickup's steering went whacko, and he ended up at his favorite bar . . . but, only for one drink.

Four hours and one dog later, Taylor returned home sometime after midnight. Maria, his fourth wife, disgusted at her husband's behavior, had gone to bed thinking that the rocking horse would not be ready for their six-year-old daughter's Christmas present.

However, to Taylor, time wasn't a problem. He still had six hours before his daughter would be allowed to get up, and he knew that he could finish the wooden horse with two hours to spare. Being the so-called genius that he was, he could do almost anything, drunk or sober, except keep his wife, or any of his former wives, happy. And that, he had decided long ago, was more than he could accomplish by himself. Even with his one hundred and sixty-five I.Q.

He was still in love, mainly because Maria remained faithful to this giant-of-a-man, and he knew that to be one difficult task. However, with six hours to go, miracles could happen. After all, he reasoned, look at what everyone's celebrating.

Lovingly, Taylor put the gift-wrapped pearl necklace he had bought for his Mexican wife underneath the Christmas tree, and then, he and the dog walked through the new snow to his immaculate shop. Once he had a fire going in the two-barrel stove, he located the Wild Turkey stashed among the glue bottles and proceeded with his daughter's present.

The saw blades were sharp, and the planes cut like laser knives through the wood. His new dog stayed right near him, watching every move and was smart enough not to get underfoot. The only thing that Taylor had forgotten that night was to feed her. But, what-the-hey, if he could go for twenty-four hours on a liquid diet, why not Christmas Dog.

It was around four o'clock when he had the tools put away. All he had to do was cut up the scraps and he would be finished two hours ahead of schedule. And then it happened. As he was thinking about crawling Santa-like into bed with his beautiful, dark-skin wife, one cut, and off came three of Taylor's fingers. They went flying through the air like trapeze artists, landing safely in Christmas Dog's mouth. One, two, three . . . three perfect basket catches, and she had them swallowed before Taylor could even turn around.

Taylor grabbed a towel, wrapped up his hand and then started looking for his missing fingers. Needless-to-say, they were nowhere to be found. That's when he became concerned, because he was beginning to get sick to his stomach. Even though he liked to brag that he was tougher than sour-owl-crap, the pain that he was experiencing was testing his mettle. He sat down on the stool and tried to remain calm.

After several deep breaths, he was able to bring his logical mind to a reasoning process and it went something like this: if the fingers are gone there's no sense going to the hospital. Right? I've got enough pain pills to make it through the night, plus, if anything needs to be stitched-up, Maria can do it. I took harder hits than this in Vietnam.

That's when he looked down at Christmas Dog, who was nervously sitting at Taylor's feet. Licking her chops.

Taylor froze. There was some blood on the dog's nose, with a streak of it going straight down her back, and there was more on the sheet-rocked wall. With his one good hand he reached into the cabinet and grabbed the Wild Turkey. One swig and then another, as he studied the blood's trajectory. The fingers, although not as aerodynamic as the blood droplets, had to be somewhere in that same line, which meant that if they were not on the floor, they must have been intercepted. And the only interceptor who could have done that was . . . Christmas Dog. Taylor knelt down and opened the dog's mouth. "Christmas Dog," he said, as he looked down her throat, "did you swallow my fingers?"

The black dog's tail was wagging thump-thump against the walnut cabinet door.

Taylor sat down and took another swallow.

The dog licked Taylor's face.

"However," Taylor reasoned, "if my fingers are in your stomach, they should be safe. At least until your digestive juices start marinating the flesh." Taylor took another drink.

There was another lick from the dog.

Carefully, he picked up the dog and the rocking horse and closed up the shop. Once inside the house, he placed his daughter's present next to the tree and wrote his wife a note.

Dearest Maria,

I don't want to distress you, but I've chopped off three of my finger on the radial arm saw, and it is my belief that my new dog, (won last night playing liars' dice), ate them. Hopefully, swallowed them whole. No need to wake you, I'll drive myself to the hospital. Don't worry, fingerless or not, I'll be back as soon as I can. I love you, and please apologize to Graciela for me, and tell her that her daddy will be a-okay.

*Your loving husband,
Taylor*

P.S. Feliz Navidad.

Once again, Taylor picked up Christmas Dog and walked through the snow to his pickup. "I think you'd better ride in the cab," he said to the dog as he opened up the door, "because right now, you're more important to me than Santa Claus." He climbed into the cab, took another swig of Wild Turkey as the dog laid her head onto Taylor's lap.

As soon as Taylor walked into the emergency room with Christmas Dog underneath his arm, he was stopped by an orderly. "No dogs!" he commanded. Taylor, who was well over six-feet-four, put his arm around the young man's shoulders, and in a paternal gesture, tried to pass him the dog. "You don't understand, son, this dog has three fingers from my left hand in her stomach."

"What?"

Taylor could tell that he was not being taken seriously. "Just X-ray her stomach . . . *por favor*."

Thinking that Taylor had imbibed in too much of the Christmas spirits, the orderly stepped back. "The next thing you're going to tell me is that this dog is Santa Claus."

Taylor was dizzy, and didn't feel much like trying to explain further. He pointed to the towel wrapped around his hand. "I've cut off three of my fingers and it is my belief that my dog ate them whole." He looked at his watch. "That was exactly twenty-eight minutes ago, and if you don't hurry up she will have digested them, and there won't be anything left but bones. *Comprende señor?*"

The orderly rang for security.

Taylor foresaw what was coming down. With Christmas Dog still under his arm, he went out to his truck, removed a highly-illegal, 4.10 sawed-off shotgun, along with a box of shells, and returned to the emergency room. The orderly and security guard froze in mid-stride.

"*Feliz . . . Navidad,*" Taylor said, as he waved the shotgun over his head. Walking backwards, he eased into the operating room, turned, and confronted the doctor. "Please don't be alarmed, doc," he said, as he sat down on a metal stool, "but, I'm not being treated the way I should be, and I would like that to change."

The emergency doctor held up his hands. "What's going on?" Taylor showed him the bandaged hand. "Well, y'see Doc, I've cut off three of my fingers using a DeWalt twelve-inch radial arm saw with a eighty-tooth carbide blade, and I believe those fingers are in my dog's stomach. And, by God, if you try anything besides the finest of your medical skills I'm going to blow this operating room to smithereens."

The doctor slowly inched himself forward. "We'll have to call a veterinarian and another surgeon."

Taylor stood up and pointed the shotgun at the doctor. "Let's just bypass the specialists, son. All you got to do is remove my fingers from my dog's stomach, and sew them back onto my hand. And that's pronto!"

The doctor kept shaking his head. "I'm not a surgeon."

Taylor aimed the shotgun. "You are now."

The doctor stood firm. "I can't stick those fingers back on with Super Glue."

Common sense finally enlightened Taylor's mind. "Call one," he instructed, "but you retrieve my fingers from Christmas Dog's stomach."

"I'll need at least two nurses."

"Okay, but keep that pimply-faced orderly out of here. We don't need anyone in this room who is severely handicapped by lack of the Christmas spirit."

Wisely, the doctor saluted. "Yes sir."

Taylor sat down, and for just a moment closed his eyes.

"Excuse me, sir," the doctor said, "I'll need your dog."

Taylor lifted the shotgun. "No monkey business, you hear! I want her treated as if she is the Savior reincarnate, so let's keep the faith on this special night." He passed him Christmas Dog.

The Bannock County SWAT Team had been summoned, but the doctor tried to relieve their fears. "I believe he's harmless, although he's got some weird notion about the dog being the Christ Child. But, stick around just-in-case."

To make certain that the hospital didn't try and take his dog away, Taylor stayed awake during the four-hour operation. Halfway through, one of the nurses told Taylor that his wife and daughter were in the waiting room.

"Tell them," Taylor said, softly, "that a miracle is taking place here tonight." He looked over at Christmas Dog who was wearing a hospital gown and face mask. "Who else, but a child of God would come into my life and then proceed to take care of me like she has."

The surgeon looked up, and rolled his eyes.

"Make fun if you like," Taylor added, "but, as you can see, this dog right here didn't even put a dent in any of my fingers." Taylor closed his eyes, as a smile came sneaking like a cat-burglar across his face. "A black, female, beer-drinking Lab, born in a bar in Pocatello, Idaho. Now that's something to get real religious about."

When the operation was over, the surgeon was confident that Taylor's hand would accept the fingers because they had been so neatly preserved in the dog's stomach. "It's a miracle," he kept repeating, "if only we could transport all organs this way."

Taylor grinned. "Well Doc, I'd loan her to you, but she's going to have a hard time trying to swallow a human heart."

The surgeon almost laughed. "What's your dog's name?" he asked.

Taylor gave the doctor his best, opiated grin. "Well Doc, I've been calling her Christmas Dog, but I think after what she's done tonight, I should call her Hayseus." He smiled, as he reached over and patted the dog's head. "But y'know, my wife, Maria, being religious in an orthodox way, would have a hard time with that handle, so I'll just call her Christmas Dog, and then say a silent prayer to Hayseus every time I do it." ■

Christmas Dog *originally was letterpress printed in a very limited edition and given away as a holiday gift from Limberlost Press in 1996.*

INTERVIEW

Gino Sky, 1980, from the dustjacket of Appaloosa Rising *(photo by Alan Minskoff)*.

STILL RIDING A BRAHMA BULL THROUGH THE THIRD EYE OF GOD: AN INTERVIEW WITH
GINO SKY

Rick Ardinger

Grammy Award-winning folksinger Ramblin' Jack Elliott once described poet Gino Sky as "An Idaho original. Mountain climber, poet, author, tracer of lost birds, keeper of the truth, horseman, scribe, whopping great liar, kind lover, high liver, old truck hero, keen observer—anything he writes, I want to read. If he leaves me a note on my wiper blades, I save it. I step around or over his tire tracks."

In his inimitable way, Ramblin' Jack summed him up well.

Gino Sky's life as a writer in the Mountain West has been shaped by his experience growing up in a small town and vast landscapes of the mid-20th century American West, by his deep involvement in the literary mimeo magazine movement of the 1960s, by the chance of finding himself in the very center of the counter-cultural, psychedelic revolution of San Francisco's Haight-Ashbury two years before the Summer of Love, and by his focus ever since on channeling through his writing an exuberant pursuit of peace, beauty, and resistance, pushing the literary envelope with humor and hallucinogenic clarity.

As an editor of the legendary literary magazine *Wild Dog* in Salt Lake City and San Francisco after poet Edward Dorn handed off the magazine in 1964, Sky helped the magazine go on to be considered one of *the* great "underground" mimeo journals of the era, as noted in the New York Public Library's major 1998 exhibition of the 1960s-era small press literary movement, *A Secret Location on the Lower East Side*.

Born in Pocatello, Idaho, in 1935, Burt Gail Clays, grew up in the mind-expansive deserts and mountains of the Intermountain West as a dyslexic Mormon kid, who, despite his reading disorder, was compelled to tell—and write down—his stories.

He changed his name, moved on to Salt Lake City, San Francisco, Bolinas, Santa Fe, Tucson, and places in between before roads led him back to Idaho and Salt Lake City again.

While writing, he made his way as a fine woodworker, gardener and itinerant handyman. He climbed the most technically challenging peaks of the Grand Tetons, canoed the entire Salmon River—more than 400 miles of undammed wild river from its source in Idaho's Sawtooth Mountains to its confluence with the Snake River—and poured all that experience into a life where he never compromised his muse.

He's the author of a dozen books of poetry, two novels, and a collection of stories, including, perhaps most notably, the novel *Appaloosa Rising: The Legend of the Cowboy Buddha* (Doubleday, 1980), now a western classic with a cult-like following. He created humorous characters within a mythology blending Eastern mysticism, a vision of freedom in the American West, and a no-holds-barred approach to the creative process that's probably most comfortable humming and hammering along on an IBM Selectric typewriter than on a word processor.

In the 1990s, he had a poetry radio show on "the lobe dial" on Boise's KBSU Public Radio called *Poetry in Commotion*, interviewing such poets and writers as Robert Wrigley, Terry Tempest Williams, Keith Wilson, Irish poet Medbh McGuckian, British travel writer Jonathan Raban, and many others. He toured with his lifelong friend, legendary folksinger Rosalie Sorrels, on seasonal holiday concerts, weaving his poems and stories with Rosalie's songs and stories for a memorable tapestry. For years he taught poetry in the schools to elementary and high school students, and he held workshops with emerging adult writers. He participated in and MC'd numerous poetry readings, and eulogized old friends as they passed.

At home today in Salt Lake City for the past 20 years after a circuitous journey through decades of friendships and landscapes, Sky tends to his projects with his wife Barbara Jensen—woodworking, gardening, occasional teaching, and writing.

It's been suggested that if he ever wrote a memoir, it should be typed out on stencils, hand-cranked on a Gestetner mimeo machine, collated, stapled, and given away on the streets for free as the Diggers would have done in the heyday of San Francisco's Free Stores.

As he eases into his 85th year, we asked Gino Sky to look back on his life and work.

AN INTERVIEW WITH GINO SKY

Ardinger: *How did a dyslexic high school kid in 1950s Pocatello, Idaho, grow up deciding he'd be a writer?*

Sky: Well, being dyslexic, or lysdexic, I learned to do things a little backwards. Some teachers probably thought I was slow, or fifty cents on the dollar, one cucumber short of a parade. But I hung with the smart kids. My father had the same condition. He even bragged that he had never read a book. My Mormon mother . . . all she read were church books. Try reading the *Book of Mormon* dyslexically. During high school, I kept going to the public library to find books that I could read without tipping off the librarians. One day after football practice, I accidentally stumbled onto a book of poetry by e. e. cummings. When I opened it up there were these skinny poems with lots and lots of white space on the page. And my brain exploded! An incredible skylight opened up. I could read the words without having a meltdown. All of that beautiful space. I was so knocked out that I stole the book because I was afraid the librarians wouldn't let me check it out. When I got home, I discovered that it wasn't a library book. Someone had left it there. Spooky no? From then on, I was going to be a poet, whether I could write poems or not. I was a jock, played the trombone, sang in the choir, and for some weird reason, I could read music. Go figure.

Ardinger: *So you were able to get into college?*

Sky: My high school choir director suggested that I study music and opera at Brigham Young University. To go there all you had to do was be a Mormon. No grade points required. I gave it a shot, but I lasted only five months. Then a theater major friend and I fled to Hollywood. He wanted to study acting at the Pasadena Playhouse. We both found jobs at a sign-art studio on Melrose Avenue that created display art for billboards, and backdrops and scenery for film studios. It was across the street from RKO, and our rented bungalow was across the street from

Paramount Pictures. I sat in on some of my friend's acting classes, but after about six months in Hollywood, I really didn't know what I was doing, so I joined the Air Force. It was a four-year commitment.

Ardinger: *But your time in the U.S. Air Force turned out to be a really eye-opening cultural experience?*

Sky: Three-and-a-half years in Europe. I was based in Germany, with most weekends off, thirty days a year leave, and as a medic, we had the best chow on the base. The Cold War was heating up big time. West Berlin was the biggest-baddest party in Europe. This was 1955, only ten years after the end of World War II, and life was finally returning to Europe. I had a lot of great experiences. I spent a month on leave in Copenhagen. One summer I bicycled from my base to the Provence region of France. Fifteen days one way, three days at a youth hostel in Aix-en-Provence, and twelve days to get back to base without being AWOL. A lot of France was still bombed out, as they hadn't rebuilt as quickly as the West Germans. I attended lots of operas during those three years. And in 1958, I saw Edith Piaf perform at the Olympus Theater in Paris. The strange and magical thing about that adventure was, when I took that night train to Paris, I didn't even know who she was.

Ardinger: *When you came home from the Air Force, you decided to go to college on the GI Bill at Idaho State University?*

Sky: A couple of months before I was scheduled to be discharged, my mother was diagnosed with bladder cancer and given six months to live. I took a military airplane back to the States, and then two days later I arrived at the Greyhound Bus station in Pocatello. For the first six months I was a mess. My left brain couldn't believe it was back in my hometown, and my right brain, a recovering dyslexic, wanted to believe that if I were cool enough, I could live anywhere. Both sides of my brain were doing the time-warp boogaloo. The triple irony to all of this identity change was that my mother lived for another 52 years. In the fall of 1958 I enrolled at Idaho State College.

AN INTERVIEW WITH GINO SKY

Ardinger: *Where you had some influential teachers?*

Sky: The enrollment at Idaho State was around 2,200 students then, which was the perfect size for my meager academic skills. At that time there were some excellent professors. Some had been fired from more prestigious schools for refusing to sign Loyalty Oaths. Lucky for us. Painter Ray Obermayr was a major influence for sure. Though I majored in English, Ray was my number one teacher and friend. He taught in the art department, but could easily have taught contemporary literature. Ray and I stayed close until he died just a few years ago. Forrester Blake, the author of five published novels, had also been a big influence in my life. He was a brilliant teacher I would compare to Charles Olson for his vast knowledge of western literature and history. He didn't hang out with his students like Ray did, but he was open to early morning visits at his office.

Ardinger: *You met poet Ed Dorn in Pocatello.*

Sky: Actually, Dorn didn't arrive at Idaho State until I had already left again—one class short of a diploma because I had failed to take freshman speech. I had over 150 credits, but still they wouldn't give me my DE-gree. So I said *adios* and went back to Europe. It wasn't until I returned to Pocatello that I became friends with Ed Dorn. Ed was Ray Obermayr's student when Ray taught in Illinois and encouraged Ed to transfer to Black Mountain College in North Carolina. Ray then helped Ed get a teaching job at Idaho State around 1961 or so. Ed was good friends with LeRoi Jones—Amiri Baraka—and many of the writers who appeared in Donald Allen's *New American Poetry* anthology. Ed was like an Italian sports car, and I was very impressed by his comportment and the way he delivered himself. He would take a conversation way beyond anything I had ever experienced. I really liked Ed's wife at the time, Helene. She was Rolls Royce cool to his Ferrari hip.

Ardinger: *So you decided to start a literary magazine?*

Sky: At Idaho State, Sheldon Newman and I started a mimeo mag called *A Pamphlet*, with political articles, artwork, poetry, and anything else we could gather that had a sting to it. It came out as often as we could crank it out for about two years. I can't remember how many issues exactly, because I've lost my copies during my too many moves. The *Monthly Review,* a Socialist journal, wrote that our magazine was one of a few truly left-wing publications coming out from colleges and universities at that time. Another one came from the University of Chicago. My last year at Idaho State, I edited and published a little literary anthology called *Portneuf,* named after the river that runs through Pocatello.

Ardinger: *When did you start editing the literary magazine* Wild Dog?

Sky: Ed Dorn started *Wild Dog* in Pocatello in March of 1963 when I was living in Salt Lake City and working at the public library for $1.25 an hour. One of the co-editors sent me the first issue. After nine issues, it stopped coming out, and the next time I was in Pocatello, I stopped by to see Ed and Helene, and Ed said that he had turned *Wild Dog* over to my friend Drew Wagnon in Pocatello. Drew needed help in putting out the next issue, so I invited Drew to move to Salt Lake so we'd crank out the mag together. After we published four issues together, a lot of libraries across the country wanted all of the back issues.

Wild Dog, No. 9, Oct 28, 1964

Ardinger: *It was an impressive canon of poets published in* Wild Dog.

Sky: Allen Ginsberg, Robert Creeley, Charles Olson, Gary Snyder, Denise Levertov, Philip Whalen, Keith Wilson, LeRoi Jones, many others.

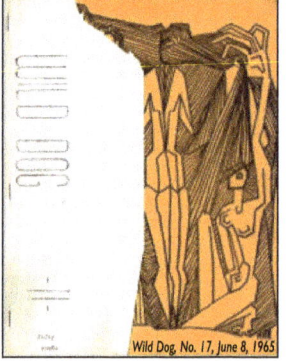
Wild Dog, No. 17, June 8, 1965

Wow, we were feeling like we had the world by the tail, but then the cops started paying attention to us. One night, at one of our famous *Wild Dog* parties, we were raided by the narcs. After the second raid, we loaded up our beater station wagon and fled Salt Lake to San Francisco in a raging snowstorm. We arrived just in time to hear Richard Brautigan

AN INTERVIEW WITH GINO SKY

give a reading from his novel *Confederate General from Big Sur*. And we inadvertently moved into the Haight Ashbury in January of 1965. Nothing was happening yet because IT hadn't happened yet. Michael McClure was the only poet living in that district, Philip Whalen on Beaver Street, Richard Brautigan on Geary Street, Gary Synder and Lew Welch in North Beach, Joanne Kyger in Bolinas, Alan Watts in Sausalito, Robert Duncan and his companion Jess in the Castro District, Jack Spicer at Gino and Carlos's bar in North Beach, Brother Antoninus, across the Golden Gate Bridge, tucked away in a monastery, Hunter Thompson in the upper Haight on Grattan Street, writing his book *Hell's Angels*.

Ardinger: *Those days in San Francisco were life-defining for you. You met a lot of poets.*

Sky: Our flat became a literary gathering place in San Francisco. There were writers coming through all the time. Allen Ginsberg, Lew Welch, Robert Duncan, Michael McClure, Philip Whalen, the avant-rock group *The Fugs*, the black playwright Ed Bullins, Diane Wakoski, Joanne Kyger —who once was a guest editor for *Wild Dog*—Alan Watts, Richard Brautigan, Donald Allen, the West Coast editor for Grove Press, the editor of *The Realist*, Paul Krassner. Buckminster Fuller showed up once and took us out to dinner after we published some of his poems. Michael McClure's play *The Beard* was put on in our living room. And then the music groups started showing up in the Haight.

Ardinger: *You started to get your own poems and stories published. When did the original stories that eventually became part of your first novel begin to come to you?*

Sky: In 1966 we cranked out a new mimeo magazine called *Out of Sight* that lasted just two issues but featured some of my work and many other *Wild Dog* contributors. My first chapbook of poems *The Year of the Fat Flower* was published in San Francisco in 1967. I was still Gino Clays then. I hadn't added Sky as my new name. The stories that later were part of my novel *Appaloosa Rising* were first published by Cranium Press, by the poet and letterpress printer Clifford Burke. He published several broadsides and two chapbooks of my poems and stories in the 1970s. The second book *Jonquil Rose (Just One More Cowboy)* featured poems and two stories that later I incorporated into *Appaloosa Rising*. I have Clifford to thank for that jump start. We're still in touch and he's one of my dear friends and always my teacher. He's one of the literary greats of that era of San Francisco.

Out of Sight *editorial board meeting (Sky in mask, poet Max Finstein to his right).*

Ardinger: *When did your vision of the Cowboy Buddha come to you?*

Sky: Aaahhhh . . . "my secret god hero," to quote Jonquil Rose in *Appaloosa Rising*. I think you're right, it was a vision, or good enough for the angels we hang out with. Since the Sixties, I've had this idea in my head of combining my love of the vast, open landscapes of the West—cowboy culture—with Eastern philosophy. The Sixties sparked huge changes in consciousness, and my cowboy-western soul became immersed in Buddhism, Taoism, Hinduism. I just needed a little nudge from whatever it was I was partaking. I'm not saying it was the drugs, but something deeper. Everything just felt right. Tibetan Buddhism and Native American religion—well, there it was. I wrote a poem, which Limberlost published in my book *Spirit Bone* expressing that exchange: "I'm thinking that the next migration must be inside the old maps. / To discover that seam where Tibet moved on to Indian land, and back again."

Sometime around 1971, I was driving from Pocatello back to Stinson Beach with Brenda, the mother of my two daughters, Nichole and Maggie, where we were living at that time. I always drove that stretch through Nevada at night so our kids could sleep, and I could blend into the night sky and the vast openness of the Nevada desert, and . . . all those stars. Just outside Winnemucca I had this vision . . . The Cowboy Buddha jumped into my head and said *let's ride. Move over, I'm taking the wheel.* Holy shit! I pulled into the first truck stop I came to, went inside, ordered coffee, borrowed a pen and wrote the first Cowboy Buddha poem on a stack of napkins. It's called "Winnemucca Rodeo Stopover, High Confessions of the Cowboy Buddha."

It just flooded out. One big psychic dump. Spiritual hurl. Whatever you call it. In Winnemucca. Back home in Stinson, I dropped off my family, and drove like crazy to San Francisco and gave the napkins to Clifford Burke. He passed them on to one of his students to print up as a broadside. And, that's the beginning of my secret god hero, the Cowboy Buddha.

In *Appaloosa Rising,* my main character, Jonquil Rose, rails after his Apache wife, Infinity Cactus, runs off to Nepal with a hippy mountain climber from Los Angeles: *"I like what I do, dammit! Being a cowboy . . . It makes me feel like I'm connected to this country and I like being part of that myth. Bein' in the center of the four winds hittin' you right in the face at the same time. The earth, cattle, horses and man. Four different creations all moving together to produce a legend. Damn! I like that!"*

Ardinger: *"The Complete Trombone History of Mankind" is a classic short story of the Mountain West, spoofing the Mormon Church and introducing*

some surrealism to a tale about growing up in a small town in the West. Where did the story come from?

Sky: Totally from my imagination—which does get out of control sometimes, like in my novel *Coyote Silk*. People say, 'Wow, you must have taken lots of drugs to write like that.' I take it as a compliment. Salvador Dali said about a similar question: *". . . Drugs? Drugs? I am drugs."* Maybe it had something to do with my learning disabilities. Where else could I go?

In my story "Complete Trombone History" a Mormon Bishop asks a kid to play his trombone in church. As a kid, I really did give a trombone solo in church once, which was one of the worst trombone solos in history, like a huge sonic fart in church. But I made up for it by writing the story that became a chapter in *Appaloosa Rising*.

When I wrote that story I was living on a farm outside Bolinas, California, and folk singer Rosalie Sorrels was living there too in an old school house that had been moved onto the property. My artist friend Elia Haworth had a studio there, the novelist Anne Lamott had a writing studio there, a six-foot-ten-inch giant of an electronic genius was living above the main house. He was the sound man for Marty Balin and The Jefferson Airplane.

It was quite the group, especially when Rosalie would throw one of her famous parties, or when we all gathered to celebrate Richard Nixon's resignation, or when we raised our glasses when the Comet Kohoutek passed overhead. How glorious a time that was. One night Rosalie and I had our own special party. It was about midnight when I finished "The Complete Trombone History of Mankind," and I ran across the quad to the school house. She was still awake, and I read her my new story. When I finished, she raised her wine glass. Can't you just see her doing that? Giving me that look. It was a winner. Approved by Rosalie Sorrels. It can't get any better than that.

Ardinger: *When did you start knitting together all your stories as a novel?*

Sky: In the late 1970s, I submitted a collection of short stories to Doubleday. The first reader for Doubleday, Wendy Jacobson, suggested that I tie all the stories together, because, at that time, the publishing world was less interested in short story collections. I was more than willing to do anything she suggested. I didn't even have an agent, but it wasn't difficult to find one because the book had already been accepted. I finished the book in a garage in Boise. And then *whammo*—soon after it was published in 1980 my new agent optioned the movie rights to Columbia Pictures. And dig this—Alan Arkin wanted to direct it. Michael Douglas also was very interested. Now that's a double whammy with a case of George Dickel thrown in. There's no preparation for that kind of sudden attention, believe me. I was so high that I floated around Boise like I had wings. Rosalie's mother Nancy Stringfellow, who managed The Book Shop in Boise, helped me celebrate and keep me grounded at the same time. It was a grand time, which helped erase all of those lonely nights spent writing in garages. There was this inner, bizarre feeling, like for some insane reason the moon chose me. And then Doubleday put out a four-foot, cardboard poster of me, standing in a fur coat, cowboy boots and hat, next to an outhouse. *Penthouse Magazine* bought two of my stories. All those cold, lonely days and nights were being erased faster than I could keep up. The movie was never made, but that's Columbia Pictures' mistake.

Ardinger: *Your novel* Coyote Silk *(North Atlantic Books, 1986) is your wildest work, featuring a vast two-page cast of mythological and historical characters, from the Mother Goddess to Confucius, Leonardo da Vinci, April Fools, Coyote, Cowboy Buddha, and characters with names like One Hand Clapping, Babe Ruth's Home Run Swing, and many more. Some say it's your most challenging work, yet it was one that was translated and published in Korea. Why do you think Koreans sidled up to that book?*

Sky: Well, after *Appaloosa Rising* was published in 1980, Doubleday wanted me to write a sequel, which I should have done, but I was too stubborn, or stupid —or maybe smart? There were lots of Cowboy Buddha fans out there, and maybe I should have followed that up. When the film artists

L to R: Rick Ardinger, Robert Creeley, Rosalie Sorrels, Gino Sky. Boise, 1990.

who did the special effects for *Stars Wars* heard that Columbia Pictures had bought the movie rights to *Appaloosa Rising,* they made up a presentation of how they would do the special effects. But by 1982 the economy was going into another recession and Columbia Pictures decided not to make the film because it was too experimental. Maybe if *Appaloosa Rising* had been made into a film that would have changed everything. I didn't play my hand very well, and I was really upset with agents and publishers at the time. I just wanted to write and keep it simple.

Coyote Silk with all those crazy characters right and left was a challenging book for a lot of readers. *Coyote Silk* is kind of like a mythical modern-day Lysistrata, where women get so tired of men and their wars that they wage war against the men. I love it all. The Great Goddess is Lucy, our first mother from Africa. One day during baseball season, I was watching a New York Mets baseball game, and the cameraman zoomed into the bullpen, and one of the pitchers, feet propped up on a bench, was reading *Coyote Silk*. And that's about as much notoriety as the book ever got. And by the way, the Mets won the game so there must be some good ju-ju there.

My publisher from North Atlantic Books was at a book fair and a Korean publisher became interested in the idea of the Cowboy Buddha. That's the reason why they translated both *Coyote Silk* and *Appaloosa Rising* into Korean. At that time in the early 1990s, I was moving around quite a bit, living all over the place, and no one knew where to find me to sign the deal. Without my knowledge or permission, the books were translated and published in Korea. When I was finally located, I received three copies of each book and a pittance of a royalty check—but enough to buy a case of champagne and hors d'oeuvres and to throw a big party.

Ardinger: *Near The Postcard Beautiful (Floating Ink Books, 1994) is another compelling collection of stories, featuring some of your most memorable work, for the most part completely different in tone than the earlier stories. They're autobiographical, quieter, with a lot of familial humor and warmth, stories about a boy and his older sister, and the boy's relationship to his grandparents in southern Utah to get away from something going on at home in Idaho for a time. Some of these stories—one about witnessing an atomic bomb test—are classic tales of the New West. Another, "The Fruitcake," was reprinted in* Chicken Soup for the Soul.

AN INTERVIEW WITH GINO SKY

Sky: All those stories are autobiographically *true* except for two, and they're part of my family's myths. What is the real *truth*, though? Although my imagination's working on super drive in *Appaloosa Rising* and *Coyote Silk,* I think there's more truth in those two novels than in any of my other writings. Listen to Miles Davis and then read his autobiography, and then try to figure out his *truth*. Someone once said "art is what takes you farther than you can go by yourself." I love my voice in those *Postcard* stories. After *Coyote Silk* I wanted my voice to be like soft jazz. A soft  dance of words—Nat King Cole singing my stories. I'll take that on a silver platter. Does that make sense? Probably not, but as my St. George grandfather would say, "I don't know much, but I do know that shit and two make eight."

Ardinger: *Over the years, you spent a lot of time teaching poetry in the classroom to kids. What did you most want to bring to the kids? What was your take-away?*

Sky: For me, the most important lesson was to tell my students that they were the geniuses of their own stories. Many times, I would walk into the classroom and shout, "How are my geniuses?" How many times do you think those kids ever heard that? And then I would praise them for everything they wrote. I thought of myself more as a conductor, begging for a little more. *Come on . . . you've almost got it . . . give me all you've got.* Second grade to adults. It works. I've never known a kid, at any age, who couldn't write a great poem. I'd print their poems as broadsides, with the Cowboy Buddha Press imprint, and gave them each stacks to pass out to friends and family. I was just barely getting by financially, but it was always worth it. Third, fourth, and fifth grades I enjoyed the most.

Ardinger: *At 84, what's next in your arsenal?*

Sky: Writing, writing, writing. I have several unpublished novels right now, including three versions of a novel called *Sweetly Adios*. Also a collection of stories, *Plum Crazy Bronco*. I should focus on getting them published, but at my age I just enjoy the writing. Our late friend Gerald Grimmett said writing was "being in a state of grace." That's where I am right now.

Ardinger: *Okay, one more question. In your long poem* Wild Dog Days *(Limberlost Press, 2010) you write about how poetry—hand-cranked on mimeograph machines—stopped a war. Is that message of peace your legacy?*

Sky: In *Wild Dog Days*, I quote Paul Reps, who wrote somewhere, "I drank a cup of tea and stopped the war." If that's my legacy, I'll take it for a red-hot balloon ride. But let me end with a story. After the poet William Everson—Brother Antoninus—left the monastery in 1969, he and his new wife moved to Stinson Beach, California, where I was living with my wife Brenda, and our two daughters. Everson and I became friends, and occasionally he would ask me to join him for walks on the beach. At that time, he was twenty years older than me and a big star, with many books published. He was a principled man, a conscientious objector during WW II, and he also was known for being extremely cantankerous sometimes, especially if he got interrupted during one of his readings. On our walks that was always in the back of my head.

After several walks and a Thanksgiving dinner together, I finally got up the nerve to ask him why he asked me to go on these walks. He looked out to the ocean for what seemed like a long

AN INTERVIEW WITH GINO SKY

time, and then turned, put his arm around my shoulder and pulled me in closer, "Oh, Gino, that's easy . . . you always make me laugh." I guess that's about as much legacy as I could ever want.

Home in Salt Lake City.

BY GINO SKY

Poems & Stories (Chapbooks)
The Year of the Fat Flower (Magdalene Syndrome Press, 1967)

The Ball Tournament Specialist (Duende Press, 1973)

Sweet Ass'd Angels, Pilgrims and Boogie Woogies (Cranium Press, 1973)

The Great Medicine Trail (Cranium Press, 1973)

Jonquil Rose, Just One More Cowboy (Five Trees Press, 1975)

Spirit Bone (Limberlost Press, 1991)

Christmas Dog (Limberlost Press, 1996)

Hallelujah Two Groundhogs & 16 Valentines (Limberlost Press, 1999)

Cowboy Buddha Christmas (Wolf Peach Press, 1999)

Now That's a Peach (Acid Press, 1999)

Double Shot, Pocatello Blend, Rare Beans (with Ray Obermayr, Blue Scarab Press, 2004)

Wild Dog Days (Limberlost Press, 2010)

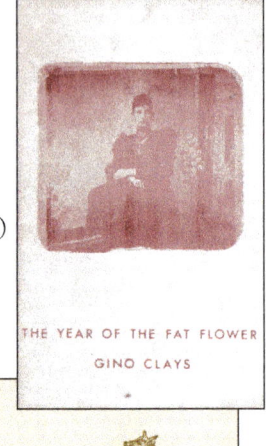

Novels
Appaloosa Rising: Or the Legend of the Cowboy Buddha (Doubleday, 1980; Reprinted by North Atlantic Books, 1987; Translated into Korean 1991)

Coyote Silk (North Atlantic Books, 1987; Translated into Korean 1991)

Short Stories
Near the Postcard Beautiful (Floating Ink Books, 1993)

As Literary Magazine Editor

A Pamphlet (Pocatello, 1960-62)

Portneuf (Pocatello, 1962)

Wild Dog (Salt Lake City, San Francisco, 1964-1966)

Out of Sight (San Francisco, Kamikaze Press, 1966)

LIMBERLOST LETTERPRESS

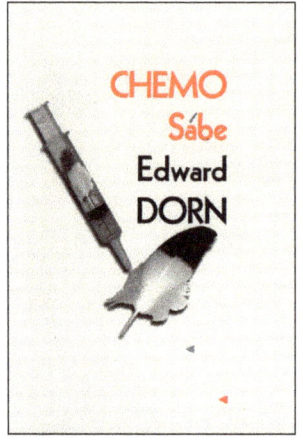

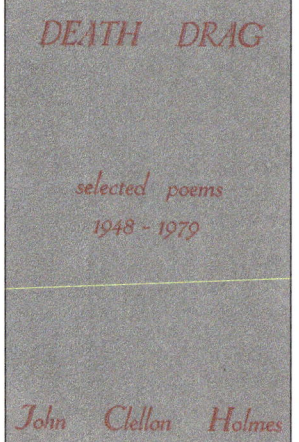
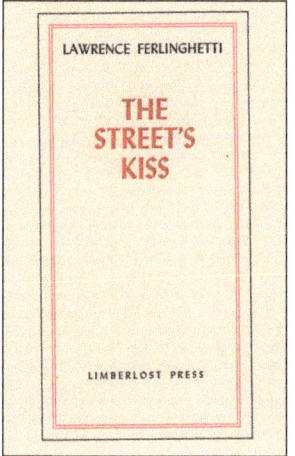

www.limberlostpress.com

GALLERY

Photographs by Glenn Oakley: (1) Rosalie Sorrels, (2) Pinto Bennett, (3) Muzzie Braun, (4) John Hansen, (5) Johnny Thomsen, (6) Ted Wells, (7) Rebecca Scott, (8) Jonah Shue.

GLENN OAKLEY

Where Music Lives

A bout eight years ago I began photographing Idaho musicians at their homes. I sought out musicians who roughly fall under the folk genre—roots music, the kind of music that seems to have a special connection with place. Our homes are the personal places we create for ourselves, and as such they reflect who we are in many ways. I thought it likely that roots musicians would have created some pretty interesting environments for themselves, and I was not disappointed. For their graciousness in indulging me in the project—and for their music—I am forever grateful.

Photographer Glenn Oakley at home in Boise, Idaho.

ROSALIE SORRELS

Yellowjackets were feeding on the warm fallen apples in front of Rosalie Sorrels' home on that October afternoon in 2011. Inside, sunlight filtered through yellow leaves illuminated her bed, above which was a canted ceiling covered with festival and concert posters: Vancouver Folk Music Festival, Ken Kesey, Ramblin' Jack Elliott, Nanci Griffith, Rosalie Sorrels. Her musical history and career appearing like a reflection while she sat below and played guitar and sang to her dog.

GLENN OAKLEY

PINTO BENNETT

Pinto Bennett was living in a sheepherder's wagon on a ranch close by the Snake River near the hamlet of Hammett, not far from where he grew up. It was a needed respite from the honky tonk life. His next album would be a gospel release. Between photo sessions he re-set the irrigation heads watering the adjacent pasture and smoked a cigarette. Afterwards we went out for a six-pack.

MUZZIE BRAUN

One of the patriarchs of the very musical Braun family, Muzzie lives far up a dirt road leading into the White Cloud Mountains. His two-story wood-heated house is designed along the lines of a rustic hotel, complete with a Western-style bar and stage.

GLENN OAKLEY

JOHN HANSEN

I did a photo shoot for John in about 1981 when I was just starting out as a photographer. He was living in this same North End Boise house then and has been since 1978. On this June evening he played his one-of-a-kind Martin guitar while his then-wife Jenny looked on. She looked like one of the stories in John's songs.

JOHNNY THOMSEN

Warm-toned, handmade and little quirky might well describe both Johnny and his home at the self-titled Loafers Glory on Mores Creek near Idaho City. On a sunny October day he took little prompting to break into song with guitar and banjo.

GLENN OAKLEY

TED WELLS

Ted is a banjo player and organic farmer who lives at the base of the Tetons in Victor, Idaho, in a craftsman house he built himself. Musical instruments and plants fill the home.

REBECCA SCOTT

Rebecca's dog seemed to dance when she played in her North End Boise living room, a space defined by house plants, wood instruments, wood floors, wooden bead curtains.

GLENN OAKLEY

JONAH SHUE

Fiddle and family life were having to coexist in Jonah's music room—a shed behind his north end home. His two sons came and went in a whirlwind, stopping for awhile to play their own fiddles.

LIMBERLOST LETTERPRESS

www.limberlostpress.com

ESSAYS & NONFICTION

"Succor Creek Canyon" by Nancy Brossman. Linoleum block print, 6" x 9."

MARY CLEARMAN BLEW

Riding Horseback with the Midwife

These days live mostly in my head, but I've been traveling recently across the rural Montana of 1925. I've been retired for a few years from my final teaching position at the University of Idaho, and I've raised four children on my own, and for the first time I can remember, I have hours of dreamtime to write and ponder. But not to writing the short stories and essays I used to fit into whatever scraps of time I could steal from teaching or child-rearing. Instead, I've begun writing the novels I've never until now had these luxurious long stretches of time to lose myself in.

So how have I come to travel through rural Montana in 1925? Where did I find this opening line? *Mildred rode west*. How have I come to know Mildred as an intimate friend, why have I ridden horseback beside her?

Answer: my old companion, Research.

*****

My first significant publication, while I was still in graduate school, was titled "Blueprint for *English Bards and Scotch Reviewers*: The First Satire of Juvenal," and it appeared in *The Keats-Shelley Journal* in 1970. In this article, based on a close reading of language and tone in the original Silver Latin, I argued which of the English translations of the cranky old satirist then available to Lord Byron had been his source for his poem. I was drawing upon the scholarship and research I had been trained for and which I expected to continue throughout my academic life.

But when I finished my dissertation, which was titled *Aspects of Juvenalian Satire in Ben Jonson's* Comical Satires," and passed my oral exams, I came up against a roadblock that would have been unimaginable even a few years before: few or no academic positions in the liberal arts. Disheartened by rejections, I finally accepted what I thought was the last assistant professorship in English in the world, and maybe it was—at a small state college in northern Montana, with a heavy teaching load, an inadequate library, and, of course, no magical internet that I draw upon today. My best research tool was a clunky, one-book-at-a-time interlibrary loan system which might or might not send me a reference within six weeks.

Oh, well. At least I had a job. And I turned to writing short fiction, which I had written as an undergraduate, drawing upon my teen-aged experiences on a Montana ranch. One publication led to another. I became something of a curiosity among my colleagues at the state college. "Where do you find those magazines you publish in, that nobody's ever heard of?" a well-meaning professor of diesel mechanics once asked. He was referring to *The North American Review.*

Life goes on, with or without scholarly resources. When hard times fell upon my small state college in Montana, I looked for another job and found an advertisement for a Shakespearean from a small college in Idaho. By this time I had published my first book of short fiction, *Lambing Out,* and the search committee in Idaho was electrified by my application, as I was told over the telephone by the dean. What? We can get somebody who can teach Shakespeare *and* teach creative writing? Whoever heard of such a person? (They hadn't heard of Marilynne Robinson). And when we've always wanted to expand our creative writing offerings? I was offered an interview and, soon, the job.

As a professor of history in Montana once remarked to me, "Life's very strange, Mary. Sometimes it goes very well, and sometimes it goes very badly." My life in Idaho went well. I discovered creative nonfiction shortly after I began teaching at Lewis-Clark State College in Lewiston, and I loved the feeling of breaking into new and unexplored territory with this strange non-genre.

And as I wrote about my own first-person experiences and the stories of my family, I discovered I was using the research techniques I had learned in graduate school, but with a difference. My close attention to the text had moved from second-century Silver Latin satires to the crabbed handwriting of grandparents and great-grandparents that I found stored in boxes in attics. To the diaries they had kept. I was less likely to be hanging out in a library than in county courthouses in Montana, searching out homestead records, records of marriages, records of birth, and feeling the thrill of finding my great-grandfather's signature, in real if faded ink, on an ancient property document. I studied old photographs, finding clues in clothing and facial expressions and the arrangements of posing. On trips back to Montana I visited places where my extended family had lived, took pictures, and talked with those whose memories went farther back than mine. My reward was the pleasure of discovery and several books of creative nonfiction.

*****

For years I had been intrigued by the 1937 murder, in the Plum Creek country of Montana, of a 68-year-old sheepherder named Jess Sample. He had been shot in the face as he stood in his cabin door, where his body was discovered by his employer, a Miss McGuire, when she arrived a few days later to bring him supplies. My father often talked of Jess Sample's murder, which to his mind never had been solved. "Oh, they arrested that Fisher kid and tried him and sent him to the state prison for a few years, but none of the neighbors ever thought he did it. Rumor was, Jess had been stealing grass for Miss Maguire's sheep in those drought years, back then. And if Jess thought her sheep needed it, he'd have stolen grass. Yeah, that might have been why he was shot. But who the hell knows?"

Jess had been a surrogate father to my father, whose own father had died before my father could remember him. In his mid-twenties in 1937, my father served as a pallbearer at Jess's funeral. He never was reconciled to Jess's death, and he impressed on me and also on my mother that it remained a mystery. In her later years, she thought my father had found the answer.

"He was vistin' with this fella he knew from Denton—"

Denton is a small town in central Montana. I think my mother spoke the fella's name, but I don't remember it. What I do remember is my mother's certainty that my father had known, and now she knew who murdered Jess Sample, and her equal certainty that someone else needed to know the truth, as she believed it, and so she told the fella's story to me.

"He said his uncle did it. Said everybody in his family knew it. It was just the way his uncle was. To ride up and shoot somebody, just because he could. People need to know the truth!"

Eventually I wrote a short story based on Jess Sample's murder, less about the murder itself than about the importance of his story to my mother and her conviction that she finally knew who had killed him. And although I still possess the old newspaper clippings I gathered about Jess's death and the trial and conviction of a John Fisher, then aged twenty-two, writing that story closed the Jess Sample chapter for me.

Instead, my attention turned to a minor character in the Sample murder—his employer, Miss McGuire, who testified at Fisher's trial about finding Sample's body.

Miss McGuire. I can still hear the tone of respect in my father's voice as he spoke her name. More than respect, reverence even. Miss McGuire is how she always is referred to in the old clippings. And to this point, my old companion, Research, is nudging me. Is listening to a speaker's tone, his or her choice of words, a form of research? As I think about what I might call aural evidence, and my further experiences with aural evidence, I'm convinced that it is.

One example, if second-hand. My sister's sister-in-law had been digging through the microfiche records of the central Montana newspapers for me and became almost as fixed on the Sample story as I had been when she realized that her neighbor across the street was a brother of convicted murderer John Fisher. The next time she visited her neighbor, she asked him about the Sample murder and the Fisher trial.

"And the first words out of his mouth," she reported to me, "were, *I'm not the one that did it!*"

I can still hear her excitement.

Miss McGuire. A woman of legend. I possess one photograph of her, from a faded copy of a 1967 newspaper article about the opening of a new nursing home in Lewistown, Montana, where Edna McGuire has been admitted as one of its first residents. First time I've found in the records that her first name is mentioned. (Was she chosen for the photograph because she already was a woman of legend?) And yes, even now, my old companion Research urges me to study the face of a very frail woman seated in a wheelchair. A little iron gray lingers in the hair that is combed into a bun on the top of her head. Large, expressive eyes, a faint smile. Gnarled hands with long fingers. I think, but am not certain, that she wears a ring on one hand.

I'm hearing a voice now. The voice of an old cowgirl named Edith Blair. I'm in Edith's living room, listening as she talks about Edna McGuire, whom she had known slightly.

"—watched her one time, she was on horseback, bringing a flock of sheep across the Judith River. By god, she could out-ride and out-cuss any man in Fergus County."

Edith's voice softens. "But she was a midwife, you know. And she had nursing training, and she'd tie her black bag to her saddle and go to help anybody that needed her, within horseback-riding range. She was all the medical help people had, down there in that Plum Creek country, miles from a hospital or a doctor. Broken bones, burns, flu, babies—"

Edith pauses, pensive. What she says next is still with me. Words from a time and custom different from the present.

"Yeah, she lived all by herself down there on that Plum Creek sheep ranch. All alone except for a man named Pete Daniels. And yeah, Pete Daniels was an Indian, but he was a good old Indian. You know, when Edna was dying in the hospital in Lewistown, Pete Daniels cut a big armful of balsamroot, her favorite flower, and carried them to her." What an obituary.

I have read Edna McGuire's actual obituary, where I learned her full name—Edna Mary Murphy McGuire—and that she was born in Blackfoot, Idaho, in 1885, came to Montana as a girl, probably following the gold camps, and lived in Montana until she died in 1969. No mention of a husband that might account for the blurred impression of a ring in her photograph or the suggestion that she might have been born a Murphy and married a McGuire.

Which is almost all I know about Miss McGuire. Almost. Like a good humanist scholar, I return to the text. An inscription below Miss McGuire's photograph, written by my aunt by marriage. I will quote in full.

"EDNA MARY MURPHY MCGUIRE the nurse that saved (Mom's Life) when she had the miscarriage on Mrs. Cunninghams place over by Christina MT. Dad got on one horse that bucked him off then us kids caught him another. Then he rode for help. Edna had just got back from a picnic. She stoped the bleeding." Then, in a side note, "Dad was on crutches at the time & could not walk without them."

Another side note: my sister's sister-in-law, an RN herself, talking in low tones to her own sister, also an RN. "Uterine massage, do you think?"

For a long time I clung to the possibility of writing a nonfiction piece about Edna McGuire, but I finally had to admit I did not have enough information even to write a short essay about her.

So that was that—but no! One of those lightning flashes! I know how to get to know you, Edna McGuire! How to get answers to my questions, like how did a relatively well-educated woman like you end up on that remote sheep ranch, alone except for the Indian named Pete Daniels? What other choices did you have? Were you ever married? What was your relationship with Pete Daniels, and how did it happen that you became a legend among your neighbors in spite of a lifestyle that your neighbors would have seen as miscegenation and immoral? By writing a novel, that's how I'll get answers!

Mildred rode west. And I rode beside her, through a 1925 Montana landscape of drought and poverty and despair. I came to know Mildred through my research, beginning with standard textbooks on Montana history, implemented by a series of email interviews with a retired professor of Montana history to get the inconsequential details that bring a scene alive.

More characters emerged in Mildred's world, including a middle-aged Roman Catholic nursing nun and a young Roman Catholic priest from Boston. (He came in handy in clarifying Western vernacular and Western actions for contemporary readers as his friends explained to him what they were doing—bucking a bronc out, taking dallies, hogtying a colt.)

I'm not a Roman Catholic, let alone one of the clergy, so how to come to know my new characters? Here I'll thank the many people who have surprised me by their generosity and graciousness in answering the questions asked them by a stranger, and their gift to me of their deepening interest in my project. To help get acquainted with my priest, I made an appointment with the local parish priest, Father Joe, who wore blue jeans and a sweater for our talk.

When I described my young priest from Boston, Father Joe's eyes lit up. After taking me through the priest's daily routine, he leaned back in his chair and mused for a moment. "I think he's a Jesuit!" he said. "Yes, make him a Jesuit. If this is his first parish, he'll be about thirty-four years old. And he'll need to have a housekeeper! Priests always have a housekeeper! Make her an Irish Catholic housekeeper!" He rolled his eyes. "Housekeepers always know *everything* about their priest and their parish!"

"Where the bodies are buried?"

"Exactly."

Then I described another character for Father Joe, a middle-aged Metis ranch hand named Renny who works for Mildred, my midwife. In his youth and in my backstory, Renny had had a passionate love affair with another man, who then was killed in an accident. Renny felt so guilty that he confessed his affair to an older priest, who was so horrified that Renny vowed to himself never to speak of his love affair again. Would my young priest, I asked Father Joe, perhaps suspecting the affair, try to seek out a confession from Renny?

"No," said Father Joe. He shook his head for emphasis. "No. Enough sin would be brought to him that he wouldn't go looking for more sin."

Something of Father Joe, his compassion, his common sense, his tone, has fused with my portrait of my fictional young priest.

To get acquainted with my middle-aged Roman Catholic nun, I made an appointment with Sister Margaret, recently retired as principal of St. Mary's School, which my grandchildren attend. Like Father Joe, she welcomed me warmly. While she is a teaching nun, she also helped me to understand the routines, duties, and clothing of nursing nuns. (I had decided that my midwife, Mildred, had earned an RN through a hospital diploma program run by my middle-aged nun). When I described my 1925 Montana, where homesteaders from middle European and Scandinavian countries had brought their incomprehensible language and religious customs to a place largely settled by earlier white Protestant immigrants who disdained the newcomers, Sister Margaret straightened in her chair. "Sounds exactly like what's happening today!" she cried.

Like Father Joe, Sister Margaret regaled me with stories and lent me books, including a chapter about a young Ursuline nun, left behind in Miles City, Montana, by her farther-reaching missionary sisters, to run a school, a hospital, a chapel. After years of writing letters begging for assistance—*I can't do all this alone!*— finally had enough. She took off her habit, folded it on the altar. and ran away with a local carpenter. The diocese searched for her for years and found her too late and unrepentant. There's a book there, maybe a novel, for someone who wants to do the research.

Research. The way the generous stranger responds to my questions, the tone of voice, the choice of words. Yes, my characters are suffused with the aural evidence. I make no excuses, make no claims for objectivity, only to point out I'm aware of the subjectivity that shapes my novel. Mildred lives. She rides horseback with her black bag through the Plum Creek country, helping her neighbors where she can. She loves, she worries, she suffers, she makes choices. She owes her existence, not just to me, but to the many strangers who lent me their time, their knowledge, their growing interest in my work, and above all, their voices. ■

MIKE MEDBERRY

Walking the L.A. River

Maybe there is a place where I could talk over this river with you, to grieve for this poor damned stretch of water that has been concreted and cursed, routed and revived, pumped, poisoned, peopled, and picked at like a war victim. We could speak of rocket testing and the nuclear meltdown that happened in 1955. We might touch on the L.A. River being a race strip for fast cars in sexy films. But let's not, let's speak triumphantly of the river's future, to tell you what I have found, maybe connive to fix some of its most serious problems and have it solve yours and mine, to come close to this river for solace and maybe even a little exercise. Or maybe we could find a coyote or cougar living and passing through the river corridor like some shadow. This river is home to many, simply a place with undoubted and evanescent value. But the L.A. River, as they say, weaves a more complicated story and it begins like this:

I have lived much of my life beside wild rivers and undeveloped landscapes in the Western outback of Idaho, but I was raised in L.A. The Los Angeles River terrified me far more than Sacramento's American River, far more than Idaho's "River of No Return," the Owyhee or the Selway, more even than the Colorado. The only thing to fear in those wild places is nature. This is not so along the L.A. River which has been wounded by men of science and re-made to protect human lives from the occasional Noachian floods. Herein lies the problem: we have not remade the L.A. River well. It is straitjacketed, the subject of laughter and pity. We've wiped out much of the original wildlife and 95 percent of the riparian areas. However, the floods were the one-dimensional problem well solved by linear thinking of engineers in our multi-tasking world.

When I grew up in L.A. in the 1970s, I lost track of the L.A. River just like almost everyone else in L.A. had; it lay so harmless, so emasculated, and so mostly hidden from sight. Now, more than 40 years later, I returned to look at what the L.A. River had become and what I thought it might become. I was curious about this switchblade river that I hadn't seen since I was a child. This time I researched its past, walked for three days along its "banks," travelling from Long Beach to the headwaters in the Santa Susana Mountains. I spoke with advocates for rehabilitating the L.A. River and tried to talk to the Army Corps of Engineers about the agency's dreams and work in the basin.

I flew into L.A. in March and found a motel somewhere in the middle of the old river plain and planned to walk the river. I talked to a man who lived under an overpass of a freeway and he suggested a place that I could find the river, just to see it. But by the time I got off the 405, the 105, the 110 and Interstate 5, I might have been almost anywhere. There was no river that I could see in this large and heavily used park. Elysian Park held many paths, many palm trees, sycamore trees, and speedy cars running through. I parked my rented camping van in a safe place with other cars and began walking on an old road. There was beauty in this part of the park as I climbed down and up a mountainside across the road seeking the river. (Where else would you look for a lost river but on the highest hill?) I stood on Angels Point, which overlooks the massive City of L.A. and Dodger Stadium—the Dodgers running merrily inside, hitting, sliding and catching the ball in Chavez Ravine—the booming voice of a familiar announcer revealing the score amidst an enormous spread of parking lot concrete that, once upon a time, was only a rural village on the banks of a small watercourse, The L.A. River.

I saw a piece of the L.A. River far, far away down below, and young hoodlums standing before me, talkin' trash and drinkin' Tuborg beer. The clean air shocked me but the beer that they offered refreshed. And there was the river which I had come to see. We talked about it and I heard wonder in their voices. These were my natural friends, these lovers of a river. The air was as sweet and pure as the blooming jacaranda trees. Forty years ago, L.A. was lousy with stinky, snaky, brown, ubiquitous smog; it stole my breath and held an acrid ozone-and-coal smell that made me lazy. I hated L.A. for the smog and was glad to leave this mess of a city for Sacramento. Now, this place pleased me enormously and I was again surprised when an owl hooted in the eucalyptus trees amidst the thrum of traffic and police whistles.

MIKE MEDBERRY

In the beginning

The Los Angeles River begins in the Santa Susana and San Gabriel Mountains in Los Angeles County and flows into the San Fernando Valley, through Los Angeles and Pasadena, through Compton, Watts, and Hollywood, emptying into the Pacific Ocean at the port of Long Beach. It runs smack-dab through the city of L.A. beside anonymous industrial buildings and railroad tracks, under overpasses and over sacred land. It issues less than a hiss on most days when it is overwhelmed by the roaring traffic. On uncertain other days, however, it howls, wrapping around bridge pylons and carrying houses on its back, muddy water rising like a troublesome tidal wave.

The L.A. River was once an ephemeral stream, growing with spring rains, but otherwise mostly a dry gulch. Swamps and lakes that existed in the early years of the 20th century dried up on the river's coastal plain because of groundwater pumping for agricultural and residential uses. Ephemeral streams, however, are notoriously sneaky; they flash-flood or sleep, flowing in a torrent or a trickle, and it was just these conditions that led to the modern incarnation of the L.A. River. The floods of 1933 and 1938 came as unexpected disasters. In 1933, 400 homes washed away. In 1938, 115 people died and 5,600 homes were destroyed. Major storms occurred in 1815, 1825, 1861, 1914, 1969 and 2005 but the floods occurring after 1960 were less damaging because of flood control projects.

People who had valuable buildings along this slow meandering river were surprised in the 1930s to see the water rising above their eyeballs and raging down the watercourse, ripping along with it lives, homes, possessions, and fragile hopes. Naturally they angered and blamed the confounded river rather than themselves as no one chooses to accept blame for building too close to the river. The U.S. Army Corps of Engineers, with growing fame for its feats of controlling nature through flood control dams, answered the calls for help in 1934 and 1938 and throughout the '40s. The L.A. River became an anonymous series of concrete ditches as the work of the Army Corps and hundreds of volunteers proceeded. The river, once slithering like a rattlesnake through town, now lay defanged by the Corps and a motivated contingency of the public. We lost the namesake river, effaced by the city of dreams and traffic jams.

Now is the time for the L.A. River

The L.A. River is coming back. While in L.A., I talked with longtime architect, Bill Coburn as he remembered the L.A. floods of 1938 at age 11. He is a sharp man and I could feel his joy and love of nature. "In the '30s we went right down by the river here behind us and there were sand dabs, frogs and birds. It was a very nice place." Coburn beamed with the memory. "In 1938 we got eight or 10 inches of rain and the water got behind the concrete that was put into the channel after the earlier flood and it ripped and tore the concrete to pieces." Bill's father's design firm had planned much of the repair work. "It was all very vulnerable and every little street had a bridge and every bridge was swept away by the water. There were even alligators loose in Lincoln Park Lake!"

Bill laughed at the thought of alligators in downtown Los Angeles and told a story about riding his bike through a raging river to deliver newspapers. He got caught on a cable in the current by some kind of good fortune and left his bike there as he finished the paper route. He said that was the last time he tried to fight the river. "Now, after the Corps controlled the river, it is coming back and has been restored. There are kayaks and canoes and ducks and geese in the Sepulveda flood basin. There are fish in the river and again it's lovely!"

Today the L.A. River is the most thoroughly urbanized and channelized large stream in the nation. This distinction is epitomized by its being jailed in an engineered-to-perfection concrete ditch channel for 40 miles of its 51-mile length. One foot-thick reinforced concrete, roughly 400 feet wide spanning 40 miles is a stunning engineering feat and the 3 million barrels of concrete used in construction is roughly the linear equivalent of pouring the concrete for Hoover Dam; the consequences, however, of allowing the growth of Los Angeles, were even greater. Today, the river only appears to citizens in occasional glances from the freeway, tucked behind fences, as if it were a prisoner, shamed, criminalized and pitied, relegated to a trickle in an expansive ditch of sterile concrete. However, the river has always been there, as if working out a plan to escape. It is said that there is a time for everything and now is the time for the L.A. River.

The next morning I parked my car at the L.A. River Garden Park, took a hectic metro train through L.A. down to Long Beach, and began hiking the first 20 miles from the Pacific Ocean to the train yards, just below downtown L.A. I began at the outlet of the river to the sea, an odd-seeming place where the WWII-era Queen Mary is permanently docked in the harbor as a symbol of something like hope. People wandered in the park beside the river's mouth. The place where the river widened and mixed with the ocean formed a rich estuary for many kinds of wildlife.

The long and hot bike path was easy to follow as I walked upriver through impoverished neighborhoods. There is little to tell for several miles except that I endured it and saw many citizen-based efforts to improve the river along the way. Several sub-watershed and recreation plans on this lower stretch of the river aim to restore the badly damaged ecosystems in L.A. Beside the river, bicycle riders are surprisingly numerous, which made me feel a growing appreciation for this place. Pelicans, cormorants, gulls, vultures, coots and mallard ducks flew along the river and kept miserable company with me in the desiccating heat of day. Occasionally, men camped on the riverbank, surviving on next to nothing, along with ubiquitous shopping carts and souped-up bicycles that lay around. Occasionally I stopped to eat or explore under one of the more than a hundred bridges along the route.

Many miles upriver, when I thought my day's hiking was near its end, I found myself locked out of the river corridor by vertical concrete river walls built by the Corps of Engineers. It reminded me of the Parunuweap fork of the Virgin River, a canyon in Southern Utah where vertical rock forces you to swim or climb above the creek. However, I really didn't want to walk in the green ooze of the L.A. River because I had already slipped on the incredibly slick river-on-concrete and had slimed my knees. So I left the river and reenergized myself with a coke and some nice greasy, yam fries.

I called Chauncey IV, my cousin who lives in L.A. is the son of Chauncey Medberry III who had been a teller in the Bank of Italy which became the Bank of America and CJ III its president and Chairman of the Board. I told him I was in Vernon, amidst industrial buildings. The sign read "Welcome" "Mike, uhm, that's not a safe place to go," CJ IV said.

"Yeh, I can see that this neighborhood doesn't seem safe."

"You can go around. Or just take a cab. Listen, why don't you just stay where you are and I'll come get you."

"Well, daylight's burning, Chaunce. I think it is safe enough. My car should be beyond the rail-yard maybe three miles. I appreciate your offer." I imagined the long trip from Chaunce's house and all of the confusing streets in L.A.. It might be midnight before he came.

"Right. It's not safe. It's dangerous and you shouldn't walk beside the river."

"I appreciate your concerns, Chaunce. It's only a little ways back to my car."

"Well, I guess that's your call. Call me when you get back to your car."

"Alright."

I didn't tell Chauncey that none of the maps that I carried would be helpful for navigating or that my magical cell phone was on the blink and soon would be out of power. I'll be careful, I told him and re-entered the canyon of this wounded river. It wasn't at all like the Virgin River, in Utah but it still flowed downhill.

MIKE MEDBERRY

I scoured several blocks for access to the concrete canal and finally found a side-canyon. I passed several tents and the gathered utensils and implements of their residents, people I came to think of as being much like the indigenous Tongva and Gabrieleno people. I climbed through a cut fence to the river path. I had read that the Gabrieleno and Tongva were killed off or held as laborers by the Spanish, Mexican Missionaries and later by the Yanks. They were the native Californians when the Spanish arrived in 1769 with weapons and firewater. Before that Native Americans had lived peacefully in the sun, in this land of milk-and-honey, drinking from the river, eating steelhead, lamprey, acorns, deer, squirrels and other game that no longer exist in L.A.. They lived close to the land and learned to respect the rhythms of the storms in this near desert climate. For that they were enslaved and killed or taught other ways to live.

These riverside campers seemed to be living a tribal life in 2016, living on the banks of the river, hiding out under the protection of bridges, foraging on city streets and bringing salvaged food to their camps. Today these nouveau Native Americans had bicycles, skateboards and other valuable modes of transportation. (After all this is L.A.) They were living in the solitude of a canyon, surrounded by millions and millions of people living a city life. I tiptoed beside and through these camps and hoped that the inhabitants were not at home because I did not feel safe there. No one came out to greet me and I assumed that they were out for a long day seeking contributions from the public or somewhere out drinking firewater. They were making a living, but not one that I would want. I moved on quickly, feeing rich, conspicuous, and vulnerable.

When twilight came I had an uncertain number of miles before I would get back to my car. I saw beautiful bridges that Bureau of Reclamation planners had designed to span the river during the years of 1910 to the late 1930s. Their design was intricate and artful and at least one of them, the Sixth Street Bridge, has been redesigned to glorify L.A. and its river.

Upon one wall above the river I found many intricate murals in a graffiti code that I didn't understand. I photographed some of the illustrations. Beside the wall, brush grew profusely and, as it turned out, provided homes for the wandering people. Two of them popped up and one walked along the wall with a spray can. I hid my camera and waved to them. The camera is worth a fortune to me and it would provide a fortune to those who have nothing, so I stuffed it in my pack and walked on into the coming darkness.

A bit further upstream, I stopped and took pictures of one of the most striking bridges I had seen. When I looked back at the men they were looking my way, holding steady at a distance. They began nonchalantly to follow me. What I had done was clear enough to me: I had shown my valuable camera. I stuffed the camera back into my pack and took off running. I looked back as one of my apparent pursuers ducked down. Looked again and another ducked. I took off again and didn't stop running until I glided into the train-yard above, scanning a long series of coupled trains on three or four sets of rails, considering my next move. I didn't know what was inside the open boxcars so I continued jogging quietly beside them and felt certain, almost certain, that no one had seen me. Then I heard the rumbling sound of a freight train and saw its brilliant maniacal headlight coming toward me. I ran faster, fearing—I don't know what. Was it the infamous "bulls" who worked for the company and beat-up strangers or the strangers who might be chasing me? Regardless, I didn't plan to find out if there was trouble lurking and ran further along the train tracks.

Trains rested above the lower canyon of the concrete river and were now isolated from it by a tall fence. I realized that I was trapped between the train tracks and the river-fence and my heart pounded like a goddamned timpani. This seemed the kind of moment where one should turn, look up to the sky, and pray. Instead I looked down the tracks for a break in the fence and ran more. I eventually found a hole in the fence. Clearly someone had run this path before me and found the way out. Perhaps this was the route of escape for the Tongva, the native tribe of Los Angeles, once upon a time, long, long, long ago. I looked over the wall, found the cement descent moderately safe despite the severely sloping canyon wall, and leapt over before the lights of the train lit my path. I felt safe again in the hardened, barren river drainage below the railyard, which I later found out was called the Piggyback Yard.

I felt safer when I found a goose, or she found me, viciously squawking in defense of the five eggs the size of pool balls safe in her nest on the ground.

Safety, I realized, was momentary, fleeting, a contingency dependent upon immediate circumstances. Those eggs would hardly last forever and the goose might learn a tough lesson. I continued searching for a way out and found another cut fence in a dark place under a bridge beside a lonely road. And then I was out and free, walking in this relentless city once again. Soon I found my car among the dark streets, called Chauncey, and fell into a weary sleep in my damned-fine-van with the curtains drawn and doors hard-locked.

The river is an idea

The L.A. River is now to be partially restored to some of its former glory with help from the most unexpected ally: The U.S. Army Corps of Engineers. The Corps has identified 11 miles of river to restore, from Griffith Park, just south of Burbank, to Downtown L.A., according to a federal and City of L.A. plan. The reason that the Corps defined those 11 miles out of the 51-mile long river is that this portion of the river has the greatest potential for recovery. Not only the bottom of the river is natural rather than concrete but these 11 miles are surrounded by parkland, including the 4,210 acre Griffith Park and 575 acre Elysian Park and it is connected to promising tributaries that will increase the biological diversity of the region. That's why this stretch has strong support for restoration from the City of Los Angeles, the State of California, Governor Jerry Brown and many environmental and local citizen advocacy organizations.

The City of Los Angeles supported the broadest alternative (Alt 20) among the Army Corps' proposals for rehabilitating the L.A. River which would cost $1.08 billion as opposed to the Corps' tentatively selected plan (Alt 13) with a projected cost of $804 million. L.A. Mayor Eric Garcetti told the *L.A. Times* that the city would give an additional $44 million to the Corps' smaller alternative to support restoring the Verdugo Wash, a critical tributary to the L.A. River, and Piggyback Yard, the place I had run from. Verdugo Wash is currently fully clad in concrete and would be opened-up while Piggyback Yard would be turned into a marshy riparian area within the city. This was a visionary plan which was nearly inconceivable to me.

One main reason that the restoration plan was finally proposed goes back to the long-time work of a poet named Lewis MacAdams, who in 1986 formed FoLAR, the Friends of the Los Angeles River. FoLAR grew like wildfire. It seemed that MacAdams wasn't alone in his longing for a return to a riverine Los Angeles; many other organizations have grown up alongside FoLAR to restore the river. FoLAR's current goal is to provide a swimmable, fishable and boatable river. The 5,000-member organization advocates for people using the river and for the birds, fish, mammals, and other life that depend on the river for sustenance.

MacAdams and I talked a few times while I was in L.A. and I interviewed him by phone after I walked up the L.A. River. "The L.A. River is raw, not refined in any sense," he said. It's raw and bruised black-and-blue, yet the L.A. River retains its persona. MacAdams once stood, literally, in the way of bulldozers in the L.A. River channel. "Desperation is what I felt at the beginning and I was just working from the seat of my pants," he said. "The river is an idea, an impression confronting what people have done to it. It's like a rape victim." And he showed compassion for it.

The Corps, which created the modern-day L.A. River, has viewed its baby a little differently than MacAdams over the years. But things change and in the environmental review, which the agency prepared, the terms "biodiversity," "connectivity" and "habitat corridors" are used lovingly and have come to have real meaning. I called and visited the Corps office and tried to talk with the spokesman for the Corps in L.A., a nice guy named Jay Field, who wrote that I should try back later when the final decision is made. The Corps of Engineers couldn't tell me how its views have changed to support the restoration of the river, but then it's never been exactly in the agency's mandate to be open.

A cougar runs through it

My feet held 50-cent sized blisters from the first day of walking up the river from Long Beach to the Los Angeles River Center near where my van was parked. Mostly I had walked on the asphalt bike trail in oppressive So Cal sunshine, along the railroad tracks, and in the river. The second day was decidedly different as I walked upstream from the confluence of Arroyo Seco, beside the Golden State Freeway, and across the river from Elysian Park. I began by crossing the river on the Figueroa/Riverside Bridge, which was in the midst of reconstruction. It was a Sunday and there were no workers on the bridge, so I trespassed and made my way across the bridge without any traffic on it. Then I walked along the L.A. River Greenbelt, which was very pretty with many trees and golden poppies. But still, it was an awfully damned long walk.

For the first time, much of the river actually looked like a river. The flow moved between vegetated islands and along the river's banks —it wasn't the classic sinuous path of the free flowing, meandering river that I know in Idaho, but it was a river of some kind. It moved within its hardened walls, rubbing on each side, grumbling and wanting out, it seemed, with ribbons of garbage hanging from tree branches, screaming: "Let me out!" It was unlike the river downstream, which ran quickly and submissively down the concrete channel of the canal. Herons, egrets, a red-tailed hawk, hummingbirds and other animals were plentiful in this second stretch of river. People enjoyed the parks as they fished in the river and fooled around beside this living portion of the L.A. River.

That is the phenomenal quality of a desert river—give a stretch of gravel a little water and life will arise.

The river ran clear in this segment and the flow seemed adequate to sustain life. Smells were pleasant (well, most of them…) and the vegetation lush. I noticed that the temperature of the water in this more natural stream was far cooler than the water running in the concrete channel above or below. There were plenty of dead trees in the flood path to assure that there would be holding water for wildlife and that the river would dilly-dally rather than race directly to the ocean. There were more butterflies and birds, turtles and squirrels in this section, a gentleness to the parks built beside the river. The river retains its natural bottom here, including rocks, gravel and sediment, which are the most honest and fundamental possessions of a living river. People recreated and the breeze cooled as the water laughed by.

One man and I pulled up a big, awkward gate that had come down the river in a flood. He grinned at this catch, his wife shook her head and I high-fived him and walked on. I thought, "one fewer gate to keep people out." This stretch includes the 11 miles of the natural river bottom that 75 years ago, the Corps claimed had too shallow a water table risk holding concrete.

That calculation led directly to this almost familiar river experience along the Glendale Narrows, the very section of river slated for restoration, complete with side drainages and new "pocket parks." Most of the homes that back the river here are open, free of iron prison bars and high barbed wire that were common in other areas along the river. A few of these homes have decks with tables and chairs looking conversationally toward the river. The place appears nicely groomed, safe, and somehow alive.

The rest of the route ran along the near-wilderness of Griffith Park, the place where an oft-photographed cougar lives, endangered by the park's smallness and roads surrounding it. The cougar's mere presence, however, is testimony to the power of reclaiming lost land. There is no better example of growing wildness in North America than the presence of a cougar here, in the middle of L.A.. Cougar are wily, untamed, usually compassionate to man, but occasionally deadly. This one is in trouble, having been exposed on film to the world by *National Geographic*

Magazine. Griffith Park looked like an undevelopable place, which could work on the cougar's behalf, but it was surrounded by a punishing city. Could the people of L.A. endure this cougar in their midst? Would they even endure this worthless river? For some reason they do. Perhaps it is a need expressed by the people of L.A. for wild space and untamed things. They've got all of this in the L.A. River basin.

I walked on the east side of the river now, having crossed to maintain a navigable route. I left the corridor just shy of Toluca Lake, where the horse path leads through the elegant L.A. equestrian center near the Warner Brothers' studio and Forest Lawn Cemetery. The vertical walls of the river soon made the route uninteresting and difficult to negotiate as property lines ran right to the edge of the river wall. There I left the river for a time, grateful for the excuse, but painfully aware that the movie studio and the golf course were on private property, property held by a class of people who choose to ignore the river. What have they done to return a portion of their immense profits to restore this river? Not a lot so far. Some have used it as the steely background for noir films, as a drag strip for racing cars, murders occur here and odd-named drugs are sold, but most have never seen the ditch in front of them as a living river. It's a peculiar thing, but can you blame multimillion-dollar corporations for wanting to hide this ugly drainage ditch while they are creating a world of enduring beauty? Someday, perhaps, the movie studios will lend a hand to create beauty right outside their doors.

A gathering place for people

I drove to the Sepulveda Basin on Monday morning to begin my third and last day of hiking up the L.A. River. The Sepulveda Dam was built in 1941 to catch floodwaters that would otherwise inundate parts of L.A. during flash floods. Sepulveda Basin is a 2,000 acre piece of open land that stands behind this dam and can be opened to release flood waters when deemed safe. It is a refuge for wildlife and recreationists as well as the mechanism for flood control. The L.A. River runs through it: the Basin is an anomaly in Los Angeles, a truly multiple-use landscape, managed by the Corps and the City of Los Angeles for the use and protection of the city's residents and wildlife. Birds were everywhere and I thought of Bill Coburn as I walked here. He was right to be so positive about this flood-catching basin that his firm had designed.

Then I came to the Donald C. Tillman Water Reclamation Plant, a facility that takes about 70 percent of the sewage from homes and businesses in the San Fernando Valley, runs it through the notoriously pure, but uncertain tertiary water treatment process and releases 60 million gallons of it into the L.A. River each day. *Voila, the L.A. River is reborn!*

No longer is it a natural ephemeral stream. The river flows all day and night, every day of the year, every year of the century, from here to the ocean. The L.A. River is now a perennial river, which is to say that the L.A. River is mostly an artificial river, with the exception of seasonal floods of residential wastewater, which flows quite copiously off streets and roofs during rainstorms and from sprinkler water overflow. However, the residential runoff is also artificially delivered as it is wasted into the river. This river is wholly a handmade, hand-watered concoction, with many impurities in its blood. It contains significant quantities of copper, cyanide, bacteria, lead, selenium, nutrients, arsenic, oil, chromium, trash and unspecified radioactive elements. Remediation of the river is expected to extend for 50 years at some areas and there are a few existing superfund sites, thanks to the long-held claims of big business to the watershed.

As MacAdams, poet and advocate of the L.A. River, said: "It was originally a seasonal river and now it's a year-round river. Like most post-modern rivers, the L.A. River is a sculpture." He explained that having water in the river helps the richness of the ecosystem and acts to change the extreme loss of riparian areas that California has experienced over the past hundred years. "It's alive with all of the creatures in it," he said, "and with all of the human population increases, we should be thinking about what to do if the City reduces the amount of water in the river. What kind of river do we want? In the end," he added, "I hope it's a gathering place for people."

Melting down at the beginning

By the time I got to the confluence of Calabasas and Bell Creeks I was tired of walking along the concrete drainage, cut off at every turn of the creek, so I called my cousin to beg a ride to the top of the drainage. I walked up beside Bell Creek, the add-on portion of the L.A. River that isn't much talked about, and I kept walking down Sherman Way, trying without success, to keep the creek in sight until Chauncey found me. The drive was spectacular as Chauncey and I wound our way up through the thin, growing developments and open rock drainages into the headwater canyons of Bell Creek.

The Santa Susana Mountains are a knobby range of sedimentary rock formed mostly of shale and sandstone that attain an elevation of 3,700 feet. Several housing developments lie on the lower slopes of this range but near the summit is the ultimate surprise, or maybe the ultimate insult in all of Los Angeles: Santa Susana Field Laboratory. This privately owned field station gained fame as the testing site for rocket engines that sent the first U.S. rockets into outer space, NASA's later and wildly successful Apollo space program. It was also the site of a significant nuclear reactor failure in 1959.

Yes, the head of the much-maligned L.A. River drainage was also once the site of a partial nuclear meltdown. In 1959 the main reactor, which was one of 10 reactors at the 850-acre site, experienced a partial meltdown that has been compared in danger to the famed Three-Mile Island meltdown. Actually, I learned that the radiation released at the Santa Susana mishap was estimated at 15 to 260 times that from the Three-Mile Island disaster, according to an April 2006 article in *California Lawyer*. Fourteen out of 43 fuel rods were badly damaged in this experimental sodium cooled reactor. The reactor provided 75 megawatts of electricity to the local town of Morepark, California, which is near the base of the mountain range.

More than 150,000 people live within five miles of the Santa Susana facility and half a million people live within 10 miles, according to the *California Lawyer.* In addition, the reactor had no containment, absolutely none, so that much of the nuclear effluvium was sent off as gas or solids into the landscape. Today little proof remains of what actually happened. Nonetheless, residents of the region were never told about the danger of the laboratory above them as the meltdown occurred. Some individuals were undoubtedly harmed and eventually killed by it. In addition, in the 325 confirmed rocket engine tests (30,000 tests were estimated but unconfirmed) the engines were cooled with TCE (trichloroethylene). The TCE is still being cleaned up in soil, streambeds, and potentially in the aquifers. A $42 million study by the Environmental Protection Agency in 2012 reported that 10 percent of the Field Station still contained radioactive concentrations that exceeded background standards. NASA and Boeing are tasked with the cleanup that was scheduled for completion by 2017.

The L.A. River will never be what it was in the 1800's: a lazy ephemeral stream wandering through a valley to the ocean. But it has survived and endured in a place that wanted to make it go away. If you're standing on the riverside when torrential rains fall one fine spring day, when the river floods from the mountains down to Long Beach and your precious belongings become splinters on the banks of this reborn ephemeral stream, when this canal is no longer the sweet, floatable, walkable waterway, when rattlesnakes (those feared and toothy venomous serpents!), are once again swept from the San Gabriel Mountains down to Long Beach, and your precious property and belongings become fond memories, recall that the river is as unpredictable and remains angrier than a nuclear melt-down. It insists on being remembered like a geological fact.

Remember that the containing walls that engineers hope to make higher are only thin, foolish, and temporary diversions. You will recognize, or perhaps you will, that this river is not going away. Appease it if you will. Pet it with compliments. Swear at it. Restore it. Walk on it. Piss in it. Respect it. Play in it. Or do what you will with it. But you gotta love it for what it is—the river that created the most beautiful and wicked City of Los Angeles in the desert. ■

TOM REA

Remembering Marc Kashnor
1951-2009

The morning of the funeral Barb and I left Casper early and drove up to Story in that uncertain light you get in April when it might or might not snow. We were glad to get this out of the way, hoping to see old friends, ready to stay the afternoon if the weather cooperated. The Woman's Club looked the same as ever, a small, comfortable log building from the thirties, on a rock foundation. It has a single meeting room with a fireplace, kitchen in back. Folding chairs were set up in rows and at the front—Christ, there was Marc. The casket was open. It was like there was a force field around it. Barb went up for a look but I couldn't. From the fourth row of chairs I could make out his forehead, glasses, top of his nose, black hair streaked with gray and pulled back neatly. The forehead and nose were a waxy yellow. This was an artifact; our friend had left it some time ago.

Barb and I first saw Story in a spring snowstorm thirty years earlier; teenage boys in pickups were turning lazy, recreational cookies in the unnamed main street. We got directions at the post office. The house as advertised was on a creek. It was a thin-walled summer cabin with two tiny bedrooms, but it had what we wanted, an attached, two-car garage with a cement-pad floor. This was space for our 1918 printing press and type drawers, out of which we would set type by hand and with the press make beautiful books of superior poetry, and sell them at regular-book prices. This was where we were going to raise our children, and jump-start the cultural revolution.

Back then Story had a population of around 400, 650 in summer; it's more now but not much. It lies halfway between Buffalo and Sheridan, Wyoming, on the east flank of the Bighorn Mountains between the north and south forks of Piney Creek, in big ponderosa pines, with houses stashed among them. The pines are tall and gloriously straight; if a fire ever crowned in their tops the town would be gone in an afternoon. Something about that possibility fits the place: beautiful and unaware of its liabilities.

Being unincorporated, the town had no government and no politics but gossip. The Ambulance Picnic did bring people together once a year for a fundraiser in a generous, public sort of way. The EMTs, all volunteers, were the leaders in town; people looked up to them. But then the picnic ended in drunken fights too many years in a row, and it was abandoned.

Four institutions held the town together: post office, Woman's Club, branch library, and school, 40 or 50 kids, k-4. The place lacked gravity, however, because it lacked commerce. Its businesses were one small store and three bars, any two of which were likely to be open in a given year. People drove to Sheridan or Buffalo for gas, groceries, and everything else. The first two years we were in Story there was a café, Mama Bear's, with a Laundromat attached. But that didn't last. The town seemed to lack a middle class. People were either poor or rich.

Within a year of our arrival my cousin Margie and her best girlfriend Lee rented a house in Story much more unusual than ours; it had thick walls of yellow stucco, light blue shutters, a cluttered porch, and an upstairs dormer room under steeply slanted eaves. Lee was recently out of art school, in San Francisco. Margie then was not long out of college. They had a cat or two. They drove old, small pickups, and filled the house with their odd stuff. In the yard was an apple tree, magnificently tall, as it hadn't been pruned for decades. It was a heavy bearer. Barb learned to make apple butter. Our first child, Hannah, was born late the first fall we were there. Our second, Adam, was born in 1982.

Somewhere along in there Marc arrived, and moved in with Lee and Margie. He had known Lee in art school. He had a thin face, thick, dark hair, dark eyebrows, a dry wit, and a hankering for solitude; in these respects he reminded me of a college friend who'd moved to Alaska to run a winter trapline with dogs and a dogsled. Marc's humor was full of peculiarities. He loved terrible movies. Time and again, he described *Plan 9 from Outer Space*—Bela Lugosi knocking over cardboard tombstones—a decade before its cult revival. He told stories about Austin, Nevada, where he'd lived after San Francisco and perfected his blackjack game. He talked a lot about Boston—a gritty Cambridge, actually, where he'd grown up. His grandparents and his sister had raised him; his grandfather was a cooper, and very old. He had a brother who was retarded, as we called it then, and in a home. Out of these lives, facts, and places he somehow constructed a place for himself, in which he walked and joked and lived in all our minds, I think. The place was a little dark, a little smoky but real nevertheless, and its jokes were kind. He was very smart. He was courteous to the children. We had other childless Story friends living so-called artist lives like ours, but they always seemed to have strong opinions about how we should raise our children. Marc had no points to make, no axes to grind. The kids liked him and took him for granted the way children will, when their affections are respected.

Marc's taste for miscellany matched Lee's and Margie's. In their house there were little setups on end tables, windowsills, and the upright piano: army guys, dinosaurs, miniature forklifts, Virgin of Guadalupe medallions. Cobwebs, sometimes, among them. The house was cold in winter. Margie bought a kerosene heater. On Christmas they hung three-pronged adaptor plugs on the tree.

Marc's friend Moro (pronounced Motto; she's Armenian) also moved to Wyoming. Since they were small, in Cambridge, she had been his best friend in the world. She had been in California when he was, and may have lived with him for a time in Austin. She came to Hanna, Wyoming, and took a job in the coal mines there. Olive-skinned, smart, black haired, black eyed, she would come up to Story once in a while and visit. It was clear Marc felt easier around her than anyone else, also clear that some old romance between them had run its course.

Marc was a good photographer. He set up his enlarger in one of the tiny bedrooms, and printed big black and whites. There was a funny one of a tail-smoking B-29 diving into—Italian hills, 1944? No, on closer inspection, a woman's rear end; Moro's, he admitted. Most of the pictures were desert landscapes from the Great Basin—those Giacometti tufa towers at Mono Lake, for example, with flat, shallow water stretching to all the bitter directions.

From time to time he contributed news items to local newspapers. This gained him the nickname Scoop, around town. Once after two men were killed at the Buffalo airport in the crash of a small plane loaded with Malathion, he told me the headline should have read, "Humans, three million; mosquitoes, two." But he didn't write the story.

He acquired Lucy, a Rhodesian ridgeback, who grew swiftly into a quarrelsome, disobedient, sharp-toothed barker. "That wretched dog," Margie still calls her, 35 years later. Marc loved the dog very much. After a while, Margie moved out. Some years later, Lee got cervical cancer, had successful surgery—and eventually she moved out too. Marc and Lucy stayed in the stucco house, with the stuff.

Those years I was often gone two weeks out of every month, teaching poetry writing in schools around Wyoming. Barb ran the press and raised the kids. Marc would sometimes show up at suppertime, as single people will when they are friends with a family. We fed him, or when I was gone Barb fed him. He was always good company, and often brought a fresh bottle of Jim Beam. Once he broke some ribs when he fell onto the newel post at the bottom of the stairs in the stucco house. Maybe years later I learned the truth, that he'd been kicked in a fight in the Tunnel Inn parking lot. How strange, I thought; a fight. And it wasn't the only time.

In 1987 I took an honest job on the Casper *Star-Tribune*. We were glad to leave Story, as it was by now clear we weren't going to start the cultural revolution, I was dead tired of teaching poetry to kids, and Story was no place to raise children. I plunged happily into newspaper life. Max, our third child, was born two years later.

We didn't hear much from Marc. I sent a postcard or two; no answer. Once he came to the paper to interview for a job, but that didn't work out. Once he visited us in our tract house in Casper with a woman who clearly liked him, and vice versa. He looked all right, maybe a little uncertain around the eyes and teeth, or maybe I'm just making that up. Once or twice on trips to Sheridan we detoured through Story and drove past his house. It looked more hidden than ever by its big spruce tree, the apple tree on the side, and the thick lilac bushes along the road. Fifteen, eighteen years passed. Marc died on March 3, 2009.

We heard about it ten days later from Margie, in an email. A friend had stopped by Marc's house, found him in bad shape and called Moro. She drove up to Story and right away took Marc to the Buffalo hospital, where he died in the ICU the following night. For the last few years Marc had done little but drink, Margie said, and managed to alienate most of his friends.

That night for some reason Barb and I watched *Into the Wild* on TV, the movie about the smart, dark-haired, thin-faced young man who turns his back on family and the world and starves in an empty bus in Alaska. Marc was one of the world's orphans, Barb said, a wanderer who never knew enough love, or how to accept it. But he was so good to our kids.

There was delay in setting a funeral date. Margie and Lee met some other people at the house to begin cleaning it out. Clearly it would be up to Marc's second-oldest friend, Tom Faulkner, a half-time sculptor and half-time Episcopal priest in New York, to do the service, but he had schedules to juggle and so did Marc's sister, Cynthia. Lee had to be in France, with her new husband. And Lucy had to be exhumed.

Marc had wanted to be buried next to Lucy in his yard, but that would have meant ensuring an easement to the grave when the house was sold. Faulkner later told us how he'd directed, by cell phone, the guy from the Buffalo funeral home through Marc's yard, past the apple tree, past the second junk car on the left to Lucy's grave. Which was a wooden stake with two crosspieces. On the top one was written, in letters now barely legible, "Good dog, Lucy." And on the bottom one, "Stay." The funeral home guy dug up the dog's remains, and they were now, we learned the morning of the funeral, waiting for Marc in the bottom of his grave.

Moro was at the funeral with her square-faced, cowboy-hatted husband and their swell 12-year-old daughter. Margie was there, an old friend of ours from Story named Dave Clarendon was there; several of Marc's barfly friends were there, and a couple of Episcopalians who'd visited Marc often the last, bedridden months of his life were there. But several other people who were friends of Marc's when we knew him, and who we knew were still in the area were absent. I kept looking around.

Faulkner started the service, asking for stories. Slightly shy, people reminisced. Then he gave an eloquent eulogy. "Marc was too smart *not* to believe in God," Faulkner said. "Let me say that again: Marc was too smart *not* to believe …" I found that unconvincing; his point was that Marc had been Bar Mitzvahed, which I'd never known, and so had to grapple in a big, meaningful way with the Old Testament. More interesting was Faulkner's observation that Marc was so open to stimuli that he was receiving input all his life—"Input, input, input"—but he never figured out how to corral his skills and make a product with them. And so he drank because it calmed him. Together we all sang "Take Me out to the Ball Game," and then Faulkner played a CD of Marty Robbins singing "El Paso."

The graveyard was south of town on a snow-swept, south-facing slope with a long view out over prairie to the south and east. The road in was muddy with fresh snow, and all afternoon the sun kept coming and going among the snowflakes. Faulkner had us lay handfuls of dirt on the coffin. Supposedly Lucy was down there too. Slowly, horizontal poles at ground level unspooled, allowing canvas straps like green-cloth bed slats to lower the coffin slowly into the grave.

Back at the Woman's Club there was a big meal ready: fried chicken, white gravy, wax beans, sweet potato pie with marshmallows. And more stories. Marc's barfly friends loved and forgave the recent Marc, who locked a dead deer for winter meat in the old, unheated enlarger room, who'd been 86ed from both Story stores for stealing booze off the shelves, the Marc who, toward the end, shit on his couch when necessary. But other old friends I'd been looking for never showed.

A few nights later, in Casper, Margie's brother Dan stopped by. Dan's been sober now 21 years. Of Marc, and the liquor, Dan said, "It's as important to him as air. What if someone said to you, here, I'll take all of the air out of the air, and then if you want some I'll sell it back to you in little bits. Wouldn't you be willing to trade me anything? That laptop there? For your next breath?"

Word circulated in Buffalo medical circles that Marc in fact was "peeled off" that couch—gangrene—and when he was brought to the hospital and put in a whirlpool bath, some of his skin sloughed off. Later he fell into a coma. Moro left those parts out, however, and told only how, riding to the hospital in the passenger's seat, Marc rolled down the window. It was one of the first days when spring seems possible after all, and the earth is releasing its smells. "Great day for a ride," Marc said. "I wish it was longer."

Friends die, and only after that do you get to look back over their lives and see arcs of meaning there. As we pulled our coats back on and said our goodbyes, I thought, maybe that's true of the West, too, which sometimes seems so intent on killing itself—that its meanings will come clear only after it finally does itself in.

I worry more about the West's chronic shrug toward the unfortunate. The kind of attitude Barb's brother Todd found, when he went to the Department of Family Services to figure out how to get his new heart. Or the attitude Marc found, in my heart, the day he showed up at the *Star-Tribune* for an interview, at 10 a.m., with whiskey on his breath. I was angry, and offended. Take your stinking trouble somewhere else, I thought. It's my clearest memory of him, except for the strange, waxy look of his skin in the coffin, from a distance, when I couldn't stand to get too close.

Idaho novelist Vardis Fisher, mid-1960s.

ALESSANDRO MEREGAGLIA

Vardis Fisher's Last Essay

When Vardis Fisher died on July 9, 1968, the Idaho novelist left behind an extensive bibliography: more than two dozen novels, collections of short stories, essays, and poetry, as well as three books written for the Federal Writers' Project. But he also left behind multiple projects in mid-process. Obituaries and memorials noted that Fisher was at work on a book called *The American West: The World's Greatest Physical Wonderland*.[1] Biographers over the ensuing decades also mentioned this incomplete project but didn't elaborate further.[2]

The following essay, which appears in print for the first time, is a surviving remnant of that project he was working on at the time of his death. It is a finished, polished piece, and likely the last essay he completed in his life (excluding newspaper columns).

The manuscript lay dormant for half a century until I came across it earlier in 2019 in Fisher's papers housed at Yale University. My interest in Fisher stems from my on-going research into Caxton Printers, a Caldwell print shop and publishing firm. Caxton published dozens of Fisher's books, including the well-regarded *Idaho: A Guide in Word and Picture* in 1937. Moreover, Caxton's founder, J. H. Gipson, was good friends with Fisher.

"The World's Greatest Physical Wonderland" started as a lecture that Fisher delivered at the College of Idaho six months before his death. For six weeks in the winter of 1968, Fisher served as writer-in-residence at the college, where he taught classes on creative writing and also gave three public talks. Delivered at 9:30 a.m. on January 12 in Jewett Auditorium, Fisher's first lecture focused on the physical beauty of the American West.[3]

That lecture was not the first time he referred to the West as a "physical wonderland." In 1966, while delivering a speech on "The Western Writer and the Eastern Establishment" at a meeting of the Western Literature Association, he described how "this Western part of our country is by far the most remarkable physical wonderland in the world."[4]

Fisher planned to turn his College of Idaho lecture into a full-length volume, similar to his final book, *Gold Rushes and Mining Camps of the Early American West* (Caxton, 1968). *Gold Rushes* was a large-format (9 x 11 inch), 466-page book, written with his wife, Opal, and filled with hundreds of photographs. In newspaper articles reviewing *Gold Rushes* in spring 1968, Fisher was already talking about his next project and how he and Opal planned to travel east to acquire photographs from libraries in New York and Washington.[5] He envisioned a "large and very beautiful book" featuring "300 or 400 of the finest photos from all possible sources."[6] There's no evidence that he produced any more material for the book than this lecture he gave.

In "The World's Greatest Physical Wonderland," Fisher acts as a booster for western geography, specifically the national parks, but also as a defender against what he called the "condescension and contempt of the Northeast for our Western land."[7] Born and raised in Annis, Idaho, Fisher lived most of his life in Hagerman, Idaho. He nursed great disdain for easterners for much of his life, based on his experience teaching in New York City.[8]

The specific impetus for this essay was his reaction against a book published in 1966 calling most of the western United States a "desert." Fisher vehemently objected to that label; he believed that reducing the West to mere desert was to ignore its beauty and natural diversity. He highlights Crater Lake, the Grand Canyon, Yellowstone, and Carlsbad parks, among others. Regarding Idaho, he spends several paragraphs describing Craters of the Moon, which he characterizes as the state's "greatest physical wonder." Drawing heavily from Freeman Tilden's *Our National Parks* (Knopf, 1951), Fisher describes why and how these natural areas are beautiful. Fisher also pulls extensively from John Muir, an early proponent of U.S. national parks, as well as several other early naturalists and environmentalists.

To be sure, Fisher engages in extreme jingoism: the West is better than the East in every way. And he leaves no room for discussion:

"We have such a wealth of splendors out here that I feel a little shame at holding a few of them up for the East to look at.

In the entire expanse of it, from Caribou in the northern tip of Maine, to Flamingo in the southern tip of Florida the East has, besides its two outstanding features, Mammoth Cave and the Everglades, only the Acadia, Shenandoah, and Great Smoky parks, which, compared to our greatest, are really nothing at all."

Fisher's boosterism, though jingoistic, is not the fluff writing found in promotional brochures from state agencies or chambers of commerce. Instead, it's brutally honest and critical, even of places in the west. Not every western national park deserved its status, Fisher thought. "Big Bend, the Rocky Mountain, and Glaciers are beautiful wilderness areas but should not be national parks." Even the Sawtooth Mountains in Idaho weren't beautiful enough for Fisher: "[The Sawtooth range] would make a nice wilderness area but it simply does not have national park status." When describing Lassen Peak in northern California, he says it, too, is not worthy of being a national park, given its location in the West. However, "it would be [a national park] in the northeast, where they have so little that is unusual in natural features, but not in the West, where we have so much."

Despite his tone, Fisher clearly has a "love affair" with the West to speak so longingly of its beauty.[9] Had Fisher not died when he did, he likely would have turned this essay into a beautifully illustrated and produced book, perhaps published by Caxton Printers. But this extant remnant serves as a fitting final word from a writer who, above most everything else, cared about the American West.

Where possible, I've added endnotes identifying the sources of the quotations and references within the piece.

Many thanks to Vardis Fisher's son, T. R. Fisher, for permission to publish this essay. ■

NOTES

[1] Fisher had also begun to write his autobiography just eight days before his death and was also revising an unpublished novel.

[2] See, for example: Ronald W. Taber, "Vardis Fisher of Idaho, March 31, 1895-July 9, 1968," *Idaho Yesterdays* 12, no. 3 (Fall 1968), 2-8; Wayne Chatterton, *Vardis Fisher: The Frontier and Regional Works* (Boise, ID: Boise State College, 1972); and Dorys Crow Grover, *Vardis Fisher: the Novelist as Poet* (New York: Revisionist Press, 1973).

[3] The other two lectures were titled "What is the Evidence? The Author Comments on His 'Testament of Man' Series" and "Vignettes of a Few Prominent Authors." "American West Is Topic for Noted Gem Novelist," *Idaho Free Press*, January 10, 1968, 10.

[4] Vardis Fisher, "The Western Writer and the Eastern Establishment," *Western American Literature* 1, no. 4 (Winter 1967), 244-259.

[5] Jan Arthur Sainsbury, "Will the Real Vardis Fisher Please Stand Up?," *Twin Falls Times-News*, May 1968, from Folder 73, Box 14, Cage 48, Inez Puckett McEwen Papers, Manuscripts, Archives, and Special Collections, Washington State University Libraries; Betty Penson, "Vardis Fisher, Gem Writer, Dies," *Idaho Statesman,* July 11, 1968, 3.

[6] "American West Is Topic," *Idaho Free Press.*

[7] "Idaho Writer Will Address College of Idaho Students," *Idaho Statesman*, January 12, 1968, 33.

[8] See, in particular, the above-referenced essay, "The Western Writer and the Eastern Establishment."

[9] "American West Is Topic," *Idaho Free Press.*

VARDIS FISHER

The World's Greatest Physical Wonderland

When about a century ago the new *Scribner's Monthly* asked Nathaniel P. Langford[1] to submit an essay on the real or legendary wonders of the Yellowstone area, and in his essay he wrote that there was a canyon with a waterfall higher than Niagara's, throats in the earth's surface out of which boiling water exploded two hundred feet into the air, eruptions of multi-colored muds, hot fountains that boiled continuously, solid brimstone hills and a mountain of volcanic glass, one reader declared to the editor that Langford was the champion liar of the Northwest, and other readers reminded him that when he founded the magazine he promised that it would have a "moral tone." A man named Cook, who had seen parts of the area in 1869, sent an article about it to *Lippincott's Magazine,* and was told that "we do not print fiction." The first national park to be established in the world is a land of such marvels that it was "discovered" and reported six separate times before the East would believe that such wonders were there, the sixth discovery was by the U.S. Government; its report must have been dismissed by many persons as a fantastic credibility gap.

This attitude towards our fabulous West is the dominant one in the East, and is now and then supported by persons with visible credentials. One of them, historian W. P. Webb of Texas published in *Harper's* in May 1957, an article called "The American West, Perpetual Mirage." According to him eight states—New Mexico, Arizona, Nevada, Colorado, Wyoming, Montana, Idaho, and Utah—are the center of an American desert; and the nine states bordering these are "desert rim states." Apparently without bothering to look up the meaning of the word desert, Prof. W. E. Hollon took up the matter where Webb dropped it, in his Oxford Press book *The Great American Desert*,[2] Hollon says that the Webb article caused a "howl of protest from western senators, governors, chambers of commerce officials, newspaper publishers, and citizens in general." Among those who howled, according to him, was Idaho's Senator Frank Church.[3]

Hollon not only calls our land desert, but true desert. Facing his Introduction he gives us a map; the inner part of it, roughly the Great Basin, he seems to regard as really appalling desert, though it includes Salt Lake City and the mountains behind it. October 12, 1966, my wife and I drove down Parley's Canyon, just southeast of the city, and for twenty miles saw the most lavish display of autumn colors that we had ever seen. In some areas the patterns of color were continuous from the canyon floor up the broad high mountainside clear to the top. One dictionary before me says a desert is "A barren tract almost destitute of moisture and vegetation." *The New Century* says it is "An uninhabited and uncultivated region . . . with scanty vegetation (as, the desert of Sahara)." I've seen a great deal of the *desert* of Sahara. It is true that our West has some spots of genuine desert—small areas of shifting sands, the alkali wastes along the Humboldt, parts of the Salton Sea region; but semi-arid regions are not desert. The thousands of lakes, the hundreds of fertile river valleys, the innumerable creek valleys, the mountainsides of luscious berries in season, the huge expanses of flowers and flowering shrubs, the ten million acres of national parks, the other millions of acres in state parks and national forest playgrounds, the millions of acres of magnificent conifer forest—what ignorance and presumption to dismiss all that as desert! What a false picture such books give of this western land, which in plain and actual fact is the greatest physical wonderland in the world.

Hollon's map gives what he calls the approximate limit of the desert influence, outside and beyond the Great Basin. It includes three-fourths of Texas, more than half of Oklahoma and Kansas, nearly all of

VARDIS FISHER

Nebraska, most of the Dakotas, all of Arizona, New Mexico, Colorado, Wyoming, all of Montana and Idaho but a small slice of area at the north, most of Washington, Oregon, and California. I don't think the world's greatest physical wonderland could exist in a desert, or in a few oases in these seventeen states; so let us now put aside the ignorance, the supercilious condescension and the arrogant books by those who know this vast western country only superficially, and have a brief look at a few of the more remarkable things that make it the world's outstanding wonderland.

In books about our national parks I found more than once the statement that a widely-traveled man who had seen all the world's major physical wonders thought that two of the greatest are in this western country. The third is the Victoria Falls on the Zambezi River between northern and southern Rhodesia, though Webster's Geographical Dictionary says it is surpassed in grandeur by the Niagara. Whether that is fact of prejudice I do not know. Let us proceed to the other two, the Grand Canyon and Crater Lake.

I suppose that millions of Americans have seen this gorge which the Colorado River in a billion and a half years, or longer, has washed out across what is now northwestern Arizona, for a distance of about 220 miles, a width of four to eighteen miles, and a depth in much of

it of a mile—a canyon that John Burroughs called "the world's most wonderful spectacle." John Muir said, "No matter how far you have wandered hitherto, of how many famous gorges and valleys you have seen, this one . . . will seem as novel to you, as unearthly in the color and grandeur and quantity of its architecture, as if you had found it after death, on some other star; so incomparably lovely and grand and supreme is it above all the other canyons in our fire-molded, earthquake-shaken, rain-washed, wave-washed, river and glacier sculptured world. . . . Every architectural invention of man has been anticipated and far more, in this grandest of God's terrestrial cities."[4]

It is now visited by more than a million persons a year, and though they may agree with Burroughs and Muir, insofar as they have seen the world's natural spectacles, few of them have done more than to look into the awesome depths and try on film to catch the magnificence of color and form. If they do not read the literature about it they do not know that they could spend months, even years, exploring the wonders in the depth of this canyon that are not visible to those who look into it. Parts of it were formerly inhabited by Indians; within this park's thousand square miles more than 600 pueblos have been found, and no doubt some of them have not yet been found. It is an amazing fact that what some have called the world's most beautiful and stupendous natural feature was for eleven years only a national monument, and that it took resolute efforts for more than thirty years to get it established as a national park. Efforts equally resolute are now being made to keep it from being debased to a series of dams and reservoirs, though it must in all fairness be admitted that dams only two or three hundred feet high, and the basins of impounded water, would appear to be small and insignificant to persons on the rims looking down.

By one enchanted visitor Crater Lake has been called "a huge flawless lapis lazuli set in a rugged wall of variegated cliffs whose predominating color is pale lavender."[5] Another, no less enchanted, who had seen Tahoe, Como, Constance, and other famous lakes, though that of them all Crater has "the deepest, strangest, loveliest blue."[6] What gives this water its deep color has long been a matter of interest to laymen and scientists alike. It is not its mineral content, and it is not reflection of the sky, for if the sky is clear or cloudy the water is of the same color. It has been conjectured that the light in water so clear and deep reflects the blue rays and absorbs those of other colors.

In recent geologic time volcanic peaks were formed near the western edge of an enormous lava plateau that covered parts of what are now Oregon, Washington, Idaho, Montana, Nevada, and California. Mount Mazama of the Cascade range was one of the highest of these peaks. It had been built by a series of lava flows and accumulations of volcanic debris. About seven thousand years ago there was an eruption so violent and stupendous that nothing that men have seen on this earth, since then, can be compared to it. Geologists estimate that ten cubic miles of boiling stuff were coughed out of the vast throat, and that seven cubic miles of materials fell back into the boiling cauldron, helping to build the rather flat floor of the present crater, six miles across and twenty miles in circumference. To put it another way, Mount Mazama blew its top off and emptied its stomach, and for quite a while it literally boiled over, "pouring out great quantities of frothing material in a series of glowing avalanches. These avalanches must have traveled at terrific speed down the valleys." Then huge "cracks developed in the flanks of the volcano, other cracks opened beneath it, draining out an estimated ten cubic miles of molten rock." What was then left of the central part of the mountain collapsed into the void, and the deepest lake in this country was formed, with neither inlet nor outlet. The rim all the way around rises above the water from 500 to 2,000 feet. The marvel of it is too much for the mind to grasp, but it helps a little to realize that long ago there was a range of fire mountains from Lassen to Baker; and that all of them, including Rainier, Hood, and Shasta were active volcanoes. The mightiest of them, rising, it is thought, to 15,000 feet. And then higher than any other peak in North America, is the one that now holds Crater Lake. A cinder cone in the lake—many persons have descended a hundred feet to its bottom—rises 763 feet above the water level.

Where did its water come from? It is, of course, in an area of abundant rainfall, and of snow depths from ten to fifteen feet all around it. Over thousands of years water slowly accumulated in the enormous pothole, until it was two thousand feet deep. Eventually the water coming in and the water evaporating balanced one another, until now the level does not vary more than two or three feet from season to season. Is it fresh water? During the long time it was becoming a lake in the sealed throat of a mountain it apparently had no fish; but trout have from time to time been planted in it, and it is now estimated to have hundreds of thousands. On mountain slopes below, visitors on the road that completely circles the lake can see more than five hundred species of flowering plant and fern. There are whole meadows of gilia and phantom orchid, hillsides of lupine, paintbrush, and mimulus, and seventy species of birds, including the bald and golden eagle.

Almost countless millions of people in this hemisphere and from nearly all parts of the world have visited Yellowstone, our largest and oldest park and the world's most famous, but most of the visitors see only a few of its wonders. Many of them don't see even all the popular features from the 153-mile motor road in the form of the figure eight. And it is possible that here, as in the Grand Canyon, no visitor has ever seen all that is worth seeing. Because many persons in the states close to it have gone to it again and again I shall mention only a few of the principal wonders in this area, which has no serious rival in the whole world.

Ancient Troy is said to have been the ruins of nine ancient cities, built one upon the other. In Amethyst Mountain are twelve petrified forests, buried one on top of another. Except the bottommost one, by volcanic eruptions; and on top of the most recent one are pine and spruce cheerfully growing, to furnish timber for a possible thirteenth. In the steep north face of this mountain, where thousands of logs jut out, the lava strata show the twelve ages. Among fossilized trees are redwood, walnut, pine oak, sycamore, fig, magnolia, and dogwood. Mineralized action has transformed many of the logs to opal. What a wonder it would be if in turn each buried forest could be laid aside, so that we could see the fantastic riches of all of them! This one feature is in an area as large as Delaware and Rhode Island combined would be worthy of national park status.

One writer on our parks says there are ten thousand geysers, hot springs, and vents of steam, acid, or gas. The number of geysers is usually given as three thousand, of which fifty-eight are listed as prominent. Among the most impressive besides Faithful are Giant, Giantess, Grand, Splendid, and Excelsior—these five all have more powerful eruptions than Faithful, to which most visitors gravitate. Faithful is said to be the most perfect of all known geysers, with exquisite sculpturing in three small pools on its north side. Into its deep hot caverns flow a quarter of a million gallons of water an hour, but this is only a trifle in the park's total hot flow. Of springs ranging from quiescent to boiling there are thousands. Though the Mud Volcano, or geyser, has been thought by some to be the most wonderful feature in the park, Chittenden fount it "uncanny, repulsive, and suggestive of everything horrible and uncouth." [7]

Park attendants say that a lot of people find some features repulsive, such as mud pots and paint pots, but this is what Muir thought of the whole geyser system: "The wildest geysers in the world, in bright triumphant bands, are dancing and singing in it amid thousands of boiling springs, beautiful and awful, their basins arrayed in gorgeous colors like gigantic flowers; and hot paint-pots, mud springs, mud volcanoes, mush and broth cauldrons, whose contents are of every colors and consistency, plash and heave and roar in bewildering abundance. In the adjacent mountains, beneath the living trees the edges of petrified forests are exposed to view, like specimens on the shelves of a museum, standing on ledges tier above tier where they grew, solemnly silent in rigid crystalline beauty after swaying in the winds thousands of centuries ago.... Here too are hills of sparkling crystals, hills of sulphur, hills of glass, hills of cinder and ashes, mountains of every style of architecture, icy or forested, covered with honey-bloom sweet as Hymettus, mountains boiled soft like potatoes and colored like a sunset sky." [8]

A poll of visitors in any year would disclose a wide range of preferences. Some prefer the lakes, of which the park has thirty-seven; no other lakes in North America lies as high as Yellowstone, or, in Muir's words, "gives birth to so noble a river." [9] The park has such a network of streams that more than a hundred and fifty have names; some of the waters flow into the Yellowstone, which empties into the Missouri, and some into the Snake, which empties into the Columbia. Thirty-seven lakes, two major rivers, and hundreds of other streams, some of which are larger than most of the rivers in the East, are a lot of water to find in a desert. The Yellowstone, with its two waterfalls, one three hundred feet high, and its magnificent canyon, is alone worthy of national monument status. Near Prismatic Spring, with its deep blue center, is the Excelsior, the largest known geyser in the world.

Some visitors prefer the animals. This park is one of the world's great wildlife preserves, its animal density being greater than any other except a few veldt areas in Africa. In some seasons Yellowstone Lake and some of the other lakes are literally covered with pelican, goose, swan, duck, crane, heron, curlew, snipe, plover, and other wildfowl. Or some visitors may prefer the flora, though this park is so high—its lowest spot is higher than the so-called mountains in the East—that it doesn't have the magnificence of tree and flower of some of the parks. Only a few of the West's wild flowers such as the columbine, lupine, gentian, gilia, and paintbrush, are at their loveliest here. But the whole park, with eighty-five per cent of it tree-covered and with its multitude of streams, is a pretty impressive two million two hundred and thirteen thousand acres of desert.

Under the Guadalupe Mountains is what one book on our parks calls the greatest of all known caves. [10] Another says the Carlsbad "are the largest and most magnificent caves in all the world." [11] If that is so, Grand, Crater, Yellowstone, and Carlsbad give us four world firsts in an area which our eastern friend sneer at as desert and frog ponds, meaning by frog ponds our reservoirs. The visitor is allowed to spend five hours covering from five to seven miles in a series of chambers and corridors, which are part of a vast complex which has been explored for thirty miles on three levels. How many miles remain unexplored no man knows. The first level is 754 the second 900, the third 1,320 feet below the surface.

About two hundred million years ago there was an enormous limestone formation in an arm of the ocean far inland. When, about sixty million years ago, the Rocky Mountains were heaven upward out of the earth's hot depths, the limestone area was raised above ocean level, and during the millions of years since then rain water has seeped down and leached the rock, leaving immense voids and sculpting amazing formations which we see today. Where limestone solutions were too large to be evaporated, huge overhanging deposits were left, which we call stalactites; and drippings from above to the floor formed stalagmites. When stalactite and stalagmite meet they form a column.

VARDIS FISHER

The tour descends by trail, sometimes fairly steep, from level to level, with concealed artificial lights, of from fifty to 2,000 watts, skillfully hidden and manipulated. There are twenty-five circuits, each illuminating about a thousand feet of the caverns. In passing the alert nose detects Bat Cave, which extends back half a mile from the trail. As the descent continues the formation become more impressive in size and color; many of them resemble totem poles, pagodas, obelisks, and other weird and ancient formations. At a depth of six hundred feet weary or frightened travelers, especially those from the gentle safe hills of the Northeast, can take a shortcut to the lunch room and from there hasten to the elevators, the highest lift of which almost equals that of the Empire State. The speleologists and others eager to see more proceed past the Iceberg, weighing two hundred thousand tons; down to the Green Room, with its magnificent sculpturing; to Green Lake, an emerald pool; past the frozen waterfalls; through the King's Palace, which some have thought most beautiful thing they have seen; to the Queen's Chambers and past cleaner cold pools to the big room a half mile long. Four hundred feet at its widest, and 348 feet high. It takes a fat person in fair health almost an hour to walk around its circumference. Under a brilliant ceiling the adventurers proceed to the lunch room, the world's largest underground restaurant, which can serve between two and three thousand persons an hour. After lunch the visitors, with their egos reduced to normal, return to the Big Room, close by elevators which can lift twelve hundred persons an hour. A few prefer to leave the depths under their own power.

These caverns were discovered by a white man when he saw a swarm of bats. It is estimated that there are between three and five million bats of five species that roost in the bat corridor. At dusk there is a vast outpouring of them; for their supper they devour about twelve tons of moths, gnats, mosquitoes, or whatever it is that bats eat in that area. In 1933 the Bat Guano Company set up in business, and in a few years took out of the cave over a hundred thousand tons of bat dung, for the citrus groves of California.

There are persons who live by preference in our Southwest not primarily for the dry climate and mild winters but for the beautiful flora—for the magenta of cactus bloom and the snow-white lily of the yucca—both yucca and Joshua tree belong to the lily family. All the flora is strange to those from lush rain areas whose houses are full of damp and mold. The ocotillo survives heat and lack of moisture by becoming dormant in certain periods; it may even shed its leaves to preserve the water in its stem and roots. The saguaro, cholla, and barrel cactus store water in their fluted stems; and the yuccas and agaves in their leaves. Some plants here have leaves of a color that more easily reflect the sun's rays, and others with delightful cunning grow their leaves vertically to offer less surface to the sun. The leaves of still other plants are insulated with a wax-like substance or with tiny hairs. Gathering moisture by its roots and storing it in its pulp, a large saguaro cactus, weighing ten or twelve tons, may store as much as a ton of water during a good rainstorm. But this plant, so formidable when mature, leads a precarious life in infancy and childhood. If a seed is lucky enough to escape the hunger of small animals it may not get its head above ground for ten years; and twenty more years will pass before it is big enough to protect itself. It is believed that the Saguaro Monument cacti will eventually all die because of bacteria rot caused by the larva of the drone-fly. One writer sees a parallel between this tree, so formidably defended that no animal on earth dares to touch it, yet at the mercy of a fly, and the human male able to blow up the planet but likely to perish in his silent springs.

  It is a long jump from the marvelous garden of plants near the pay station at Carlsbad to El Capitan, upon whose sheer granite face of thirty-three hundred feet some daring climbers recently lay in nylon hammocks suspended from pitons, while hundreds of tourists on the canyon floor stared up at the tiny specks, two thousand feet above. Yosemite has also been called by world-travelers "one of the principal scenic wonders of the world."[12] It is remarkable not so much for one or two features as for the variety of its wealth in all its twelve hundred square miles. It has scores of lovely alpine lakes in basins of solid stone, sculptured by glaciers, time, and weather; many streams, with two unusual rivers, whose waterfalls have vertical drops of 2,300, 600, and 300 feet, the Yosemite fall having the height of nine Niagaras. The Merced flows "among stupendous and astounding glacial landscapes," and through the "matchless Yosemite gorge," which, as all who have seen it know, is less a gorge than a narrow valley seven miles long.[13] On a weekend in 1966 every parking place in campgrounds and elsewhere in this valley was taken, and from the entrance cars stretched down the road for five miles, bumper to bumper. Because the litter in this alley's campgrounds after a weekend has to be seen to be believed, it is easy to imagine what will happen to the lakes, streams, and flora in the less accessible areas when hordes of tourist reach them.

Because Yosemite, like Sequoia and King's, is a part of the four million acres of beautiful mountains and trees of the western Sierras, all of which Prof. Hollon puts within his "desert influence," it is best to let John Muir speak for it, because no man ever lived who loved it more or wrote about it with greater eloquence, while confessing that it was a "hopeless task" to put even Yosemite into words—the noblest forests, loftiest granite domes, deepest ice-sculptures canyons, brightest crystalline pavements—"Nowhere else will you see the majestic operations of nature more clearly revealed beside the frailest, most gentle and peaceful things."[14]

The Sequoia Gigantea was for him "the greatest of living things," a tree that once flourished in what is now the arctic and in parts of Europe, but is now found only on the western slopes of the Sierras— a tree without a tap root but with a root spread of two hundred feet or more—that may ripen millions of seeds, so amazingly small that except the gauzy wig that enables them to leave the parent they are no larger than your fingernail—a tree that does not reach maturity for fifteen centuries, and cannot be said to be old before thirty centuries—some four thousand years old show no sign of decay. It is said that they never die of age but only when "burned, blown down, undermined, or shattered by some tremendous lightning stroke." Muir saw a silver fir "two hundred feet high split into long peeled rails and slivers down to its roots, leaving not even a stump, the rails radiating like the spokes of a wheel from a hole in the ground where the tree stood." But it takes a lightning bolt of celestial size to shatter a mature sequoia. "It is a curious fact that all the very old sequoias have lost their heads by lightning." The wood of this noble tree is so impervious to time and change that when fallen it lies in the forest mold for centuries without rotting at all. One of the largest trees Muir examined had increased only ten feet in diameter in the last seventeen hundred years of its life.[15]

According to this naturalist no other coniferous forest on earth had so many species of tree—from sequoia, king of conifers, to the sugar pine, king of all pines, living or extinct, and the yellow pine, next to it in majestic size, as well as six other species of pine, and the Douglas fir and two other firs, the Paton hemlock, which some think the most graceful of evergreens—all those and many kinds of oak, maple, poplar, dogwood, and a vast flowering undergrowth of rhododendron, cherry, rose, chestnut, manzanita, ceanothus, lilies ten feet high, whole meadows of gentian, several kinds of orchid—there is not space here to name even half the wild flowers. Let us say simply that taken all in all this area of four million acres does indeed show the influence of areas practically without moisture and plant life.

With rain-soaked cultures in mind I now go beyond Hollon's desert to the Olympic Park, which, according to Tilden, is not only unique but one of the world's wonders.[16] Its eight hundred thousand acres in the center of the Olympic peninsula is kept so primitive that except in dangerous places the trails must be no more than eighteen inches wide, the bridges must be of logs, the shelter cabins must have split-spruce bunks. There are no ranges but only deep canyons, high meadows, and peaks covered with glaciers or snow. On the western slopes are the great rain forests, where Douglas and silver fir, red cedar and western hemlock all reach size rarely equaled in other forests. There is tropical luxuriance because of the rich soil, heavy rainfall, and a climate softened by ocean winds and warmth. From high crests whose sides drop almost sheer for two or three thousand feet fall gossamer veils of water, like those in Yosemite. All the glaciers, about fifteen in number, and ranging in color from white to clear blue, are slowly moving downward to polish the mountainside, as at Rainier.

Because there is fantastic variation in the rainfall—within fifty miles east-west are one of the areas in the United States, and the driest on the Pacific coast north of southern California—there is a bewildering variety of plant life. Up to about fifteen hundred feet the flowering plants are at their spectacular best, and the trails are cool and deeply shaded by the jungle of fir and hemlock, pine and cedar. Flowering shrubs here include several berries, grape, vine maple, salal, trillium, and Solomon's seal. In the next zone above are tiarella, dogwood, twinflower, tway blade, and alpine beauty. Still higher, above thirty-five hundred feet, are the most gorgeous meadows; the flowering shrubs here include white and pink heather, spiraea, and mountain ash. The flowers are avalanche lily, western anemone, valerian, arctic lupine, larkspur, gentian, and many others. In the fourth zone, the arctic-alpine, are still other species of shrub and flower. It is said that there are twenty flowers in this park that grow nowhere else in the United States.

This is tremendous country, our western land, all the way from the Mexican border to northern Alaska, but I have pointed to only a few of its wonders. It would take a book to do justice to all of them. The most picturesque and fantastic of all our parks with the possible exception of Carlsbad, is Bryce, a small area of only two by three miles, lying a thousand feet below the surrounding walls. There are no words know to me that can describe this basin, where erosion is so rapid that formations literally disappear in a generation and new forms appear. The Cedar Breaks National Monument not far from it is even more brilliantly colored. Indeed, southwest Utah and northeast Arizona, where we have almost a dozen national parks and monuments, is a wonderland without a rival of its kind in the world. What a joy it would be to spend years exploring and photographing it! Zion Park, not far from Bryce, was for the geologist Captain Dutton, a man not easily impressed, in its Temples

and Towers of the Virgin "the most exquisite of its kind which the world discloses," and the colors—chocolate, maroon, purple, magenta, and broad bands of toned white—truly amazing.[17] For F.S. Dellenbaugh, "The delicacy of merging tints of red and white and yellowy cream, with tones of soft vermillion spread here and there athwart the white like alpenglow transfixed, is discouraging enough to the brush of the painter."[18]

May 30, 1914, Lassen Peak at the northern end of the Sierra Nevada, with no warning at all, belched skyward a part of the boiling contents of its belly, and in the weeks that followed steam and ashes rose twenty thousand feet above it and were visible all the way down the Sacramento valley. A year later, after periodic vomitings, the volcano spilled a lava flow down the mountain. It then took an inventory of its power and buried a forest. Lassen is only one of the outstanding volcanoes on the edge of a lava field that extends across Oregon and into Washington and east across southern Idaho to Yellowstone park, but like the two hot springs park in Oklahoma it is not worthy of national park status. Oh, it would be in the northeast, were they have so little that is unusual in natural features, but not in the West, where we have so much. Big Bend, the Rocky Mountain, and Glacier are beautiful wilderness areas but should not be national parks.

Glacier, with its 900 miles of trails, its primitive mountain masses, its many lakes, waterfalls, pure cold streams and sixty glaciers is a marvelous area for persons who need to get away from the stinks and poisons and lunacies of the big cities; and so is the smaller Rocky Mountain Park, with its 218 miles of trails, its glaciers, flowered meadows, and abundance of wild life. But there's nothing unique about either park. Nor about Big Bend, one of the three major canyons scooped out by the Rio Grande. After learning that some of the western states had parks, and that Washington had two, Utah two and California four, a group of Texans was outraged. How ridiculous it was that Texas, which had the biggest of everything, didn't have a single national park! Politics being what it is they got one—seven hundred thousand acres, sixth largest, 300 miles downstream from El Paso; but the area across from it in Mexico surpasses it in natural features. Some persons in Idaho with a case of Texas fever have been clamoring for a national park in the

Sawtooth area. It would make a nice wilderness area but it simply does not have national park status.

Idaho's Craters of the Moon is its greatest physical wonder. It is dead now, or seems to be—that vast spread of lava flow, once incredibly hot when it came gushing and roaring out of the Great Rift—an area of fissures in the earth's crust that allowed the tumultuous and imprisoned molten masses to boil up from their depths. A thousand years ago, or even a few hundred, what a scene this huge expanse of southern Idaho must have been!—as an ocean of flowing stone hurled white-hot blobs of magma high into the heavens. What an area of cinder, spatter cones, and bombs that rained and rolled and cooled to form the round-stone bomb fields of today! The tremendous flow engulfed forests, encasing trees with white-hot envelopes, and leaving perfect casts of consumed tree trunks, and even roots. For centuries this huge area has been cooling in its death throes, with a few dwarfed trees and other plants getting a toe-hold of sorts and standing twisted and distorted in the winds, but never wholly defeated. The whole area is a terribly beautiful field of lava ropes and pillows in all possible shapes and contours. Down under are ice and wind caves, and parts of unfilled old river beds of the North Fork of Snake River, down which flows for nearly two hundred miles a part of the waters of that river, to issue as the Thousand Springs for sixty miles up and down the Snake River gorge, a half-dozen of which are just outside my window as I write these words.

We have such a wealth of splendors out here that I feel a little shame at holding a few of them up for the East to look at. In the entire expanse of it, from Caribou in the northern tip of Maine, to Flamingo in the southern tip of Florida the East has, besides its two outstanding features, Mammoth Cave and the Everglades, only the Acadia, Shenandoah, and Great Smoky parks, which, compared to our greatest, are really nothing at all. California in itself is more than enough to abash any easterner and send him back to his oak grove and magnolias and low monotonous hills. There is no area on earth of comparable size that can match the Orange State in the variety and magnificence of its flora, its natural features, and the range of its climate. It is a fact that while hundreds of thousands of persons are bugging their eyes at the superlative loveliness of the tournament of flowers, in the same state at the same moment motorist on a transcontinental highway are driving between snowbanks thirty feet deep on either side. That fact alone ought to be enough to rebuke the supercilious condescension and silence the critics.

A wise man said long ago that those who have great power should use it gently. We who have so much more than our share of the world's wonders can afford to be indulgent towards the motives of those who call our great reservoirs frog ponds and beautiful land a desert. ■

NOTES

[1] "The Wonders of the Yellowstone," *Scribner's Monthly* vol. 2 no.1 (May 1871), 1-17; "The Wonders of the Yellowstone: Second Article," *Scribner's Monthly* vol. 2 no. 2 (June 1871), 113-128.

[2] W. Eugene Hollon, *The Great American Desert: Then and Now* (New York: Oxford University Press, 1966).

[3] Church wrote a letter to the editor, which appeared in the July 1957 issue of *Harper's* on page 4.

[4] John Muir, "The Wild Parks and Forest Reservations of the West," *The Atlantic Monthly* vol. 81 (January 1898), 28.

[5] Thomas D. Murphy, *Oregon, the Picturesque* (Boston: The Page Company, 1917), 86.

[6] Ibid., 87.

[7] Hiram Martin Chittenden, *The Yellowstone National Park: Historical and Descriptive,* 7th ed. (Cincinnati: Stewart & Kidd Company, 1912), 216.

[8] John Muir, "The Yellowstone National Park," *The Atlantic Monthly* vol. 81 (April 1898), 509.

[9] Ibid., 513.

[10] Freeman Tilden, *The National Parks* (New York: Knopf, 1951).

[11] Nelson Beecher Keyes, *America's National Parks: A Photographic Encyclopedia of Our Magnificent Natural Wonderlands* (Garden City, NY: Doubleday & Company, 1957), 81.

[12] Eastman Irvine, ed., *The World Almanac & Book of Facts* (New York: New York World-Telegram, 1947), 104.

[13] Enos A. Mills, *Your National Parks* (Boston: Houghton Mifflin Company, 1917), 67.

[14] John Muir, "The Yosemite National Park," *The Atlantic Monthly* vol. 84 (August 1899), 146.

[15] John Muir, "Hunting Big Redwoods," *The Atlantic Monthly* vol. 88 (September 1901), 304-320.

[16] Tilden, *The National Parks.*

[17] Clarence E. Dutton, *Tertiary History of the Grand Cañon District,* Monographs of the United States Geological Survey (Washington, D.C.: Government Printing Office, 1882), 57.

[18] As quoted in George Wharton James, *Utah: The Land of Blossoming Valleys* (Boston: The Page Company, 1922), 178.

LIMBERLOST LETTERPRESS

www.limberlostpress.com

RE-READINGS

THE ATLANTIC $5,000 PRIZE BOOK FOR 1935

OLD JULES

BY MARI SANDOZ

MARC C. JOHNSON

Back to the Sandhill Country

My Grandfather—unfortunately I never knew him—homesteaded around 1905 in what my father always called the Sandhill country of northwestern Nebraska, a starkly rugged, beautiful, and unforgiving swath of high plains grassland bisected by the meandering Niobrara River.

The hills here really are sand, but the grass is so thick that the dunes are stable, but not much good for farming. Cowboys could make a go of it, however, with lots of work and more luck. Grandfather moved west from Missouri as a young man, looking for opportunity and 160 acres. He found something worth staying for in Sheridan County. I was born in a tiny hospital in the county seat a half-century after the family's pioneering homesteader arrived.

I did not live long in or around the Sandhills, as a quest for opportunity drove my father further north and west, but the memory of the rolling hills, the wind, and the slow-moving sandy-bottomed river is a bit like being tethered to a long leash. You can wander a long way, but still be connected.

The late, great Jim Harrison wrote about the Sandhills in his classic novel *Dalva* and he captured in a sentence what haunts me about the place and gnaws at my memory all these years later. "I remember something Grandfather had said when he found me after my walk in the hills one the far side of the Niobrara," Harrison wrote, "how each of us must live with a full measure of loneliness that is inescapable, and we must not destroy ourselves with our passion to escape the loneliness."

As well as Harrison is able to conjure a sense of place in his description of this remote patch of western Nebraska, the Sandhills truly belong to Mari Sandoz, and it is her masterpiece—*Old Jules*—that I read and re-read, not so much for the vivid, occasionally demonic depiction of Sandoz's brilliant and idiosyncratic father—also a pioneering homesteader—but for how she connects a reader to the courage and determination that it took to live in this place—the Sandhill Country.

And it is impossible not to admire Mari's own years of determination to gain an education and write.

"For more than a decade and a half, Sandoz filled a scrapbook with rejection letters from magazines and book publishers," Nebraska historian David L. Bristow wrote. "She was poor, staying just above starvation—and not always by much. She looked painfully thin and unhealthy. She wore old clothes, mismatched and threadbare, and was often seen walking briskly across campus, an enormous pile of books under one arm. Her friends suspected that she lived on the tea, sugar, and crackers that were freely available in the university dining hall."

Published in 1935 when Sandoz was 39 years old, and after the old man died, *Old Jules* was rejected time and again by publishers until the manuscript found its way into the *The Atlantic* non-fiction book contest. Sandoz won the $5,000 prize, and with the book well reviewed she was off to the life of a writer, first in Denver and then New York City.

Mari Sandoz, 1920s.

Jules Ami Sandoz, Mari's father, came to the Sandhills some years before my Grandfather, but my dad said everybody knew old Jules either by reputation or unpleasant encounter. The old man, born in Switzerland, big and unpredictable as a Nebraska thunderstorm. He fell, or was pushed down a well, a tumble that resulted in a crippled foot. On another occasion he shot off part of his own hand to stop the advance of a snake's venom. He terrorized his first three wives, with wife number three, a mail order bride, leaving him after two weeks. Wife number four, Mari's mother, was picked up by Old Jules at a Nebraska train station when the husband she was supposed to meet failed to show up. That union, remarkably, lasted.

Old Jules disparaged Mari's literary aspirations and discouraged her desire to learn and teach. "You know I consider artists and writers the maggots of society," he told his daughter long after she had committed to such a life.

Considering the man's meanness—misogynist doesn't quite adequately explain him—it's easy to imagine that Mari would want to get away as fast and far as possible, but she too was tethered to the rolling hills hard by the Niobrara. When her father's health began to fail in 1928 she went home to help her mother and, eventually, to write about the man who had frightened her to silence as a youngster.

As Sandoz wrote in the foreword to *Old Jules*, she grew up hearing the stories of death, life, and barely surviving in the Sandhill Country during "silent hours of listening behind the stove or in the wood box, when it was assumed that of course I was asleep in bed." She knew, she said, "the droughts, the storms, and the wind and the isolation."

As unspeakably awful as Old Jules was to almost everyone around him, particularly the women, Mari understood the importance of his story. Jules Sandoz was a builder, a promoter, but not an exploiter. When he first got settled in the Sandhills he wrote to his young friends, farmers, professional men, immigrants all, urging them to leave their disappointments behind and come to what Mari called the Running Water. A place where, as she wrote, "the days brought pale, wind-streaked skies, yellow coyotes sinking into gullies, and endless small game: rabbits, grouse, quail."

Mari admired her father's native brilliance, his ability to study the land until he knew just where the best soil was for an orchard and his expertise with a rifle and shotgun, often a decent meal in the balance. Old Jules was skeptical of everything except his own ability to navigate the land he and his daughter loved.

Old Jules searched for and found his home ground in the bluffs above the Running Water.

"Every day the wind's song was louder," Mari wrote of this time, "the air drier, the sun glare brighter on the sandy stretches. Squinting his eyes over the map he fought to hold together in the wind, he moved his finger westward along the Niobrara. The country was getting high, approximately 3500 to 4000 feet, and still the sunflowers grew and the grapevines were knotted with flower buds along the river."

Old Jules, his daughter remembered, taught her to shoot and hunt, but at one point he "developed a tendency to undershoot and let a yearling antelope get away before he could reload. A little lift to the sight remedied that. A good rifle this Vetterli [a Swiss Army rifle], for now, but a Winchester repeater—that was the gun. With it a wolf or a man could be killed a long way off; never know what hit him. Who needed the protection of law and government with such a gun?"

Mari wrote that the most impressive stories of Old Jules' country—a title of another of her books—were those told to her by the old man himself, "perhaps on the top of Indian Hill, overlooking the spot where a man was hung under his leadership, and the scene of six years of lawing that drove the second wife to the insane asylum. Perhaps he limped through the orchard as he talked, with me close behind, my hands full of ducks or grouse or quill. Perhaps I followed among flowering cherry trees, carrying plats to the orchard. Perhaps I drove the team on long trips while he smoked and talked of his own dreams and his joys and his disappointments."

And, of course, Mari was always "too frightened of him to voice either approval or surprise."

At some level my revisiting of Sandoz's book about her crusty, crazy old father scratches my own itch to know more about my own ties to this country. I read the story, think about the landscape and wonder why I wasn't smart enough to ask my own father more questions about his origin story. What did he make of the Niobrara country? Why did he always speak of it with a certain awe and respect?

He told a story of my own Grandfather, the tenderfoot rancher, who built a sod house, dug a well, planted a few trees, fenced a pasture, and waited for, what? Not to be lonely, perhaps, or to find someone to share the burdens and blessing of such a hard place. He once, according to dad's memory, went months without laying eyes on another human until one night two tired cowboys rode on to his ranch and within his sight. He went running after them to demand that they stay for dinner so he could finally have someone to talk to.

My Grandmother was the cook at a neighboring ranch, a single mother of two young boys when she married the only rancher ever in our family. I've always thought she knew something about loneliness, too.

Mari Sandoz went on to write 20 books, including enduring classics about the American West. Her *Crazy Horse: The Strange Man of the Oglala's*, originally published in 1942, is a brilliant study of a man and a military leader, as well as another fitting reminder of her father. Old Jules respected and admired the Native Americans he knew and lived with more than most of the settlers he had encouraged to come to western Nebraska.

Sandoz was fighting the cancer that would end her life when she finished *The Little Bighorn*, a study of the famous battle that at the time was almost always referred to by the name of the narcissistic 7th Cavalry officer who died along the Greasy Grass in Montana.

Unusual before her book appeared, Sandoz put the victors of that encounter at the center of her story. The book, still one of the best accounts of the battle, was posthumously published.

Mari Sandoz was buried in the Sandhills not far from where I was born and even closer to where my Grandfather claimed his own piece of the Running Water country.

One copy I have of *Old Jules* says it's a first edition and it is signed with Sandoz's looping signature. When I take it up I also read a tattered and yellowed newspaper clipping that was slipped in the back of the book long before I acquired it. The story, I think it's from the *Nebraska State Journal*, the paper in Lincoln, the town where Sandoz worked for a time at the state historical society, is about John Peters, who had a run in with Old Jules.

Peters once jerked a rifle pointed at him from the hands of Jules Ami Sandoz and, as the newspaper reporter noted, "lived to tell the tale." Mari recounts the incident in her book and Peters told the *Nebraska State Journal* that she got the story right. "People out in the Sandhills get a great kick out of the book about the man they knew so well," John Peters said. He added that he had nothing but words of praise for the book and its author. He was right.

*****

As Old Jules lay dying he was still thinking about the land and the future. He mumbled to his daughter "the whole damn Sandhills is deserted. The cattlemen are broke, the settlers about gone. I've got to start all over—ship in a lot of good farmers in the spring, build up—build—build— "

I'm left with Mari Sandoz's words, words that remind me again and again why this place and the woman who wrote so well about the Sandhill Country continue to command my fascination.

"Outside the late fall wind swept over the hard-land country of the upper Running Water, tearing at the low sandy knolls that were the knees of the hills, shifting, but not changing, the unalterable sameness of the somnolent land spreading away toward the East." ∎

MICHAEL CORRIGAN

Re-reading The Sound and the Fury

> *It is a tale*
> *Told by an idiot, full of sound and fury,*
> *Signifying nothing.*
> (Macbeth, Act 5, Scene 5)

Every Easter I re-read *The Sound and the Fury* by William Faulkner. I am not sure when this yearly ritual started. I remember in 1983 on Easter Sunday walking down a Boise street when someone asked me if the small hardbound book I held was a bible. I said no, it was the *The Indispensable Faulkner*, a collection of stories and chapter excerpts carefully edited by Malcolm Cowley. At the time the volume came out in 1946, much of William Faulkner's work was out of print. In 1949, he received the Nobel Prize for literature.

There are other great novels that I admire: *The Stranger* by Albert Camus, *Gravity's Rainbow* by Thomas Pynchon, and Faulkner's other great novel, *Light in August*. It is *The Sound and the Fury,* however, that I re-read time and time again. I have four copies of the book, including an eBook and a 1959 paperback released to publicize a very bad film of Faulkner's work starring Yul Brenner.

Easter is a good time to read the novel since it is in four sections, three of which take place on the Easter weekend of 1928. That doesn't answer the question why even an ardent fan would re-read the same challenging novel, however acclaimed and brilliant, once a year. I could dramatically declare that I started *The Sound and the Fury* while traveling through France, and while reading beside a Toulouse swimming pool, a pretty French girl saw the title and said in French, "*Il est mort.*" I knew "mort" meant dead. William Faulkner had died that very July day, a year after the other great American writer, Ernest Hemingway. I still remember that young woman's face.

I finished the book, perhaps the most impressionistic fiction I had ever read, and though moved by the Southern gothic tale of the decadent Compsons, I wasn't quite sure what I had just read. I decided to re-read

the novel with its varied styles from lyrical stream of consciousness to straightforward prose. Like any great work of art, there was a mystery that a second reading would never completely reveal. I was also fascinated by a story about William Faulkner finishing his masterpiece and drinking himself into a stupor. The next morning, friends found Faulkner on the floor, the manuscript sitting by his typewriter.
While attending college and drinking heavily, it thrilled me to think I might also create a great novel despite creative writing sessions fueled by wine and whiskey.

My university professors extolled Faulkner's courage or arrogance to start his novel "from the viewpoint of an idiot," then an acceptable term. Faulkner does begin the novel with the remarkable line, "Through the fence, between the curling flower spaces, I could see them hitting" (Faulkner, pg. 23).

This is Benjy observing a golf course; he is the first of three unreliable first-person narrators. Benjy is mentally disabled and his fragmented memories jump ten to fifteen years from moment to moment. The reader can eventually determine the timeline by who is watching Benjy: Versh when Benjy is a child, TP when Benjy is in his 20s, and Luster when Benjy reaches 33 on his birthday. Quentin, driven with an incestuous desire for his sister, Caddy, is the second narrator, and ironically, his poetic surreal narration on the day he drowns himself is more disjointed than Benjy's. Jason, the third narrator, is cold and resentful, though he has a corrosive humor. He steals from Caddy's child—also named Quentin—and is outraged when the rebellious teenager robs her own money back and disappears. Jason will eventually commit Benjy to an asylum. The three Compson brothers all either love or—in Jason's case—hate and fear the wild beautiful Caddy. Faulkner does not give Caddy a section of her own but only says that Caddy (Candace) was "Doomed and knew it; accepted the doom without either seeking it or fleeing it" (Faulkner, appendix, pg. 744).

The last section of the novel is in the third person. The parents of the siblings, an eloquent alcoholic father, and an ignorant selfish mother, complete a disintegrating family that Dilsey, a black servant, struggles to preserve. She speaks in the Mississippi black dialect of the time. In a poignant moment after taking Benjy to an Easter service in a black church, since Benjy isn't good enough for a white church, Dilsey reveals her despair: "I seed de first en de last," she said, looking at the cold stove. "I seed de first and de last" (Faulkner, pg. 537).

If Faulkner's synopsis were pitched to an editor or film director, today, it would be rejected as a bizarre story of ugly people who deserve oblivion, although James Franco made a second film of the book that failed with the public and critics. Why does anyone read or reread such a difficult work about depraved characters? A simple answer is the evocative language.

William Faulkner's intense prose elevates the novel, much like Shakespeare's verse in *Othello* raises a play about jealousy and spousal murder above the level of police news. A mid-80s stage production by the Pacific Resident Theatre of *June 2* showing Quentin's last day was extremely effective, and Faulkner's expansive prose and dialogue worked well on the stage. Quentin's father has a classic line when he tells Quentin that "watching pennies has healed more scars than Jesus" (Faulkner, Chapter 2, par.1008). Quentin, obsessed with his sister, time and death, doesn't want his scars to heal.

The novel ends on a positive note. Luster is driving Benjy into town in a horse-drawn buggy and turns left at a Confederate statue when he should turn right. Pandemonium erupts as Benjy panics. True to form, Jason jumps into the buggy, punches Luster, and pulls the horse to the right. Things then settle down.

> "Queenie moved again, her feet began to clip-clop steadily again, and at once Ben hushed. Luster looked quickly back over his shoulder, then he drove on. The broken flowers drooped over Ben's fist and his eyes were empty and blue and serene again as cornice and façade flowed smoothly once more from left to right; post and tree, window and doorway, and signboard, each in its ordered place" (Faulkner, pg. 336).

It is this rich language of an unfolding tragedy that explains why I became haunted by the mad Compsons and just couldn't stop reading and re-reading their sad story. Easter, a time of new growth and redemption, is a fitting time to read *The Sound and the Fury*.

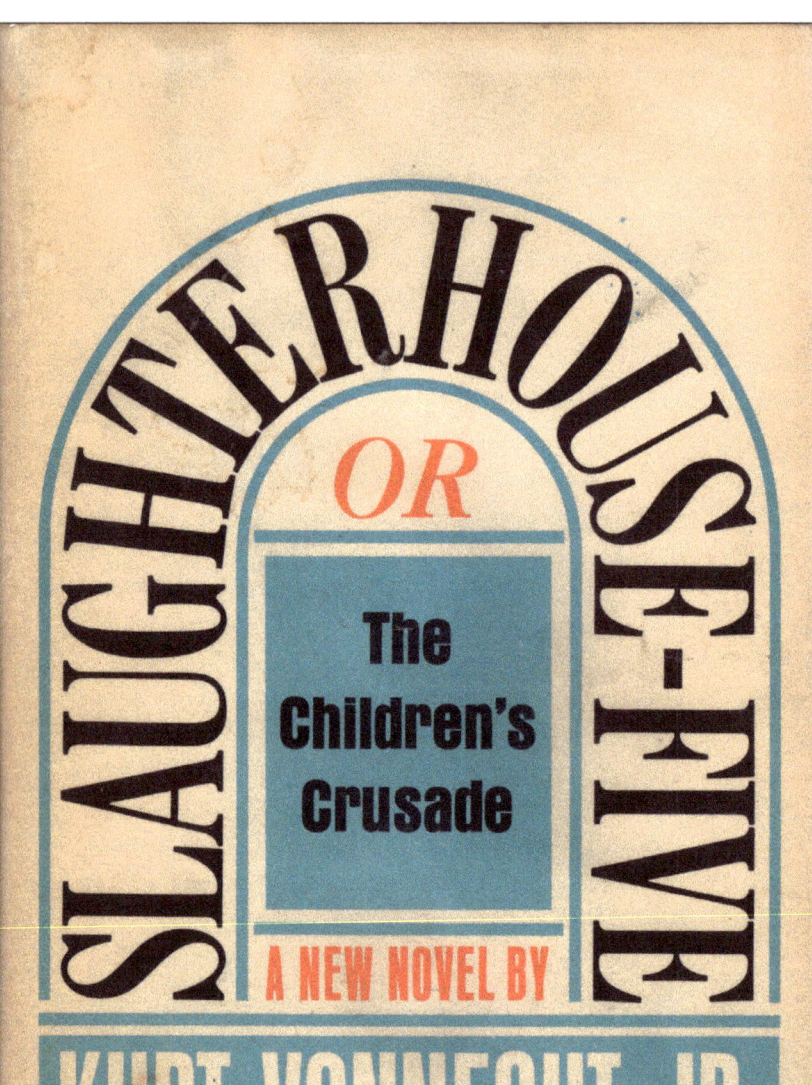

HANK NUWER

Re-reading Kurt Vonnegut's Slaughterhouse-Five

I first read *Slaughterhouse-Five* in 1969, when my chances of living another year had dimmed. I was a news reporter in eastern New York and classified immediately draftable by the draft board, which meant the U.S. Army or Marines had dibs on me for cannon fodder.

I had helped a soccer buddy load his possessions out of a Buffalo State College dormitory into a Plymouth Barracuda hatchback so he could report to Officer Candidate School. My father had fought five years under General Patton. He urged me to immigrate to Canada, but I demurred.

The news stories I covered in those years amaze me now in reflection. I reported on the 1967 March on the Pentagon, where police tear-gassed me along with Yippies burning a flag. At Woodstock, I interviewed a nurse in the drug overdose tent and reported that a sleeping boy had been run over by a farmer's tractor. I took my notebook to the New York ticker-tape parade for the moon-landing astronauts. I interviewed photographer Boris Yaro, who snapped the iconic photo of a dying Robert Kennedy at the Ambassador Hotel.

I took my physical at a Buffalo armory. I believed that I could not kill another human being, and this belief solidified after I met Cassius Clay, AKA Muhammed Ali, at a small gathering even as his own induction refusal went before the U.S. Supreme Court. Ali repeated his controversial statement that no Viet Cong had ever called him the N word.

At the armory I stood in briefs to get my shots from a rotating gun administered by a second lieutenant who was distracted while talking with a friend. The device glanced off my left bicep. Blood spurted.

I offered my other bicep. "You want to try again and get it right?"

He cursed, spittle dribbling down his chin. We stood toe to toe like boxers and he took the first swing and connected a solid hit.

We traded punches until military police pushed through a crowd of guys encircling us and led—no, carried—him away. "Wait 'til we have you, Tough Guy," he screamed.

A single MP took me to a psychiatrist's office. I sat, subdued and worried, while the shrink read my draft-board file. He raised his eyebrows and smirked.

"I see you applied for Conscientious Objector status?"

I nodded and shrugged. I recalled lines from *Alice's Restaurant* when Arlo Guthrie had been in my exact position. "*Shrink, I want to kill. I mean, I wanna, I wanna kill. Kill. I wanna, I wanna see, I wanna see blood and gore and guts and veins in my teeth. Eat dead, burnt bodies. I mean kill, Kill, KILL, KILL.*"

I stayed silent. I truly—then and now—feel I cannot kill a human, but boyhood in Buffalo required occasional fistfights. If the lieutenant hadn't taken the first swing in front of a couple dozen witnesses, I might have been sitting that moment on a jail cot.

The shrink took me to a grizzled sergeant with a salt-and-pepper buzzcut. My fight with an officer had become the main event of the interminable afternoon. Old Sarge's back-clap telegraphed that he approved.

Two hours later, Sarge gave me my graded test. "You're assigned to Army infantry," he said.

That week I read, or should I say devoured, Kurt Vonnegut's *Slaughterhouse-Five*. I had read *Welcome to the Monkey House* and *Cat's Cradle* the previous year.

Vonnegut's fans had anointed him antiwar status. Personally I love a line in *Slaughterhouse* uttered by film producer Harrison Starr. Paraphrased, Starr says that wars are about as easy to stop as glaciers.

Slaughterhouse opens in characteristic Vonnegut style, to wit in short, simple sentences. He writes that "The war parts, anyway, are pretty much true."

It turned out that some parts were fiction though not on purpose. Vonnegut relied on a later discredited but popular claim that Dresden suffered more casualties than Hiroshima: "135,000 Hansels and Gretels . . . baked like Gingerbread men."

The Dresden incendiary bombing by Allied planes did kill about 25,000 persons in horrific fashion. Some melted in puddles of fat. Some ended up charred like a roast forgotten in an oven. Others died in basements where all the air had been sucked out. One of the world's

Dresden after the February 13-15, 1945, incendiary bombing by Allied forces.

artistic and architecturally exquisite cities lay wasted. Vonnegut and his fellow U.S. prisoners of war lived because their captors housed them in a slaughterhouse that had an underground bunker. Otherwise, Vonnegut, himself of German ancestry, would have lived without publishing a word, save for news items in school papers.

I interviewed Kurt Vonnegut in a Dallas hotel lobby in 1985. If he had hostility toward the Allies that nearly took his life as collateral damage, he kept the feelings hidden.

That war had to be fought, he said, and explained. "I was in Japan a couple of years ago at an International P.E.N. Congress. I was invited to go as a guest, and I went. We were invited to express our regrets at Hiroshima *(chuckles)* and hope that it never happened again. Well, it was the militarism of Japan in the early Thirties that turned us into a garrison state. If we are a military monster now, we certainly were not headed in that direction. We were proud of our pacifism and wanted nothing more to do with foreign entanglements. We were corrupted by the Germans and the Japanese, who had gone insane."

Vonnegut, as he so often did, gave a long and thoughtful interview. I sold two pieces to magazines and published the transcript in the *South Carolina Review*. What I will always treasure is that he invited me to have lunch after our conversation. I mainly was a freelance magazine feature writer back then but had an ambition to write a piece of literary journalism about hazing deaths. Vonnegut couldn't have been warmer. He asked if I was selling my articles, and I told him yes, about 60 a year.

He said I was lucky to be able to make a living that way, but when he started writing magazine fiction in the late 1940s, he said a writer could make a good living by writing only a handful of stories. "That time is long over," he said.

* * * * *

By happenstance Vonnegut and I both spoke on the same night at the University of New Hampshire in 1993. It was a little surreal to see posters announcing our talks hanging on the same campus wall. His had his famous Vonnegut moustache and bushy hair. My poster was a photo of my first serious book, *Broken Pledges*, about the horrors of college hazing. That evening was the NCAA Finals with North Carolina and Duke. I ended my presentation and made a beeline for the campus hotel bar and camped in front of the TV alongside about a dozen male viewers. Almost immediately I heard a familiar booming voice and a trademark chuckle. "Where are all the broads?" he boomed.

He walked right up to my stool.

"Do you recognize me, Mr. Vonnegut?"

"You're the guy who wrote that I walked like a man who had cheese in his shoes," he said. "I hate you."

But he took an empty stool next to me. I told him I had written the hazing book we had discussed years before over lunch. "Do you want a copy?" I asked.

I left my coat on the stool to keep my place and ran to my hotel room get him a copy.

He flipped through the book's photos.

"Every now and then I think about returning to journalism," he said. "I think about writing the story of Eddie Slovik, the only soldier to be executed for cowardice in World War Two."

I never had to serve in the Army. On December 1, 1969, the Selective Service National Headquarters held a lottery for registrants born between 1944 and 1950. My birthday of August 19, 1946, the same day and year as Bill Clinton's birthday, drew number 311. Neither of us had to serve. The soccer buddy whose car I had helped pack died in Vietnam. His name is on the memorial in Washington.

I have written many books and articles. One now-in-progress is a biography of Kurt Vonnegut. I particularly enjoyed interviewing his son Mark at his pediatrician's office in Massachusetts, as well as his daughter Edie at her house, inherited from her father, on Cape Cod. Much of the thrust of the book concerns Vonnegut's time in Dresden, and I spent weeks there conducting research. Most moving, I interviewed several of Vonnegut's fellow prisoners who survived the bombing and later labored with him to unearth and bury the grotesque victims.

When Vonnegut died on April 11, 2007, I was chosen to write one of the tributes to him for the editorial page of the *Indianapolis Star*, his boyhood hometown newspaper. I predicted in that column that the book posterity will remember in a century or more will be *Slaughterhouse-Five*. ■

"Brautigan on the Yellowstone" by Greg Keeler. Acrylic on canvas, 28" x 22."

WILLIAM JOHNSON

Throwing Rocks in the Basement of Time: Re-Reading Norman Maclean's A River Runs Through It

When a trout turns flashing just under the surface to sip a floating insect, my adrenaline kicks in. If I'm fishing I cast in that direction. But hurry is the enemy of luck. The first time I read Norman Maclean's now well-known book, hurry owned me. As chair of an English Department, I strove to keep up—with administrivia, teaching, grading, tending a marriage and three kids. It was the mid-1980's. Maclean was in the wind, or water, that carried his story. My college Dean, also a fisherman, was co-editing the first collection of essays on Maclean. Scholars and the public were curious about the one-time logger and forest service buck turned litterateur who fashioned a career teaching English at the University of Chicago before writing the masterpiece some believe matches *Huck Finn* or *Moby Dick*.

I grew up flyfishing and one of my sons had caught the bug. What's more, Maclean was coming to campus to give a talk; I wanted to get his book under my belt. I was an academic after all. I needed something smart to say. I read the book hastily, but in time, with successive returns, the story grew on me. It was rollicking, bawdy, cornpone funny, intimate, deeply tragic and sublime. And it raised biblical hackles—Maclean's father was a Presbyterian pastor, a path I had nearly taken myself, only to be converted by literature into teaching and writing too.

I learned flyfishing as a small boy trailing my father and uncle. During the second war they worked for Armour's in Spokane and saved gas-ration coupons for summer trips to west Montana rivers. In the 50s riding a tall man's shoulders, I was prince of fords bobbing under willows flanked by the Bitterroot mountains, getting a bird's eye view of paradise.

My uncle and father were not expert fishers like Paul Maclean. They pretended to read the water, but fishing, especially the Bull River (a stretch that now lies drowned by the Clark Fork Dam at Noxon), they used the same fly all day, every day, each year. It was a grey-hackle peacock that could imitate numerous insects that floated a river. When I read the canny episode in which Norman and Paul try to outfish each other, and Paul, with his ability to think like a trout, figures out the big ones are feeding on yellow stone-flies, I realized I was a half-assed fisherman at best and probably always would be. Norman might have said I'd have been better off as a bait fisherman. But his book had me hooked. The story characterizes fly-fishing expertly, not as technique merely, but as a reflective, inward disposition that turns on brotherhood, fishing and a river. Early on I was drawn to Paul's shadow-casting, or Norman's sublime presentation of it, those rainbow vapors lifted off a line to etherealize in sun. But over time, the humanity of the book took me deeper. Fishing for others, especially for his brother, comes as a troubled beauty, twined as if by a flyline with love, loss and responsibility, the mysteries that most haunt us.

Eventually I recognized Maclean's art, its earth savvy, and the subtlety of its felt observation. If a line connects us to strange truth, it may be a flyline. Maclean no doubt felt a line of writing would do almost as well. His evoking of Paul's discovery—fishing in sun then fishing in shade; not catching them then hooking big ones—that trout are feeding on drowned stoneflies just under the surface, is funny, masterful and shrewd. The mingling of hunch and observation, getting skunked then feeling a trout slam your hook, gets its upshot in a single sentence: "All there is to thinking, he said, is seeing something noticeable which makes you see something you weren't noticing, which makes you see something that isn't even visible" (92). I sensed a profound truth rising to the surface, and realized that no matter how good I thought a cast was, half the time I couldn't even see the line, let alone the fly, which I guess is the point: you hope the fish doesn't either. Your success depends on deception, or better, the artful making of an illusion that mimes the actual then quietly hints that the actual may express time's other side.

Maclean's use of the verb "make" in the sentence above is no accident. He's a maker, and in this passage the word lends Paul's reading the water a supernal agency. When you think you know what you're looking at, hints of what you don't know are made (who or what does this?) to enter the field of observatory flow and, however indirectly, become partly catchable, if not keepable.

Like Paul's casting, the book has masterful strokes. In one scene Father Maclean looks up from his Greek New Testament to watch Paul fish. Norman is watching them both, and the familial aesthetic of the *logos,* Maclean's natural theology of the divine piscine Word, breaks through:

> I looked to see where the book was left open and knew just enough Greek to recognize *logos* as the Word. I guessed from it and the argument that I was looking at the first verse of John. While I was looking, Father said, 'He has one on' (96).

This is one of several places where, for me, "all things merge into one, and a river runs through it" (104). The argument between Norman and his father was over what Paul believed. Did he think words are formed out of water, Norman's view, or that water runs over the words, the father's (96)? The arrival of the divine Word coincides with Paul's hooking a fish, and more subtly, with tragic resonance, Norman's own fishing for his brother, wondering, always after the fact, 'Could I have helped him'? This is Maclean's twist on the question of brotherly love, a refrain that remains unanswered. Not, am I my brother's keeper, but can I be, and if so, how—in this troubled lovely world, where, for a moment, a hooked trout, or a glance at your brother, epitomize the sacred word, its generative possibility.

Then there's rock-throwing. In *A River Runs Through It* rocks are emblems of geologic prehistory and a means of friendship the brothers "throw" at each other, a habit they learned from their father, the preacher of (brotherly) Christian love (96). There may be "a lot to say across a river" (90) but most of it isn't quite hearable and the river often says No. These fishers (of trout and men) love and respect each other. In the spirit of competitive "out-fishing," they throw rocks in each other's holes. For Maclean rocks are at once cosmic and local, and throwing them may reveal, like the story itself, an arc of intimate contact, or the attempt, however problematic, to make it.

When he fishes Father Maclean imagines ancient geologic forces, the rain that makes mud, which in time, through primordial pressure, becomes the bedrock of a river. Norman recalls how the boys and their father built the family fireplace using stones from the river bank. The closest we get to brotherly love may be an image of young men throwing rocks in each other's fishing holes. When I'm on a river myself, I now hear Maclean's words inflect, and deflect, my casting—for fish and for thought. The book has taken hold and gifted a felt change that in spite of water seems indelible.

In the novella's haunted, and haunting, end, rocks are the basement of time. Maclean suggests that words of the *logos,* the divine-creative Word, lie under the rocks, under the waters that flow and the earth we walk. A fisher-person's version of the tablets of Moses perhaps, the human articulation of ancient rains and the primal flood, and the mythic if palpable stones of the river we wade. Beneath these run words that make art, and help make us what we are and what, with imaginative discipline, we may become. Maclean's novella caught, and still catches me; it hooks and holds. I can't think of fishing or cast a fly without his haunted waters moving through.

GROVE KOGER

Looking Back with John O'Hara: Reading Imagine Kissing Pete *in Context*

T he appearance of John O'Hara's *Sermons and Soda-Water* in November 1960 was only one of several important events in the author's life that year. He'd already published a major novel, *Ourselves to Know,* in February, but within only a few months he let it be known that he had also completed some novellas that *The New Yorker* might want to consider. However—and it was a big however—it would be necessary for the magazine's fiction editor, William Maxwell, to read them at O'Hara's oceanfront house on Long Island.

Now insisting that an editor come to you rather than the other way around was unusual in itself, but there was more than chutzpah involved. Between 1928 and 1949, O'Hara had published frequently in *The New Yorker,* and the connection had become a defining factor for both parties. He's usually credited, for better or worse, with creating "the *New Yorker* story"— one that, as critic Charles McGrath describes it, "turns on a tiny alteration in tone or mood." McGrath adds that O'Hara "paved the way for Salinger, Cheever, Updike and even Carver."

So distinctive, in fact, were the stories O'Hara wrote for *The New Yorker* that he believed no other market would print them. That concern led him to start insisting on a sizeable kill fee for every story it turned down—a condition that the editor of course rejected. Then, when the magazine carried an unfavorable review of his long 1949 novel *A Rage to Live,* he broke off relations altogether. But he didn't stop writing, instead completing three more major novels over the following years, including *Ten North Frederick,* which won the National Book Award.

But now it's July 12, 1960, and William Maxwell has arrived at O'Hara's house with his wife. After dinner, he's left alone to evaluate the typescripts. He reads one, then another and doesn't care for either.

315

Undoubtedly sweating badly at this point, he turns to the third—*Imagine Kissing Pete*—and, by the time he's reached the last page, realizes that it's a "masterpiece" (his word) and offers O'Hara $10,000. The novella duly appears in the magazine's September 17 issue.

(Maxwell would later remark, by the way, that "being a fiction editor at *The New Yorker* was like being an animal trainer.")

Later that year, *Pete* and the other two novellas—*The Girl on the Baggage Truck* and *We're Friends Again*—were published by Random House in an attractive boxed set as *Sermons and Soda-Water*, a title taken from Byron's *Don Juan*: "Let us have wine and women, mirth and laughter, / Sermons and soda-water the day after." All three are narrated by a middle-aged man named Jim Malloy who has occasion to remember and revisit various people and events from his early life. But to understand their significance and Malloy's reaction to them, we should consider the early life and character of his creator.

First off, John O'Hara was a difficult individual. Born in the predominantly WASP town of Pottsville, Pennsylvania, in 1905, he was inordinately sensitive about being Irish Catholic. In his second novel, *BUtterfield 8*, he gives his alter ego—that would be Malloy—a little speech on the subject:

> "I want to tell you something about myself that will help to explain a lot of things about me. You might as well hear it now. First of all, I am a Mick. I wear Brooks clothes and I don't eat salad with a spoon and I probably could play five-goal polo in two years, but I am a Mick. Still a Mick."

Another sore point with O'Hara was his failure to attend Yale, even though the university had apparently accepted him. It seems that the young man had gotten drunk with two friends and a pair of policemen (!) the night before his graduation from prep school, prompting the school to pull his diploma and his angry father to pull his financial support. The father's death the following year left the O'Hara family in reduced circumstances, and that was that.

Besides his taste for alcohol, which he indulged until he almost killed himself, O'Hara had a fragile ego, a famously combative disposition, and an interest in sex that he didn't see any reason to hide.

GROVE KOGER

John O'Hara wrote about 400 short stories, of which 247 were published in The New Yorker *over several decades.*

But he also had a gift for putting words together, and, after a period of largely aimless apprenticeship, a growing sense of where that gift might take him.

O'Hara began his professional career in 1924 writing for local Pennsylvania papers before moving on to New York City a few years later. In short order he was contributing sketches and the like to *The New Yorker.* Coupled with the acute lessons of small-town life he'd learned in Pottsville, his experiences in the big city were teaching him the crucial importance of social signs or signifiers—the kinds of shoes people wore, the makes and models (and years) of cars they drove, the schools they might or might not have attended, the fraternities they were invited to join. Such things mattered a great deal to him, which is surely a failing on a personal level, but understanding them was invaluable to a writer wanting to suggest character and status in a few quick words.

There's no end of gossip about the early O'Hara's bad behavior. One of many anecdotes concerns New York City's Stork Club, where the writer routinely drank and where waiters routinely seated him near the door so that they could throw him out more easily when he (routinely, it seems) started a fight. It's no surprise, then, that the protagonist of O'Hara's first novel, *Appointment in Samarra*, throws a drink in someone's face in a moment of anger, precipitating, within three eventful days, the fatal rendezvous announced in the title.

Appointment was published by Harcourt, Brace in 1934 and was an instant success. It's set in Gibbsville, a scarcely disguised version of Pottsville, and features Jim Malloy in a bit part. He shows up again in *BUtterfield 8,* in which he delivers that speech about Micks, and again in *Hope of Heaven,* which draws on O'Hara's own stint in Hollywood in the mid-1930s. Subsequently he puts in occasional appearances in O'Hara's many stories and novellas.

And I do mean *many.* By the time he died in 1970, O'Hara had written some 400 of them, of which 247 were published over time by *The New Yorker*—still a record for the magazine. And it was Maxwell's recognition of the quality of O'Hara's novella in 1960 that made that record possible.

As *Imagine Kissing Pete* opens, it's 1929 and Malloy is registering his surprise that an old Gibbsville schoolmate, Angus "Pete" McCrea, has written him in New York City asking him to be an usher at his wedding in June. It seems he's marrying Bobbie Hammersmith, whom Malloy himself had dated for a time, and the surprise is due in large part to the seeming mismatch of the prospective bride and groom, as the unattractive Pete had been known as "Ichabod" by his fellow students.

Looking up Kitty Clark, another schoolmate who's also moved to the city and who's to be the bridesmaid, Malloy learns that Bobbie has just broken off her engagement to a far more desirable young man. "Ichabod McCrea and Bobbie Hammersmith," Kitty intones with wonder. "Beauty and the beast.... Imagine *kissing* Pete, let alone any of the rest of it."

Over the following hundred or so pages, Malloy records what he learns from time to time about the McCreas and other Gibbsville figures, including characters we may remember from *Appointment in Samarra*. His tone is casual and unhurried, as if he were chatting with friends, and he turns frankly sentimental as they (and he himself) grow older.

Not too long after the wedding, Malloy revisits Gibbsville to discover that Pete has lost his job at one of the town's banks and that he and Bobbie have moved into his mother's house. But the couple have serous personal issues as well, as Malloy learns from Bobbie. Pete, it seems, was a virgin at the time of his marriage, but his discovery of sex has turned him into a violent and abusive man, and when he nearly rapes a mutual friend, the couple are shunned.

As the conversation continues, Malloy considers the age he and his generation have grown up in, bracketed as it is at one end by the beginning of Prohibition in January 1920, and at the other by the early years of what we now call the Great Depression, which began in late October 1929:

> We had come to our maturity and our knowledgeability during the long decade of cynicism that was usually dismissed as "a cynical disregard of the law of the land," but that was something else, something deeper.... Prohibition, the zealots' attempt to force total abstinence on a temperate nation, made liars of a hundred million men ..."

But he doesn't stop there, going on to argue that the disregard, cynical or not, made "cheats of their children" as well, and enumerates:

> the West Point cadets who cheated in examinations, the basketball players who connived with gamblers, the thousands of uncaught cheats in the high schools and colleges. We had grown up and away from our earlier esteem of God and country and valor, and had matured at a moment when riches were vanishing for reasons that we could not understand. We were the losing, not the lost, generation.

Over time, Malloy learns that the McCreas have fallen further still, moving to parts of Gibbsville "that were out of the way for their old friends," and when he revisits his hometown briefly in 1938, he encounters Pete running a poolroom. "A lot of changes," Pete allows, "but this is better than nothing," adding, a little surprisingly, that Bobbie would "love to hear from" him. That night, as Bobbie and Malloy share a bottle of whiskey, she tells him that Pete "has his women," adding that she hasn't "been the soul of purity, either."

As we approach the present, Malloy (who's O'Hara's alter ego, remember) admits that he has become "reconciled to middle age and the quieter life." But that's not all:

> I made another discovery: that the sweetness of my early youth was a persistent and enduring thing, so long as I kept it at the distance of years. Moments would come back to me, of love and excitement and music and laughter that filled my breast as they had thirty years earlier.... I wanted none of it ever again, but all I had I wanted to keep.... In middle age I was proud to have lived according to my emotions at the right time, and content to live that way vicariously and at a distance. I had missed almost nothing, escaped very little,...

The reverie concluded, Malloy mentions that, as time passed, he "would sometimes think of Bobbie McCrea and the dinginess of her history," but then adds, almost as an aside, that he's going to provide his readers with "a happy ending." It's as if a skilled composer has rearranged the notes of his somber theme to produce a sweet variation. I could provide the details of that variation, and of how Bobbie and Pete manage to reach it, but I'm going to leave the experience to you. I'll add only that, after all the misery that's come before, it's understated but deeply moving.

In one way or another, *Imagine Kissing Pete* and the other novellas in the set touch on virtually all of O'Hara's themes and interests: the ruinous drinking and the destructive anger, the interest in sexual behavior and the strife that it can produce, the preoccupation with class, the workings of fate. They also showcase his ear for what people say (or don't say) and—a rare trait among male writers of his generation—demonstrate his sympathetic treatment of women.

In the Foreword to *Sermons and Soda-Water,* O'Hara had already explained his goals, using some of the same words he gives Malloy:

> I want to get it all down on paper while I can. I am now fifty-five years old and I have lived with as well as in the Twentieth Century from its earliest days.... The Twenties, the Thirties, and the Forties are already history, but I cannot be content to leave their story in the hands of the historians and the editors of picture books.
>
> I want to record the way people talked and thought and felt, and to do it with complete honesty and variety.

After his pivotal return to *The New Yorker,* O'Hara entered the most productive period of his career. He published another sizeable novel, *The Lockwood Concern,* in 1965, several shorter ones, and six substantial collections of stories dealing with an impressively wide range of characters in an equally wide range of social and geographical settings. (The stories themselves were more substantial, too, as if O'Hara had realized the limitations of the *New Yorker* story he had created.) Two more original collections appeared after his death, and since then there have been reprints and new selections aplenty, including two in the prestigious Library of America, one of which, simply titled *Stories,* includes *Imagine Kissing Pete.* ■

CAMERON WATSON

Re-Reading Robert Laxalt's Sweet Promised Land

Browsing in a San Francisco second-hand bookstore in the early 1990s, I came across an unassuming, obviously well-used pocket edition of *Sweet Promised Land*, Robert Laxalt's 1957 memoir of the journey he took with his Basque immigrant father, Dominique, to his homeland. Laxalt's work was a milestone in the literature of the American West, but more so, it gave a voice to Basque Americans and other immigrants impacted by their adaptation to American society as well as to the landscape they settled. It serves as an elegy to the immigrant experience in America, reclaiming the figure of the sheepherder in Western mythology, giving Basques a place in the West. Most of all, *Sweet Promised Land* is a tale of realization and acceptance that home, for Dominique, was now America. Only by returning to the homeland did he grasp that it was no longer home, that the American West's landscape had become a part of him.

I myself had gone in the opposite direction at that time, from Europe to the American West, to attend graduate school in Nevada to study Basque history and culture. My interest was first and foremost in the old country and the West was just a temporary stop, a practical way, so I thought, to secure a qualification that would help me settle in the Basque Country. After the initial wonder of the new had worn off, I had already begun to dream about returning to Europe from my self-imposed Nevada exile. But I knew that Laxalt's book was important. It spoke of place and identity, twin interests in both my personal and professional life, and that Laxalt was the literary voice of Basque Americans.

Originally conceived as a series of magazine articles about his father's return after forty-seven years in the United States, he structures the book in three easy-to-follow parts: the setting, the idea, and the return. Place is key to the work, as revealed in its opening sentence: "My father was a sheepherder, and his home was the hills." Here, in eleven carefully chosen words, Laxalt pronounces the themes of lifestyle and landscape that suffuse the simple yet elegant narrative like gentle warm evening light, a reassuring hue even if the reader has never stepped foot in the American West. The peaks, hollows, ranges, and deserts of the

Nevada landscape are portrayed in a vivid poetic language that creates an immediate bond between reader and location. Recalling the first time he crossed the Rockies, Dominique observes that, "The country got bigger and the mountains was higher, and you could look for miles without seeing a fence. Even the people had a different look to them. They had color in their faces, and they didn't dress very fancy."

The story then turns to the idea of the Laxalt family encouraging the aging Dominique to make a trip to his birthplace and visit with his family there. Heated discussions ensue, with Dominque's Basque wife, Theresa, warning that he should not be left to go alone: "You don't know these Basques like I do. Once he is there where he began, he will forget he ever lived in this country!" As she herself lacked any interest in returning, it is thus decided that Robert will accompany his father, to make sure he both arrives safely, and comes back to America. And here begins a storyline that, on my first reading, I took in very straightforwardly without much deeper consideration: namely, the father-son journey. In this sense, the book is as much about Robert Laxalt's discovery of his own father—the old sheepherder who had spent most of his adult life, as underscored in the book, in the mountains and deserts of the Far West, both physically and emotionally distant from his family—as it is about Dominique's realization that home means Nevada.

And so to the denouement, which comes as some surprise in that Laxalt does not choose to complete the cycle. There is no Homeric return here. Instead, more dramatically, more poignantly still, the chronicle ends high up in the opaque green Pyrenees. "I can't go back. It ain't my country any more. I've lived too much in America ever to go back," says Dominique, even in the face of relatives pleading for him to stay. The young Robert tries to understand, and does so by framing his thoughts in terms of the impact of the West, of its landscape and promise, on his father: "Then I saw the cragged face that the land had filled with hope and torn with pain, had changed from young to old, and in the end had claimed. And then I did know it."

When I first read *Sweet Promised Land*, twenty-five years ago, I was almost overcome with grief at the ending. For someone who felt isolated and out of place in the American West, and who was dreaming of going to the Basque Country, this was a sad story. I had not gone to the United States to make my fortune. I had made a pragmatic decision to go there, gain some qualifications, and return to Europe; all of which I did. Taking out that old second-hand copy of the book, it is interesting to look at three passages I highlighted back then: "Somewhere in the darkness beyond loomed the beginning of the Pyrenees, and high in those mountains the home of my father," "Forty-seven years and ten thousand thoughts of home, and here was where it had all begun," and "This was the moment of reward he could never have known in America." In short, my thoughts were clearly about yearning to return to the Basque Country. In re-reading the book for the first time in all these years, however, so many things have changed. On a very immediate personal level, I can now better comprehend the sentiment in statements like "For the first time, I didn't feel like a stranger to the land" and "What a wonderful thing that you could have gone to America!" I, too, dream of a lasting return one day, to the country that educated me and with where I have maintained a close bond all these years. Indeed, on my first trip back there in many years, relatively recently, I was overcome, suddenly and powerfully, with a sense of belonging, of being in *my* place.

As Laxalt's book demonstrates, though, in the multiple stories recounted by the old-timer—transcribed almost in the form of oral history, with an air of listening while gathered round a camp fire— landscape alone does not instill a sense of place. In Dominique's case, people also helped to plant those roots still deeper. Likewise, people are central to my own quest to return. Laxalt's father was a sheepherder and his home the hills; my father was a mariner, and his home was the sea. Though my father lived far from the village of his birth, and had spent almost an entire lifetime in exile from his own country, he talked often of returning there without ever realizing that dream. He passed a few years ago and I now appreciate more deeply the opportunity Robert Laxalt had to spend time with Dominique and see him in the land of his birth. His is a story of a son's love and respect for his father, and re-reading the book was a powerful and moving experience for me in prompting recollections of my own relationship with my father.

Sweet Promised Land is a testament to a landscape, the American West, and a way of life, sheepherding, which helped create America. The book is grand in scope but human in scale. Therein resides the magnitude of its impact. It is a universal and timeless book; a chronicle that still, to this day, captures the endurance of the human spirit and acknowledges that we are but part of a land, *the* land. As I write these lines, I value even more how we all must find our own sweet promised land. ■

Father and son: Dominique Laxalt and author Robert Laxalt.

THE LAST WORD

"Untitled" by Dennis DeFoggi. Pencil, colored pencil, acrylic and thinset on mat board. 18.75" x 15.5," 2020.

RON PADGETT

Big Anniversary

It's October 9th,
a day that means nothing
to me. I can't think
of a single thing associated
with it, no birthday
or disaster, no holiday
or date of death.
It will be replaced
by October 10th, another day
with no resonance
other than the resonance of everything,
which, come to think of it,
is a lot.

Depth Charge

I add words to
and take away weeds from
the world. If
only my words would come back
and say, "Heh, heh, try again"
the way the weeds do.

Peppermint Air

Only twenty minutes and
I already don't smell
the peppermint oil
on the cotton balls
I have placed in this cabin
to keep the mice out.
I sit here in a cube
of peppermint air,
a big non-mouse.

"Untitled" by Jinny DeFoggi. Ink on paper, 14" x 17," 2005.

CONTRIBUTORS

"Family Album," No. 5, by Alberta Mayo. Gel pen on sketchbook black paper.

CONTRIBUTORS

SHERMAN ALEXIE has published 26 books including his recent memoir *You Don't Have to Say You Love Me* (Little, Brown), just out in paper. He has won the PEN/Faulkner Award for Fiction, the PEN/Malamud Award for Short Fiction, a PEN/Hemingway Citation for Best First Fiction, and the National Book Award for Young People's Literature. Born a Spokane/Coeur d'Alene Indian, Alexie grew up in Wellpinit, Washington, on the Spokane Indian Reservation. He's been an urban Indian since 1994 and lives in Seattle with his family. *A Memory of Elephants*, a letterpress-printed, limited edition chapbook of his poems, is forthcoming in 2020 from Limberlost Press.

SANDY ANDERSON is the author of *Jeanne Was Once a Player of Pianos*, a letterpress-printed chapbook of poems from Limberlost Press. She was the longtime organizer and inspirational force behind CityArt, Salt Lake City's longest-running literary reading series (currently presenting 25-30 readings a year), and which also delved into small press publishing. She also edited *Fragile Constructions,* an occasional anthology of creative work that evolved from writing workshops she conducted and participated in. She has been a mentor to many and a tireless promoter of the Utah writing community.

MARY CLEARMAN BLEW has written or edited 13 books of fiction and nonfiction. Her short fiction collection *Runaway* won a Pacific Northwest Booksellers Award, as did her memoir *All But the Waltz: Essays on a Montana Family*. Her novel *Jackalope Dreams* won the Western Heritage Award. Her most recent memoir is *This Is Not the Ivy League*. Her latest two novels, *Ruby Dreams of Janis Joplin* and *Sweep Out the Ashes*, were published by the University of Nebraska Press in 2018 and 2019 respectively, with another forthcoming. She lives in Moscow, Idaho.

NANCY BROSSMAN is an award-winning Boise artist who has produced prints and paintings for over 40 years. Botanical and high desert subjects run through most of her work, with images of southwest Idaho and eastern Oregon dominating her sizable output. She has worked as an artist in the schools, and her prints and paintings are in many public and private collections. She received her BFA in art at the age of 50, and specializes in etching, engraving, and carving plates and blocks.

BOB BUSHNELL was raised in Wilder, Idaho, and attended the University of Idaho, Stanford University, the University of Washington School of Law, and the Harvard Business School's Small Company President's Program. He returned to Boise in 1972 to practice law before becoming a full-time businessman and a single parent, nourished by a membership in the Boise Great Books Club for four decades. He now devotes most of his time to reading, writing, and cultivating old and new friendships.

ROYDEN CARD was born in Canada and raised in Utah, introduced to the desert at the age of eight. Drawing and then painting desert landscape has been his primary focus for over 50 years. Of his vocation, he says, "You do the work, learn, teach, keep painting, maybe win an award or two (or not), but you love the work and go on painting. Lately, I seek out those views that get overlooked; not the scenic viewpoint. Though I love slick-rock and towering red cliffs, I think I love the multiplicity of grays, siennas, pale ochres, blue-green of Morrison hills, purples and faded umbers of the badlands, even more. They seem to be what I tend to paint these past years. Love of the desert, refuge, contemplation ... an ongoing search for beauty... and the desire to paint something 'worthy.'"

MICHAEL CORRIGAN is a San Francisco native who holds an M.A. in Creative Writing from San Francisco State. He taught English and Speech Communications at Idaho State University for many years, and has authored more than a dozen books, including his memoir *Confessions of a Shanty Irishman*, and *These Precious Hours*, a collection of connected stories. His novel Brewer's Odyssey is available on Kindle and in softcover. He lives in Pocatello, Idaho.

GERALD COSTANZO is the author of nine collections of poems, including *Badlands, In the Aviary, Nobody Lives on Arthur Godfrey Boulevard* and, most recently, *Regular Haunts: New and Previous Poems*. He has also edited six anthologies of poetry, and is Director of the Press at Carnegie Mellon University, where he has been a professor of English for 50 years. He is the recipient of The Devins Award for Poetry and two creative writing fellowships from the National Endowment for the Arts, as well as fellowships from the Pennsylvania Council on the Arts, the Coordinating Council of Literary Magazines, and two Pushcart Prizes. A graduate of Harvard and the Writing Seminars at Johns Hopkins, he lives in Mt. Lebanon, Pennsylvania, and Nehalem, Oregon.

DENNIS & GINNY DEFOGGI are two Boise-based artists who have been passionately dedicated to their art for more than a half-century. Encouraged by mentor artist and friend Ray Obermayr at Idaho State University in the 1960s, they have in turn been great encouragers of writers, artists, readers, thinkers, and creative believers and welcomed them into their home and their fold. They've had many shows together, and both have exhibited at the Boise Art Museum's juried Idaho Triennial shows of outstanding work by the state's contemporary artists. Dennis' work again is featured in the BAM 2020 Triennial.

ROBERT DEMOTT's recent books are *Angling Days: A Fly Fisher's Journals* (essays, Simon & Schuster, 2019), *Conversations with Jim Harrison, Revised and Updated* (interviews, University Press of Mississippi, 2019), and *Up Late Reading Birds of America* (prose-poems, Sheila-Na-Gig Editions, 2020). His poetry has appeared in many journals, including *Ontario Review, Georgia Review, Southern Review, Hiram Poetry Review, Southern Poetry Review, Lake Effect, Windsor Review*, and elsewhere. From 1969 to 2013 he taught at Ohio University. He serves on the editorial board of *The Steinbeck Review*, and directorial board of *Quarter After Eight*, a literary journal. He lives in Athens, Ohio, with his partner Kate Fox, a poet and editor.

JENNIFER DUNBAR DORN was born in Moscow and grew up in London. Married to late poet Edward Dorn for thirty years, she collaborated with him on the magazine *Rolling Stock* (1980s) and edited his *Collected Poems* (Carcanet 2012). She taught for many years at the University of Colorado, Boulder, and now lives in Denver. Her books of poetry include *Manchester Square* (with Ed Dorn), *Galactic Runaway* and *Eastward Ho*.

DANIELLE BEAZER DUBRASKY holds M.A. and Ph.D. degrees in creative writing from Stanford and the University of Utah respectively. She is an associate professor at Southern Utah University. Her work has recently appeared in *Chiron Review, South Dakota Review, Ninth Letter, Main Street Rag, Pilgrimage, saltfront, Sugar House Review, Cave Wall, Open: Journal of Arts & Letters, Under a Warm Green Linden*, and Terrain.org. Her chapbook *Ruin and Light* won the 2014 Anabiosis Press Chapbook Competition.

VARDIS FISHER (1895-1968) was perhaps Idaho's most prolific writer of the 20th century, authoring more than 25 novels, a collection of short stories, a collection of poetry, and nine books of nonfiction, including *Idaho: A Guide in Word & Picture,* the first state guide published in 1937 as part of the WPA "Guides to the States" series during the Great Depression. Highlights of his career include the 12-volume series of novels he called his "Testament of Man" series, and the novel *Mountain Man* (1965), which was the basis for the 1972 Hollywood film *Jeremiah Johnson,* directed by Sydney Pollack and starring Robert Redford.

JUDITH FREEMAN is the author of a short story collection and several novels, including *The Chinchilla Farm* and *Red Water,* as well as a biography of Raymond Chandler, *The Long Embrace,* and most recently a memoir, *The Latter Days.* The recipient of a John Simon Guggenheim Fellowship in fiction, she was also awarded an Erle Stanley Gardner Fellowship from the Harry Ransom Center, and the Western Heritage Award for her novel *Set For Life.* Her essays and reviews have appeared in *The New York Times, The Chicago Tribune, The Los Angeles Times, The Washington Post,* and *The Los Angeles Review of Books,* among other publications. She lives on the Camas Prairie near Fairfield, Idaho, with her husband, the artist-photographer Anthony Hernandez, and is at work on a new novel.

JOHN GARMON once served as president of Berkeley City College in California and is now a writing assistant at the College of Southern Nevada. Now in his 80th year, his poems and stories have appeared in *Prairie Schooner, Ploughshares, Southern Poetry Review, Southern Humanities Review, Florida Review, New Mexico Humanities Review, Radius, West, Commonweal, Southwestern American Literature, Paradise Review, Phantom Drift, Aji, Spoon River Poetry Journal, Passages North,* and elsewhere.

GARY GILDNER says he "threw far too many curveballs in his youth, grew up to break bread in Paris, gave underground readings behind the Iron Curtain, and survived Transient Global Amnesia in the arms of a ballerina in the foothills of the Santa Catalina Mountains of Arizona." He lived for 25 years in the Idaho panhandle before moving to Arizona. He's the author of numerous books of poetry, memoir, and fiction, and winner of the Walt Whitman Prize and the William Carlos Williams Prize for poetry, the Iowa Prize for memoir, and other awards. He's also the recipient of Fulbright Fellowships to Poland and Czechoslovakia.

SHAUN T. GRIFFIN is the co-founder and development director of Community Chest, a rural social justice agency serving northwestern Nevada since 1991. Southern Utah University Press released *Anthem for a Burnished Land*, a memoir, in 2016. *This Is What the Desert Surrenders: New and Selected Poems* came out from Black Rock Press in 2012, and Limberlost Press released his letterpressed chapbook of poems *Driving the Tender Desert Home* in 2014. His most  recent books include a collection of essays, *Because the Light Will Not Forgive Me* (University of Nevada Press in 2019), and *The Monastery of Stars* (poems, Kelsay Books 2020). He lives in Virginia City, Nevada, in the shadow of the former home of novelist Walter Van Tilburg Clark.

CHUCK GUILFORD is a winner of the Western Literature Association's Willa Cather Memorial Award and the author of the novel *Spring Drive: A North Country Tale*; *Altogether Now: Essays on Poetry, Writing, and Teaching*; and the collection of poems *What Counts*. He is also the creator of two popular websites, Paradigm Online Writing Assistant (powa.org) and Poetryexpress (poetryexpress.org). He taught literature and creative writing at Boise State University for  more than two decades and founded BSU's Idaho Writers Archive. His poems, stories, essays, and reviews have appeared in a many magazines and anthologies, including *Poetry, Kansas Quarterly, Coyote's Journal, Redneck Review of Literature, Crab Creek Review, Idaho Humanities*, and elsewhere. A collection of his poems is available at https://www.forthislife.org.

DAVID GUIOTTO is the author of *Sawtooth Country* (Limberlost Press) and *Holocene Trail Guide to the Boise Front* (Wolf Peach Press). His work has appeared in the *San Francisco Chronicle, Cycling Tips, 3 Syllables, The Cabin*, and *Street Mag*. His blog *Sawing Wood* (sawing-wood.blogspot.com) explores the crossroads of art, travel, and family life. He currently lives with his wife and daughter in Boulder, Colorado.

JIM HEYNEN was born on a farm in northwest Iowa and received his first eight years of education at one of the state's last one-room school houses, Welcome #3. He's the author of several collections of poems, including *A Suitable Church* and *Standing Naked* (poetry), and several collections of stories, including *You Know What Is Right, The One-Room Schoolhouse*, and *The Man Who Kept Cigars in his Cap*. Since 1992, he has been Writer-in-Residence at St. Olaf College in Northfield, Minnesota.

JAY JOHNSON is a lawyer and writer working in Moscow, Latah County, Idaho. After college, he lived in Oregon, Colorado, Washington, and California before settling in Idaho in 1995. He repaired automobiles and logged for twenty-five years prior to law school. Most of his law practice is criminal defense, generally for indigent clients. His short fiction has appeared in *Talking River Review* and *Ramblr*.

MARC C. JOHNSON has worked as a broadcast journalist and served as a top aide to Idaho's longest-serving governor, Cecil D. Andrus. His writing on politics and history has been published in the *New York Times, California Journal of Politics and Policy*, and *Montana the Magazine of Western History* and appears regularly on the blog and podcast *Many Things Considered*. He writes a weekly column on politics for the Lewiston (Idaho) *Tribune*, and he's the author of *Political Hell-Raiser: The Life and Times of Senator Burton K. Wheeler of Montana* (University of Oklahoma Press, 2019), a biography of a colorful New Deal-era Democrat who supported landmark legislation during the Great Depression. He lives with his wife Pat in Manzanita, Oregon.

WILLIAM JOHNSON is Professor Emeritus of English at Lewis-Clark State College in Lewiston, Idaho, a former Writer-in-Residence for the state of Idaho, author of *A River without Banks*, a collection of essays from Oregon State University Press, and several collections of poetry, including, most recently, *Dogwood* (Limberlost Press). He lives with his wife Cheryl and their cat Manu in a house surrounded by trees, flanked by the Lewiston hills and sky.

GREG KEELER is the author of two memoirs, *Waltzing with the Captain: Remembering Richard Brautigan* (Limberlost Press) and *Trash Fish: A Life* (Counterpoint Press), and eight collections of poetry, including, most recently, *The Bluebird Run* (Elk River Books). He writes, paints, and composes irreverent songs in Bozeman, Montana, where he taught in the English Department of Montana State University for 30 years.

GROVE KOGER is the author of *When the Going Was Good: A Guide to the 99 Best Narratives of Travel, Exploration, and Adventure* (Scarecrow Press, 2002), and Assistant Editor of *Deus Loci: The Lawrence Durrell Journal*. He has published fiction in such periodicals as *Cirque, Danse Macabre, The Bosphorus Review of Books, La Piccioletta Barca*, and *Punt Volat*, and blogs at worldenoughblog.wordpress.com.

ANNIE LAMPMAN teaches creative writing at the Washington State University Honors College. Her essays, poetry, and short fiction have recently appeared or are forthcoming in *The Massachusetts Review, Orion Magazine, High Desert Journal* and elsewhere. Her work has been awarded a Best American Essays "Notable," a Pushcart Prize Special Mention, an Idaho Commission on the Arts fellowship, and a wilderness artist's residency through the U.S. Bureau of Land Management. She lives in Moscow, Idaho, with her husband and three sons. *Burning Time*, a letterpress-printed chapbook of her poems, will be published by Limberlost Press in 2020.

DAVID LEE is the author of more than two dozen books of poetry. His collection *News from Down to the Café* was nominated for the Pulitzer Prize in 1999, and in 2001 he was a finalist for the position of United States Poet Laureate. He served as Utah's inaugural Poet Laureate from 1997-2002 and later received the Utah Governor's Award for lifetime achievement in the arts. His poems have appeared widely in literary journals, including *Poetry, Ploughshares, The Missouri Review, Narrative Magazine,* and *JuxtaProse Literary Magazine*. His first book of poems, *The Porcine Legacy*, was published by Copper Canyon Press in 1974, and he is the subject of a PBS documentary *The Pig Poet*. A former seminary student, semi-pro baseball player, and hog farmer, he served for 30 years as Chairman of the Department of Language and Literature at Southern Utah University.

LESLIE LEEK is the author of two collections of short stories, *Heart of a Western Woman* (1987) and *Unsettled Territory* (2012), both from Blue Scarab Press. Her work has appeared in *Plainswoman, The Redneck Review, The Limberlost Review, Black Rock & Sage, Slackwater Review,* and in several anthologies. She's the winner of prizes for Best Fiction from *Willow Springs* and *Idaho Mountain Express*, and she's the recipient of a Creative Writing Fellowship from the Idaho Commission on the Arts. An Idaho native, she grew up in the small towns of McCammon and DuBois, where her parents published weekly newspapers. She taught speech communications at Idaho State University for nearly 30 years, and remains in Pocatello, near her son and grandson, where she has directed plays and organized literary events for many years.

ALBERTA MAYO says "The gift of a book of poems by Lawrence Ferlinghetti, an interest in the biological sciences, and typing skills helped launch me on a trajectory through the museum world." Along the way she found kinship with artists, visitors, and others whose expansive sense of curiosity and friendship have inspired her and her work. After ten years in the Southern California desert, she abandoned palm trees for the conifers of the Pacific Northwest where she lives "happily ever after."

RON MCFARLAND retired from the University of Idaho English department in 2018 after "47 years of blithe self-indulgence." He's the author of 20 books and served as Idaho's first State Writer-in-Residence (1984-1985). Current projects include a new collection of poems tentatively titled "A Variable Sense of Things" and a book-length study of the poetry & prose of Chicano writer Gary Soto. His most recent book is a biography of Colonel Edward J. Steptoe (1815-1865), *Edward J. Steptoe and the Indian Wars* (2016).

CHARLOTTE MEARS received her MFA in writing from the University of Arkansas, where she studied with John Clellon Holmes, James Whitehead, and Miller Williams. She has taught writing and literature in eight colleges and universities, received ten awards for her poetry, and published two books of poems, *Sweet Air* (2013) and *Winds of New York* (2014). As often as she can be, Mears is in New Orleans at the Maple Leaf reading series, the longest-running poetry reading series in the South. She currently lives in Madison, Mississippi.

MIKE MEDBERRY has been a freelance writer, blogger, and conservationist for nearly four decades. He has worked for The Wilderness Society, Idaho Conservation League, and Hells Canyon Preservation Council. A Boise resident, he holds an MFA from the University of Washington. His memoir *On the Dark Side of the Moon* was published by Caxton Press in 2012.

ALESSANDRO MEREGAGLIA is an assistant professor and archivist at Boise State University. He holds a degree in American Studies from Hillsdale College, and an M.A. in history and an MLS from Indiana University. His research on Vardis Fisher stems from a larger, archival research project examining the history of Caxton Printers (of Caldwell, Idaho) and its founder James H. Gipson, supported, in part, by grants from the Idaho Humanities Council and Boise State University's Osher Lifelong Learning Institute.

E. ETHELBERT MILLER is a literary activist and author of two memoirs and several poetry collections. He hosts the WPFW morning radio show *On the Margin with E. Ethelbert Miller* and hosts and produces *The Scholars* on UDC-TV. In 2018 Miller was appointed an ambassador for the Authors Guild. His latest book *If God Invented Baseball* (City Point Press) was awarded the 2019 Literary Award for poetry by the American Library Association's Black Caucus.

HANK NUWER is a prolific journalist and author. His main in-progress projects are varied, including a sweeping 175,000 word treatment of hazing in American culture, a forthcoming biography of Kurt Vonnegut, and his second historical novel set in the American West. He retires in 2020 from teaching at Franklin College in Indiana.

GLENN OAKLEY is a Boise-based photographer and filmmaker specializing in outdoor projects. His work synthesizes the aesthetics and lighting of landscape photography with the story-telling impact of photojournalism. A three-time winner of the Banff Mountain Photo Competition, he has shot feature stories for *Smithsonian, Sunset, Outside, Life and Time*, as well as advertising shoots for Sierra, LL Bean, Yakima, Giant Bikes and Dagger. A former contributing editor to *High Country News*, he has written and photographed several books, including *Frommer's Bed & Breakfast Guides to New England, Wolf!* and *The San Luis Valley: Sand Dunes & Sandhill Cranes*. His work with NBCNews.com on the multimedia project *In Plain Sight* garnered a Peabody Award. His film *The Falconer* was an official selection for the Wild & Scenic Film Festival.

RAY OBERMAYR (1922-2014) was born in Milwaukee, Wisconsin, to become an artist, writer, teacher, and mentor to many artists and writers throughout his life, particularly in Pocatello, Idaho, where he taught in the Idaho State University Art Department from 1955 to 1968, and lived again from 1979 until his death. A U.S. Army veteran during World War II, he participated in the Normandy Invasion and the Battle of the Bulge, and was twice wounded in action. After the war he studied in Paris, and his early paintings were reproduced in *Time Magazine* and *Art News* in articles featuring young American artists. Ray exhibited paintings in galleries and museums throughout the world, and at the age of 90 he had a retrospective show in Pocatello. He also wrote several collections of poetry, three published by Limberlost Press. He was a respected and cherished member of the community of Idaho writers, did many public readings, and read every year at Pocatello's Rocky Mountain Writer's Festival. Of the many honors he received during his lifetime, he especially valued the 1998 "Limberlost Cup" for lifetime achievement in the arts.

RON PADGETT's *How Long* was a Pulitzer Prize finalist in poetry and his *Collected Poems* won the *LA Times Prize* for the best poetry book of 2014 and the William Carlos Williams Award from the Poetry Society of America. His translations include *Zone: Selected Poems of Guillaume Apollinaire* and, with Wang Ping, *Yu Jian's Flash Cards*. Padgett has collaborated with artists Jim Dine, George Schneeman, Joe Brainard, Bertrand Dorny, and Alex Katz. Seven of his poems were used in Jim Jarmusch's film, *Paterson*. His most recent collection is *Big Cabin*.

KIRSTEN PORTER earned an MFA in creative writing from George Mason University and has taught creative writing, composition, and literature studies at Marymount University. Her poetry and teaching focus on women, cultural diversity, community, and the ability for all to repair what is broken in themselves and the world. She is the assistant to poet and literary activist E. Ethelbert Miller and the editor of *The Collected Poems of E. Ethelbert Miller*.

TOM REA is the author of *Bone Wars: The Excavation and Celebrity of Andrew Carnegie's Dinosaur* (University of Pittsburgh Press, 2001), winner of the Western Writers of America Spur Award for contemporary nonfiction, *Devil's Gate: Owning the Land, Owning the Story* (University of Oklahoma Press, 2006), *The Hole in the Wall Ranch: A History* (Pronghorn Press, 2010) and two chapbooks of poetry, *Man In a Rowboat* (Copper Canyon, 1977) and *Smith*, (Dooryard Press, 1985.) With his wife Barbara he founded Dooryard Press in 1979, in Story, Wyoming, and for eight years they published beautifully letterpress-printed books by such poets as Alberto Rios, Sam Hazo, Edward Harkness, Richard Hugo, and many others. Later he worked for a dozen years as a reporter and editor on the *Casper Star-Tribune*, Wyoming's largest newspaper, and since 2010 has edited WyoHistory.org, a state-history website published by the Wyoming State Historical Society. He lives with his family in Casper.

JOHN REMBER has lived in Idaho's Sawtooth Valley since 1953. He is the author of three collections of short stories, *Coyote in the Mountains* (Limberlost Press, 1989), *Cheerleaders from Gomorrah: Tales from the Lycra Archipelago* (Confluence Press, 1993), and *Sudden Death Over Time* (Wordcraft of Oregon, 2011); a memoir, *Traplines: On Going Home to Sawtooth Valley* (Alfred Knopf, 2003); and a book about writing, *MFA in a Box: A Why to Write Book* (Dream of Things, 2011). His latest nonfiction book, *A Hundred Little Pieces on the End of the World* has just been published by the University of New Mexico Press, a book that *Population Bomb* author Paul Ehrlich refers to as "A brilliantly written, deeply thoughtful, and even humorous book about a very dark topic."

JUDITH ROOT, during a lengthy career, taught at universities in El Paso, Columbia, Boise, Des Moines, Long Beach, and in the Summer Seminars in Prague. Her collections of poems include *Little Mysteries, Weaving the Sheets* and *Free Will and the River*. She lives in Portland and Nehalem, Oregon.

ED SANDERS is a poet, inventive musician, publisher, and longtime member of "The Fugs" rock and roll band. Born in 1939, he has produced dozens of books of poems, CDs, a novel, and several works of nonfiction, including *FUG YOU: An Informal History of the Peace Eye Bookstore...and the Counterculture in the Lower East Side* (2011). Author of the manifesto *Investigative Poetry* (1976), he has composed several biographies in verse, including *Chekhov* (1995) and *The Poetry and Life of Allen Ginsberg* (2000). In 1998 he began work on *America, A History in Verse,* a multi-volume history in poetry. Student of Greek, participant exorcisor during the 1967 March on the Pentagon, editor/publisher of *Fuck You: A Magazine of the Arts* ("published from a secret location on the Lower East Side"), editor of the online *Woodstock Journal*, husband of Miriam R. Sanders for a half-century, Ed carries on poetically and politically, bridging the Beat generation to the Hippie generation, to a contemporary insistence that poetry matters and will change the world. *This Morning's Joy*, a letterpress-printed volume of his poetry, was published by Limberlost Press in 2007.

GINO SKY is the author of the novels *Appaloosa Rising* (Doubleday, 1980) and *Coyote Silk* (North Atlantic Books, 1987), the story collection *Near the Postcard Beautiful* (Floating Ink Books, 1994), and a dozen collections of poetry, including, most recently, *Wild Dog Days* (Limberlost Press, 2015). He was an editor of the legendary 1960s literary magazine *Wild Dog* that began in Pocatello, Idaho, and moved on to Salt Lake City, and then to the Haight-Ashbury district of San Francisco prior to the Summer of Love, publishing many of the great poets of the day. His story in this issue, "Christmas Dog," was published as a letterpress-printed pamphlet in a very small edition by Limberlost Press in 1996 and given away as a holiday gift. This is the story's first publication in a literary journal.

KIM STAFFORD is the current Poet Laureate of Oregon. He grew up in Oregon, Iowa, Indiana, California, and Alaska, following his parents as they taught and traveled throughout the West. He is the author of more than a dozen books of poetry and prose, and the director of the Northwest Writing Institute and the William Stafford Center at Lewis & Clark College in Portland, where he has taught since 1979. He has worked as a visiting writer at a host of colleges and schools.
His most recent letterpressed chapbook of poetry, *How to Sleep Cold* is available from Limberlost Press. His latest book-length collection of poems, *Wild Honey, Tough Salt* is available from Red Hen Press.

CAMERON J. WATSON is the senior editor for the Center for Basque Studies Press, University of Nevada, Reno. He received a PhD in Basque Studies (History) from the University of Nevada, Reno (UNR), where he subsequently taught in the Department of History. He then relocated to the Basque Country, where he has taught at the University of the Basque Country, Mondragon University, and the University of Deusto. At the same time, he has been an instructor for
study abroad programs affiliated with UNR, the University of Washington, and the University of Delaware. He is the author of several books and articles, including *Modern Basque History* (2003) and *Basque Nationalism and Political Violence* (2007).

O. ALAN WELTZIEN, longtime English professor at the University of Montana Western (Dillon), is retiring from teaching in June 2020, and looks forward to more time to hike, travel, and write. He has published dozens of articles, two chapbooks, and nine books including three poetry collections and a memoir, *A Father and an Island* (2008). He's also just completed writing the biography of neglected Montana novelist Thomas Savage, forthcoming from the University of Nevada Press.

HOWARD WILKERSON is a retired engineer, 31 years in flight simulation. His poems have appeared in a number of literary magazines, and he serves on Salt Lake City's City Art board of directors. He's also active as a photographer and painter and has exhibited his photographs nationally. He currently serves on the Board of Directors of Utah Independent Living Center, a non-profit organization for those with disabilities. He lives in Salt Lake City.

NEW RELEASE

Legacy of War
A Novel by Ed Marohn

Psychologist John Moore is shaken when his PTSD Vietnam War patient reveals war crimes committed with a CIA agent and a South Vietnamese Army colonel. Moore, who served in the Vietnam War commanding an infantry company with the 101st Airborne Division, flashes back to his own war demons while still grieving his wife's recent death. The following day the patient is found dead—an apparent suicide. Stunned, Moore begins investigating the dead patient, the rogue CIA agent, and the lethal Vietnam War apparatus—the CIA's Phoenix Program—in which 81,740 communists and innocent Vietnamese civilians were killed. An attempt on Moore's life forces him to return to Vietnam to assist officials of the Socialist Republic of Vietnam and the CIA in capturing the CIA agent and the South Vietnamese Army colonel, who fled to Vietnam during Tet, the Vietnamese New Year, to blend and disappear among 80 million Vietnamese to recover buried loot, hidden since 1973. In the sweltering jungles of mysterious Vietnam, Moore pursues them to Laos on the old Ho Chi Minh Trail.

"*Legacy of War* is a military thriller that delivers all the goods...once the story gets going, it moves with the speed of a piano falling out of a thirteen-story window."
—*Vietnam Veterans of America Review Magazine*

"A well-researched and tightly-plotted novel. Fans of the military thriller genre will find a lot to enjoy in the pages of *Legacy of War*.
— *The Booklife Prize*

About the Author: Ed Marohn served in the Vietnam War with the 25th Infantry Division and the 101st Airborne Division. He was Assistant Professor of Military History at the University of Nevada and an executive with Continental AG, an International Fortune 500 company. Published in many magazines, he and his wife Cathie live in Idaho Falls.

$16.95 – Order directly through Amazon.com

Website: www.writingsfromed.com

NEW RELEASE

Lekuak: The Basque Places of Boise, Idaho
By Meggan Laxalt Mackey

Published by University of Nevada, Reno Center for Basque Studies Press

"Lekuak" means *places* in the Basque language. *Lekuak* analyzes the evolution of place through multiple generations of Basques in Boise, Idaho. Laxalt Mackey reveals the Old World value of community or neighborhood, the *auzoa,* and the maintenance of auzoa through communal work, or *auzolan*. This principle helped Basque immigrants resettle their lives in

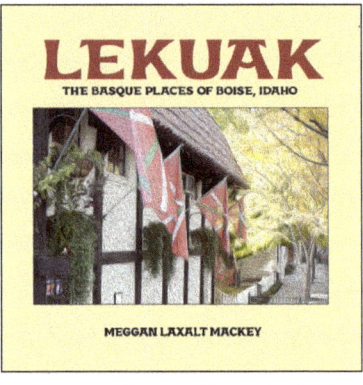

new places such as Boise, Idaho, and continues into today. Well-researched and written, *Lekuak* is scholarly, yet easy-to-read, filled with stories, color photos, and visual timeline that correlates Basque history with world, U.S., and Idaho events. This journey reveals the indelible mark of the Basques on the city's cultural landscape: yesterday, and today.

About the Author and Book Designer: Meggan Laxalt Mackey is a third-generation Basque who has dedicated over 30 years to Basque studies. Besides researching and writing *Lekuak*, Meggan also designed the book. A life-long lover of books, she has produced hand-made books, letterpress printed books and broadsides, and calligraphic pieces. She also designs books for authors in her creative services studio, Studio M Publications & Design.

$26 Order directly through University of Nevada, Reno
Center for Basque Studies Press Bookstore:
https://basquebooks.com/products/lekuak-the-basque-places-of-boise-idaho

Also available at the Basque Museum & Cultural Center
611 Grove Street, Boise, Idaho 83702

FROM LIMBERLOST PRESS

John Thomsen & Friends: Songs from Loafer's Glory
AUDIO CD

In commemoration of his 80th year, Limberlost Press has released a CD by longtime Idaho folk musician John Thomsen, of Idaho City, featuring an impressive list of musicians from the region backing up their musical mentor, friend, and collaborator. *John Thomsen & Friends: Songs from Loafer's Glory* features an array of favorites by Hank Williams, Hank Snow, Roger Miller, Tex Ritter, Sean McCarthy, and others, as well as a couple of Thomsen originals. Despite decades of making music at folk festivals, weddings, birthdays, political events, plays, dances, funerals, and backyard barbecues, *Songs from Loafer's Glory* is Thomsen's first CD.

Recorded by Sam Aarons of Idaho City Sound over several daylong sessions, the long overdue recording offers a sampling of Thomsen's musical versatility. The CD, which includes a colorful booklet of photos and tributes by admirers, features Thomsen's own "Idaho Spud," a bitingly satirical song-story about nuclear waste, the Atomic Energy Commission, and raising kids on "nuclear taters."

Limberlost Press publisher Rick Ardinger likens the recording to the work of Smithsonian folk music preservationist Alan Lomax, who saved from obscurity so much American folk music during the 20th century.

"Johnny has set the bar for being an authentic folk treasure. I am very fortunate to have had so many great times with 'the Golden Voice of the Boise Basin.'"
  —*Dave Daley, fiddle player and longtime More's Creek String Band collaborator*

"I have never failed to be impressed by his repertoire and his abilities on guitar, concertina, and Dobro. He was, and is, the complete folklorist and musician. His wit and sense of humor are unmatched."
  —*Jake Hoffman, veteran musician, and lap steel guitar artist*

"Johnny is a walking library of songs. He knows so many verses and choruses and the stories that go with them that he has to keep his interest by rewriting some with words most clever and slightly scandalous . . . I've been honored to play along, harmonizing on the fly."
  —*Beth Wilson, Idaho City folk musician and collaborator*

$12 (*plus $3 shipping; Idaho residents please add 6% sales tax*) **from www.limberlostpress.com, or send check to: Limberlost Press, Rick & Rosemary Ardinger, Editors, 17 Canyon Trail, Boise, Idaho 83716**

FROM LIMBERLOST PRESS

Waltzing with the Captain: Remembering Richard Brautigan
By Greg Keeler

Teaching English at Montana State University, Greg Keeler met *Trout Fishing in America* author Richard Brautigan in 1978 and opened a wildly memorable chapter in his own life. Having secluded himself on a 40-acre ranch in Paradise Valley, Montana, in the mid-1970s, Brautigan needed a friend with whom to talk and carouse. Attracted like a moth to the flame, Keeler became that friend and confidant, driver and clumsy co-conspirator in a number of escapades on the trout streams and rivers, at bars and cafes, and along the back roads of Montana. Together they waltzed through many late nights, until Brautigan took his own life in Bolinas, California, in 1984.

Two decades after Brautigan's death, Greg Keeler recalls those times with haunting clarity. Illustrated with photographs and the author's cartoon-like drawings at the head of every chapter, *Waltzing with the Captain* is darkly funny and poignant in its revealing portrait of an important contemporary American writer, and in its candid story of an often-tested and bumbling friendship between two poets.

Keeler taught English literature and Creative Writing at Montana State University for 30 years. A prolific painter and musician, he's written several musicals and published a dozen books of poetry, including *American Falls* (Confluence Press, 1987), *Epiphany at Goofy's Gas* (Clark City Press, 1991), and *Almost Happy* (Limberlost Press, 2015). He's recorded more than a dozen CDs of his satiric and flat-out funny collections of songs and poems, including *Live from Nowhere* (Troutball Productions). Winner of a number of awards for teaching and writing, he was awarded the Governor's Award for Outstanding Achievement in the Humanities from the Montana Committee for the Humanities in 2001.

$15 *(plus $3 Media Mail shipping; Idaho residents please add 6% sales tax)*

Quality paperback original first edition, 168 pages, from www.limberlostpress.com, or send check to: Limberlost Press, Rick & Rosemary Ardinger, Editors, 17 Canyon Trail, Boise, Idaho 83716

FROM LIMBERLOST PRESS

Of Your Passage, O Summer
By John Haines

Of Your Passage, O Summer is a collection of poems from the late-1950s and early-1960s thought lost, then found by the poet decades later, and published by Limberlost in honor of the poet's 80th year.

John Haines, once the poet laureate of Alaska, homesteaded in the wilderness near Fairbanks, working and living off the land. Written in relative isolation, the poems in this collection reflect news of the time — the Cuban missile crisis, confrontation with the Soviet Union, the threat of nuclear annihilation, the early stages of the Vietnam War.

Influenced by his readings of classical Chinese poets, Haines' poems quietly confront great questions about the very nature of existence, a plea for survival from a solitary survivor on a vast, beautiful, lonely and formidable landscape. Haines dedicates the book "to the time, the place, and the life lived—that which gave me the poems— and now to the reader of them."

"Dear Rick Ardinger: In publishing John Haines' Of Your Passage, O Summer, you have performed a very great service to the whole world of art and literature. His poems are beyond beautiful; they are important, uniquely valuable, and a destination for the hopes and ambitions of us all."
— Hayden Carruth, Unsolicited Letter, November 24, 2004

500 copies letterpress printed on Mohawk Superfine paper and sewn by hand into Stonehenge paper covers.

$20 *(plus $3 Media Mail shipping; Idaho residents please add 6% sales tax)*
from www.limberlostpress.com, or send check to: Limberlost Press, Rick & Rosemary Ardinger, Editors, 17 Canyon Trail, Boise, Idaho 83716

FROM LIMBERLOST PRESS

This Morning's Joy
By Ed Sanders

Here is a collection of anti-war poems that also offers elegies to friends (Allen Ginsberg, Robert Creeley, Harry Smith, Charles Olson), and reflects on memories of revolutionary times and the joys of carrying on despite "war-mongering sleaze" of governments.

Born in 1939, Ed Sanders is a poet, inventive musician, publisher, and founding member of "The Fugs" rock and roll band. Student of Greek, participant exorcisor during the 1967 March on the Pentagon, founder of the Investigative Poetry movement, editor/publisher of *Fuck You* magazine ("published from a secret location on the Lower East Side"), editor of the online *Woodstock Journal*, husband of Miriam R. Sanders for more than a half-century, he carries on poetically and politically, bridging the Beat generation to the Hippie generation, to a contemporary insistence that poetry matters and will change the world.

350 copies letterpress printed and sewn by hand into paper covers.

$20 *(plus $3 Media Mail shipping; Idaho residents please add 6% sales tax)*
**from www.limberlostpress.com, or send check to: Limberlost Press,
Rick & Rosemary Ardinger, Editors, 17 Canyon Trail, Boise, Idaho 83716**

FROM LIMBERLOST PRESS

Juniper
By Nancy Takacs

This collection of poems is infused with sage and juniper, images of the Great Basin, a horizon edged by mountains, where every word is measured and matters. Here is a poet whose lines grip the page like desert plants, windblown and enduring, whose quiet stories of family and wildlife and gardens are as if from a friend who logs the arrival of birds and shares coffee in a kitchen on a winter afternoon.

A former wilderness studies instructor and creative writing professor at the College of Eastern Utah, Nancy Takacs lives in Wellington, Utah, and is the author of a half-dozen books of poetry, including *Pale Blue Wings* (Limberlost Press, 2001), which was a finalist for the Utah Book Award and sold out quickly. She's the recipient of several awards, including The Nation/Discovery Award. She's held residencies at the Ucross Foundation in Wyoming and Vermont Studios. Her work has appeared recently in *Diner, Red Rock Review, Cutthroat, Plainsongs, Adirondack Review, The Spoon River Poetry Review,* and *Weber Studies.* She holds an MFA from the University of Iowa.

"Add Nancy Takacs's name to the list of Utah's best-kept secrets. These are beautifully crafted, well-made poems drawn from deliberately lived, introspective experience . . . Her truths are clothes in the silk of well-drawn imagery and are revealed in a manner that produces a life enhancing afterglow."
— David Lee

400 copies letterpress printed on Mohawk Superfine paper and sewn by hand into Stonehenge paper covers.

$15 *(plus $3 Media Mail shipping; Idaho residents please add 6% sales tax)*
from www.limberlostpress.com, or send check to: Limberlost Press, Rick & Rosemary Ardinger, Editors, 17 Canyon Trail, Boise, Idaho 83716

FROM LIMBERLOST PRESS

Don't have the 2019 revival issue of *The Limberlost Review?*

The 280-page anthology revives a literary journal of the 1970s and 1980s and features poetry, fiction essays, artwork, translations, and other personal writing by some award-winning contributors from Idaho, the West, and beyond, including **fiction** by Mary Clearman Blew, Jim Heynen, Gary Gildner, and Peter Anderson; **poetry** by Bill Studebaker, Star Coulbrooke, Gary Holthaus, Tom Bennick, Greg Keeler, Gino Sky, Larry Goodell, Bethany Schultz Hurst, Annie Lampman, Alan Minskoff, Jan Minich, Nancy Takacs, Diane Raptosh, Bill Johnson, Judy McConnell Steele, Martin Vest; **essays/nonfiction** and **"re-readings"** by Chuck Guilford, Kim Stafford, John Rember, Joy Passanante, Robert Wrigley, Jim Hepworth, Shaun T. Griffin, Brandon Schrand, and Stephen Richardson; **translations** of poems by Chilean poet Raúl Zurita by Mac Test; **artwork** by Dennis and Jinny DeFoggi, Greg Keeler, and Jackie Elo, an **interview** with Clay Morgan; and a brief, reflective history of *Limberlost Press* by the editors, colorfully illustrated with a montage of photographs and book covers.

"It was time to revive *The Limberlost Review* as a literary journal," Rick Ardinger says in the introduction. "The convener in us thought it was just time. Despite dramatic proliferation of *online* literary journals throughout the world, there are fewer and fewer print venues for writers in the Mountain West, and we miss the creative stir that comes from creating the mix, and bringing together the work of writers and artists in a print journal that can be passed around, talked about, and read in the bathtub."

The Limberlost Review (2019 Edition) retails for $16
(plus $3 Media Mail shipping; Idaho residents please add 6% sales tax)
through the Limberlost Press website
www.limberlostpress.com

What's next for

The Limberlost Review
A Literary Journal of the Mountain West

**NEXT DEADLINE
AUGUST 1, 2020**

Re-Readings
Have a favorite book you've read more than once?
Consider submitting a "Re-Reading."
Who were you when you first read it?
How did it have an impact?
Why return for a second or third read?

Remembering
Remember a friend, a writer, a journey,
an experience

Volkswagen Stories
Those old bugs and buses carried us and our dreams
over mountains and deserts, through rain and snow with
ineffective windshield wipers and little or no heat.
They were our homes, our identity
back in the days when we bought one tire at a time.
Have a VW story? We'd like to read it.

Plus
Idaho Vietnam veteran Ed Marohn on going back to 'Nam
Gallery: The Art of Fred Ochi
Robert DeMott on Thomas McGuane

Poetry, fiction, essays, memoir, artwork
and more

Details at: www.limberlostpress.com

www.ingramcontent.com/pod-product-compliance
Lightning Source LLC
Chambersburg PA
CBHW062021290426
44108CB00024B/2728